Contents

Acknowledgements

I wish to offer sincere thanks to a number of institutions and people who have helped this project come to fruition. Making books is never a solitary pastime, even though actually writing them is. I am very dependent on a far-flung as well as a local community of friends and colleagues who patiently give their time and their insights in ways that I could never hope to reciprocate.

This book grew out of ideas first explored in meetings about religion and the postmodern in the early 1990s. One was in the Unicorn Guest House in Glastonbury, UK, where the New Age was the theme, and another was in the British Sociological Association Study Group on the Sociology of Religion, meeting at Bristol. Kind invitations to deliver lectures, first the Birks Lectures at McGill University in 1994, and then the Murrin Lectures at the University of British Columbia in 1995, plus an all-too-brief stint as *professeur invité* at the École des Hautes Études en Sciences Sociales in Paris in 1996 and a conference in Sydney, Australia, in 1997, gave me opportunities to try to pull the materials together in a coherent form. In addition, involvement with the Research Unit on Religion and Society at Queen's University, and with my long-suffering co-director, Marguerite Van Die, stimulated work on this title, as did critical responses to *Postmodernity*, to which I see this present book as in some ways complementary, and teaching sessions at summer school at Regent College in Vancouver in 1996 and 1998.

I acknowledge several intellectual debts, particularly to Nancy Ammerman, Zygmunt Bauman, James Beckford, Manuel Castells, Anthony Giddens, Danièle Hervieu-Léger, David Martin, the late George Rawlyk, and Robert Wuthnow. Many people have read chapters, sections, or the whole book, and I am profoundly grateful to all. They include Phil Apol, Gary Bouma, John Bowen, Alan Bryman, Tony Capon, Les Casson, Danièle Hervieu-Léger, Mark Hutchinson, Margaret Poloma, Greg Smith, and especially Grace Davie, David Ley, Philip Sampson, and Bill Van Groningen. Zoë Ezinga and Jenn Poudrier helped me prepare the bibliography. abi lyon prepared the index. Some students in my sociology of religion class at Queen's also gave me very insightful and honest feedback. Gill Motley, Lynn Dunlop and Pam Thomas at Polity have been consistently helpful and patient with me. Thank you. I take responsibility, of course, for what use I have made of this kind help.

Sue, Tim, abi, Mynh, and Josh – who first brought to my attention the Jesus in Disneyland event – also contributed more than they know by way of encouragement, support, and love.

Every effort has been made to trace copyright holders, but if any have been inadvertently overlooked, the publishers will be pleased to make the necessary arrangements at the first opportunity.

David Lyon
Kingston, Ontario

Preface

This book is about the changing fortunes of religion in postmodern times. That first sentence may already have you worried or irritated. The "changing fortunes" sounds like a secular sociological account, unpalatable to those with sincere religious commitments. "Religion" smacks of conventional, organized religiosity, inappropriate to today's world of spiritualities and seekers. And as for "postmodern" – it is a passing philosophical fad, so why waste time trying to force false connections between it and serious stuff like religion?

Not so fast. What follows is a sociological account, but it is not unsympathetic to faith. Indeed, it suggests that faith has been underplayed and underestimated in sociology. "Religion," admittedly, is a shorthand, just to give some sense of what the book is all about. I use the term mainly in the context of institutional religiosity, which is indeed in pretty poor shape in contexts most directly touched by the postmodern. But I argue that the religious *realm*, including faith and spirituality, is far from dormant, let alone dead. Religiosity does find different modes of expression, however, and this relates to context. In premodern times, religiosity was often expressed in very traditional ways, which were upset by the coming of modernity. However, modernity itself is currently in the throes of remarkable and profound changes, but, because it is not clear that we shall ever be able adequately to encapsulate those changes in one concept, the more tentative "postmodernity" is used to sum up a movement, a debate, a set of tendencies: much more, in other words, than a philosophical fad (though I do not deny that its faddish features also exist).

All books have biographical as well as bibliographical genealogies, and it may help some readers to understand the family tree of this one. Over a decade ago a book of mine appeared bearing the title *The Steeple's Shadow: On the Myths and Realities of Secularization.*[1] Its central metaphor – the steeple's shadow – raised questions about the reach and scope of institutional religion. If once the steeple's shadow stretched over much social life in medieval and early modern Europe, what has happened in the modern era? A strong version of the secularization thesis suggests that, not only has the shadow contracted significantly, but, with that diminution of churchly influence, societies are simply less religious than they once were. There is something to this, of course. If one assumes that religion must take institutional forms, and that those institutions will exert social, political, cultural, economic impacts, then contracting institutions – seen in declining pew-populations and diminishing financial bases – will spell shrinking social shadows.

But there are other ways of considering the question. The idea of secularization, if taken to refer beyond institutional religiosity to the attenuation of all forms of faith, spirituality, and belief, is plainly mistaken. Even if one holds to the institutional definition, it is clear that on a global scale the fortunes of Christianity, not to mention other faiths such as Islam, are far from feeble. Much secularization theory is rooted in a more general theory about the modern world, that the latter has become progressively less hospitable, at least to certain kinds of religiosity. But this may be modified, in multiple ways. For a start, modernity is in part the product of religious activity and belief, so setting the one over against the other in a simplistic fashion is very misleading. For another thing, religious phenomena are never static; a constant process of renewal, relocation, restructuring, and resurgence appears to occur. Huge variations exist today between patterns of practice in Europe, North America, Africa, Latin America, and the Pacific Rim, and it becomes increasingly hard to see how one theory can fit all cases. At any rate, in *The Steeple's Shadow* I showed how secularization theory was being questioned, and argued that alternatives to its most misleading variants were becoming available. Among other things, I argued that the chief cause of secularization – modernity – was itself in question.

In the mid-1990s I involved myself more directly in the debate over modernity, publishing a small book that introduced and analyzed the concept of postmodernity.[2] In particular, I stressed that postmodernity refers to changing social conditions and not only to the well-known playfulness, parody, and pastiche of postmoder*nism*. The changing social conditions have to do especially with the expansion of new communication and information technologies (CITs), along with the spread of consumerism, in the later part of the twentieth century.

These two together have grown so fast and so far that they have altered the contours of what was conventionally thought of as modernity. The latter condition has not somehow gone away or been superseded; rather it has been reshaped, and seen in quite new ways. The indicators are varied, and include global tourism and travel, as well as television and the Internet. These have to be seen in the context of the restructuring of corporations and of cities, the increasing obsolescence of the nation state, and the fragmentation of labor and of lifestyles, as the single-occupation career declines and as cultural identities and alignments proliferate.

Seen this way, some connections with postmodern*ism* become more evident, particularly insofar as CITs and consumerism encourage a relativism of belief systems. For postmodern*ism*, as understood in this book, concerns the intellectual and aesthetic dimensions of life. TV helps to dissolve the boundaries between high and low culture, and to turn simulation into a major aspect of cultural production. Questions of ideology, belief, and culture are raised here, and, above all, ideas associated with classic modernity are challenged. Indeed, at one level, postmodernism is all about the demise of the grand narratives, the superstories of modern times, the decline of ideological commitment to big ideas like the nation state or progress. Within postmodernism, Reason loses its capital R, science softens its hard edges, and knowledge is seen – and felt – as (con)textual, local, and relative.

In *Postmodernity*, as in *The Steeple's Shadow*, I accent the importance of the everyday, the mundane, the ordinary. Despite the popularity of some rationalistic accounts of religion, secularization cannot sensibly be viewed as the steadily rising superiority of science over traditional beliefs. This is one "metanarrative" that has fallen on hard times. Nor is the postmodern challenge to faith best understood cognitively. Postmodern relativism may eat corrosively into the belief-content of some theological formulae at an elite intellectual level – and this threat ought not to be underestimated – but the gauntlet is more deeply and definitively thrown down by the social currents of postmodernity. It is in the commodification of everyday life and the impact of mass consumer cultures, facilitated by the CITs, that the impacts on faith and practice are felt most deeply. That is, they are experienced here, even if they are not necessarily understood.

This is why I chose the metaphor of Jesus in Disneyland for this book, because it neatly links together social and cultural features of the postmodern, while at the same time retaining some thoroughly modern characteristics. The world of simulations, which disturb or destroy a (modern) sense of reality, is seen delightfully in Disneyland.

Yet those simulations are highly dependent upon the highest of high technology. They are products of modernist rationality that are celebrated in their shrine at Disneyland, the EPCOT (Experimental Prototype Community of Tomorrow) Center. Disneyland, Disney World, Disneyland Paris, Disneyland Tokyo, and so on are also global tourist magnets, but, once there, one can also indulge in virtual tourism in almost any country you care to name. Heritage becomes instant and the immediate purges the historical memory, even as it is simulated in film footage and hands-on interactive experiences. Farewell to Hugo's hunchback; hello to safe suffering.

In this book, then, the themes examined in *The Steeple's Shadow* and in *Postmodernity* are explored further. I draw on many kinds of evidence, and rely on many other writers and sources, in order to paint the picture that I present here. As far as history and sociology are concerned, it seems important to listen to two kinds of voices in particular – those that allow themselves to be expressed in major surveys and opinion polls, *and* those that speak in more intimate settings of the small-scale case study. I refer to several of the latter, and also to the results of some large-scale surveys, which offer some impressions of overall situations. In particular, I make occasional reference to a major survey carried out in 1996 entitled "God and Society in North America," which garnered some data for a research project that I co-direct with Marguerite Van Die.[3] Among other things, this showed very clearly how much religious activity – often relating to orthodox belief – goes on *outside* conventional settings of churches and, for that matter, mosques and synagogues. This is a tremendously important aspect of contemporary religiosity, central to religion in postmodern times.

The picture I paint is done with a broad brush. It is impressionistic, relying on image and intimation as much as on the kinds of evidence mentioned above. Despite the definitive sounding subtitle – religion in postmodern times – readers seeking a comprehensive or detailed account will have to look elsewhere. But for those curious about the hints, the reports, the rumours of religion in the emerging postmodern landscape, I hope that what is caught in my wide-angle 'scope will help you see the world in a different way.

David Lyon

1 Meeting Jesus in Disneyland

It is Disneyland that is authentic here! The cinema and TV are America's reality! The freeways, the Safeways, the skylines, speed, deserts – these are America, not the galleries, the churches, the culture.   Jean Baudrillard[1]

The scene is Anaheim, California, home of Disneyland. Not unusually, 10,000 people are streaming through the turnstiles. Only today they are heading for a Harvest Day Crusade. In place of the regular attractions and rides, Christian artists perform at several stages through the park, and an evangelist, Greg Laurie, preaches a gospel message. While some find the juxtaposition somewhat incongruous (has not the Disney Corporation expanded its family values to include gays and lesbians? is beer not sold here?) the organizers have no qualms about it: "We saw Disneyland as an opportunity to bring God's kingdom to the Magic Kingdom. We felt that, as they opened the door to us to share Christ, we wouldn't turn down the opportunity just because other things take place there. Jesus is the example for this."[2]

Jesus in Disneyland. A bizarre sounding collaboration. Or is it? Just why does it appear so odd? At first blush, the objection could be that an ancient, premodern religion is found side-by-side, or, more accurately, *interacting* with, the epitome of postmodern culture – the artificial, simulated, virtual, fantasy world of Disney. It is not as if this religious group is merely using the park as a stadium for its event. To a considerable extent they adopt the styles, the fashions, even the attitudes of Disneyland. And they are not alone. Other groups – such as at the annual evangelical Spring Harvest weeks at Butlin's

Holiday Camps or at Christian events at Legoland in the UK, and at numerous Christian theme parks, such as Logosland in Ontario – use similar venues and methods.

It seems like an anachronism. Two vastly different historical eras are telescoped incongruously into one, within the gates of a theme park. Not only do the two seem historically out of place; culturally, too, they clash. The simply-dressed, sandal-clad, travelling rabbi who quietly admitted to close associates that he was God's promised Messiah – Jesus – also has connections with the self-advertising, technologically complex, consumer culture of comfortable California? Anachronism or not, such things occur, especially in America.

But the problem is not just one of oddity. This collusion – or collision – of cultures also takes place in a context that was once supposed to have erased most traces of conventional religion from daily life. It is often said that when premodern religions met modernity, from the seventeenth century onwards, relations were less than cordial. The scientific-technological revolution, the burgeoning of industrial capitalism, and the rise of urbanism and democratic polities often had an abrasive and corrosive effect on organized religion. The mathematician LaPlace took the trouble to inform the French emperor that he "had no need of the hypothesis" of God.[3] For many others, the process was implicit, whereby the "hypothesis" was for all practical purposes quietly dropped. Religious vestiges gradually succumbed to the evolutionary forces of modernity. Or so the story goes.

All this, and more, makes it hard to account for the Jesus in Disneyland event. Yet it occurred. And, apart from a few raised eyebrows, it was not treated by those involved as an anomaly or an isolated California quirk. Perhaps the difficulty is in the eye of the beholder? Those accustomed to the predominantly secular discourse of contemporary politics, mass media, or academe apparently have a harder time coping with Jesus in Disneyland than those who actually attended this event. This is not meant to imply that there is no anomaly, or that the view from below, which cheerfully harmonizes the surface contradictions, is in fact superior or correct. Nor do I mean to propose, however, that the secular discourse has it right either. Rather, I suggest that both perspectives should be problematized – held up for serious and careful examination – as a prelude to a better accounting for the event.

In what follows, I offer just such a problematizing account, as an introduction to the broad themes of this book. While the Jesus in Disneyland event is interesting in its own right, it also opens a fascinating window on contemporary religion and society. Conventional religion – in this case Christianity, but similar analysis can be made of other religions – is caught at a curious cultural juncture. Disneyland captures several crucial features of this, as the theme parks epitomize the tensions of modernity. Both modern and postmodern elements may be discerned at Disneyland, and today religious life is drawn by the pull of both gravitational fields.

Disneyland is a social and cultural symbol of our times. In particular, Disneyland is a trope for the democratization of culture, including religion.[4] An event like the one noted here raises questions about the deregulation of religion. Disneyland also points up the ambiguities and ironies of modernity and postmodernity, as well as their sources, the proliferation of new communications media, and the growth of consumerism. Disneyland as a cultural symbol also hints strongly at questions of authority and identity, and of time and space, each of which is crucial for a contemporary understanding of religion, spirituality, and faith.

Disney's social impact

There can be little doubt that Disney's influence is universal. Wherever it is possible to see a television or a cinema screen, Disney characters will not be strangers. And in more and more world tourist destinations, a Disney theme park is within reach. Plans for the latest are currently under way in Hong Kong.[5] Disney's impact extends far beyond films or parks made by the Disney corporation. By the end of the twentieth century Disney had become a byword for commercial culture, a symbol for animated cartoon lives, a model for tourist activities, and a mode of imagination. But it was also a way of communicating, a herald of technological futures, an architectural inspiration, and a guide to city planning. In Melbourne, Australia, a recent festival celebrated a Disneyfied Winnie-the-Pooh as a "United Nations ambassador for international friendship!" Under these conditions, it would be surprising if Disney did not have a religious relevance.

There are two main concepts used in exploring Disney's social influence, Disneyfication and Disneyization. Each has something significant to offer, but it is worth distinguishing between them. Disneyfication tends to be used critically. *Spy* magazine, for instance, defines Disneyfication as "the act of assuming, through the process of assimilation, the traits and characteristics more familiarly associated with a theme park ... than with real life."[6] The same magazine reported a telephone interview with Walt Disney World, in which it asked about the possibility of laying on a "Fantasia wedding," featuring a transparent box of mice, with pinned-on ear enlargements. The Disney receptionist balked at this, explaining that Mickey himself would attend. "Why simulate it with a real mouse when you can have the genuine article there?", she asked. The author of this piece also observed that "Genuine Disneyfication must be tawdry, contrived, useless, and dripping with class panic."

More sociologically Chris Rojek focuses on the moral and political culture represented by the Disney leisure industry, coming to the caustic conclusion that Disney parks "encourage the consumer to relate to America as a spectacle rather than as an object of citizenship."[7] Disneyfication makes social conflict temporary and abnormal, emphasizes individual rather than collective action, and generally acts as a mouthpiece for the American Way. The Disney world view fails to make sense of the present or to provide a plausible vision of the future, sacrificing "knowledge for staged spectacles organized around soundbites of history and culture."[8] Thus for Rojek Disneyfication subtly organizes our lives, even while letting us think that we are in a realm of release and escape.

Umberto Eco takes a similarly critical line, applying it to the ongoing uncertainty generated by Disney in order to perpetuate consumption. Deep questions of good and evil are rendered shallow through this process. The cynical shows through all too readily. Eco thinks of America as the prominent hyper-reality, whose ideology "wants to establish reassurance through imitation. But profit defeats ideology, because the consumers want to be thrilled not only by the guarantee of the good but also by the shudder of the bad." Thus there must be metaphysical evil, "both with the same level of credibility, both with the same level of fakery. Thus, on entering his cathedrals of iconic reassurance, the visitor will remain uncertain whether his final destination is heaven or hell, and so will consume new promises."[9]

Such critical approaches to Disney have much to commend them. Disneyfication may be viewed as a process that diminishes human life through trivializing it, or making involvement within it appear less than fully serious. No wonder Neil Postman wrote of "amusing ourselves to death."[10] Yet the Disneyfication thesis also has limits. The negative approach is not necessarily helpful in all contexts. With no pretence at neutrality, the term Disneyization has been proposed as an analytical alternative. Alan Bryman proposes that it should be defined as "the process by which *the principles* of the Disney theme parks are coming to dominate more and more sectors of American society as well as the rest of the world."[11] He isolates four elements of Disneyization, which are outlined below. As I shall show, each principle also resonates in significant ways with some major themes of this book.

The first aspect is "theming," which can of course be found in many contexts not directly touched by Disney. Thus cafés and bars may be themed, along with hotels and shopping malls. Well-known examples include the Hard Rock Café and the Subway outlets. Theming lends coherence to a site, giving it a story line. Theming creates connections and thereby gives a particular ambience to a complete environment. Today, that environment may be physical, at a permanent theme park site. But it may also be virtual. All computer users have become aware of particular kinds of "environments" that are themed in idiosyncratic ways, the "Mac" environment, or the "Netscape" one, and so on. Theming may be seen as postmodern surrogates for narratives (even "metanarratives") which, however fragmentary or temporary, tell tales within which lives may be located.

Bryman's second aspect is the "dedifferentiation of consumption." This technical term refers to ways that "forms of consumption associated with different institutional spheres become interlocked with each other and increasingly difficult to distinguish."[12] It is a breaking down of conventional cultural differences between kinds of consumption and between consuming and other activities. In the World Showcase of the EPCOT Center, visitors to Disneyland think they are sampling cultures from around the world, whereas in reality they are entering a thinly disguised shopping area. Conversely, sites where one expects to shop seem to spawn attractions. You can find rides and leisure zones within shopping malls. Airports and train stations provide evidence of the same phenomenon. Authentic crafts and current CDs can be bought, haircuts and massages obtained, tickets bought and checked. Increasingly, then, in more and more daily life contexts, one may expect to consume across a broad range of items. Such dedifferentiation accentuates the consumer culture, in which consumption becomes an order of life. The dedifferentiated environment privileges consumer outlooks and consumer skills.

Thirdly, Disneyization means merchandising. Images and logos are used to promote goods for sale, or are themselves for sale. The parks are both places where such merchandise is sold and the source of images and logos. Likewise the films are a source of images and logos that appear on merchandise, sometimes even before a film has been released. Many others, from sports teams to universities, have learned the Disneyesque techniques and advantages of merchandising. From our point of view, merchandising points up the power of an image, both in its own right and as something that can be bought. Merchandising also refers to itself and thus connects with a more general trend towards self-referentiality, which is a prime component of the post-modern. A recent example of this is the picture of the classic Coke bottle that appears on Coke cans, to reassure imbibers that it is the "real thing."

Fourthly, Disneyization involves emotional labour. Rather as McDonald's restaurants attempt to control the ways their employees view themselves and how they feel, so the Disney Corporation encourages scripted interactions using its staff. Theme park employees are well known for their smiling friendliness and helpfulness. Disney employees are supposed to give the impression that they are having fun too and not really working.[13] This focus on the self, and how the self is expressed, is again a feature of the postmodern. As we shall see, the modes of self-expression in postmodern times relate to the religious realm in interesting ways.

Bryman explores the possibility that while McDonaldization exudes some very modern features associated with bureaucratic organization, Disneyization portends a shift into the postmodern. Disneyization spells consumerism and a concern with the sign value of goods, with style and identity projects. Disneyization breaks down differences, is depthless, and deals in cultivated nostalgia and in playfulness about reality. These are certainly themes that I think are deeply significant, both for the worlds of Disney and for the worlds of the postmodern. How far these features are affecting – and are affected by – contemporary religious spheres remains to be seen.

Modern and postmodern

The Jesus in Disneyland event may be used as an exemplar for understanding religion and society relationships at the turn of the twenty-first century. In several significant respects, religion is being both Disneyfied and Disneyized. This is what makes Disneyland such a good trope for contemporary culture, both modern and, increasingly, postmodern. Disneyland encapsulates in concentrated form some leading trends, especially the preoccupation with consuming – fashion, film, and music – and the experience of spectacles made possible by high technology. While Disney's simulations by electronic media raise doubts about reality, and thus connect neatly with the postmodern, there are many other features of Disneyland that still seem thoroughly modern. High technology, to take the most obvious example, is also explicitly linked, through the high-tech EPCOT Center, with classic modern notions of progress and linear time.

How, after all, does one enter the Magic Kingdom? What sustains this world? Well, all major credit cards are accepted and these, along with the whole massive theme park system, are entirely dependent on the highest of high technology. Night and day, electric power flows into Disneyland to support the operation of machinery and its finely tuned computer-controlled system. Moreover, McDonaldization, which epitomizes principles of modernity such as bureaucratic organization and scientific management, is also present in the theme parks.[14] Whatever else postmodern means, at Disneyland or elsewhere, it emphatically does not mean that consumer capitalism has collapsed or that modern technology has been jettisoned. Just the reverse. The modern and the postmodern are equally characteristic of Disneyland.

It is crucial to dispose of the idea that modernity has somehow ground to a halt, to be replaced by postmodern conditions. Rather, the prefix "post" is attached to "modernity" in order to alert us to the fact that modernity itself is now in question. This does not mean that the sense of an ending – evinced in much postmodern literature – is insignificant, only that it can be over-extended. Sociologically speaking, although the rediscovery of deep cultural influences has helped to balance the analysis of social structure, the danger is to imagine that somehow social settings are irrelevant to the emergence of new cultural landscapes. Postmodernity is a kind of interim situation where some characteristics of modernity have been inflated to such an extent that modernity becomes scarcely recognizable as such, but exactly what the new situation is – or even whether any new situation can become "settled" – is unclear.

The inflated characteristics of modernity, which give rise to postmodern premonitions, relate above all to communication and information technologies (CITs) and to the tilt towards consumerism. Both are bound up with the restructuring of capitalism that has been under way since at least the last quarter of the twentieth century. Some such as Manuel Castells focus on the former, arguing that present trends are best summed up in the notion of an "information age."[15] Others such as Zygmunt Bauman center their analyses on the social consequences of the shift towards consumer capitalism.[16] But as the social and cultural converge, not least under the influence of these trends, it makes more sociological sense to hold the two together.[17] The growth of CITs and new media augments the power of the image, while encouraging such developments as positional pluralism. But the dynamic of the whole system may be traced increasingly to the demand that consumption levels be constantly raised.

So phrases like the end of modernity, though arresting, can be very misleading. When Italian philosopher Gianni Vattimo used this phrase as a book title[18] he was referring to the exhaustion of modern *ideas*, a modern *ethos* or a modern *world-view*. For him, modernity starts with Descartes, and is characterized above all by a belief in progress.

But this is undercut, especially by Nietzsche, when progress is shown to have become just routine, severed from its old religious roots in Augustine. For Nietzsche, the realization that "God is dead" breaks the spell of "higher values" or purposes that drive history. Consequently, some form of nihilism is all that is left. Modernity's dynamic lies dead.

Much postmodern writing, especially in literary contexts, picks up these philosophical threads and weaves them into a story of the cultural collapse of modernity. But a sociological understanding of modernity would be rather more ambivalent about its incipient demise. If, for example, one takes the pulse of transnational capitalism or of technological development – each encapsulated in the Disney empire – the patient would appear to be in thoroughly healthy shape. True, the once cherished hopes that modernity would reduce global disparities of wealth or diminish the likelihood of war are seldom mentioned today. Yet, to change the metaphor, much of modernity's machinery hums on as efficiently as ever.

Religion and social change

The Jesus in Disneyland event demonstrates how religion may spill over its older (modern) institutional boundaries, taking new and changing shapes, with a corresponding diversity of meanings. But, as I shall argue later, some traditional religious resonance with Disneyland also exists – the strong sense of a story line (what Jean-François Lyotard called metanarratives[19]) and of hierarchical organization being perhaps the most palpable. Understanding this involves exploring the reality of religious phenomena, the characteristics of the social-cultural context in which they are located, and the relationships between the two. The background to this is the debate about religion and modernity, classically understood within overarching theories of secularization. Such theories were once the standard means of coming to grips with the fortunes of religion in modern conditions.

Secularization theories provided a handy catch-all concept within which all kinds of phenomena could be interpreted, from the emptying of church pews to the decreasing references to God in political speeches (except maybe in the USA or Islamic nations). Despite the arguably powerful contribution of religion to the rise of modernity, it was widely assumed that Max Weber was right to see Christianity thus acting as its own gravedigger.[20] So an event like Jesus in Disneyland could be seen in the light of such secularization theory as an instance of the inner secularization of the churches (given that the

USA still has high rates of church attendance), in which the church becomes less and less distinguishable from the rest of the world, and entertainment rather than obedience its real dynamic.[21]

Although the secularization thesis still calls for critical attention (the burden of the next chapter), it is slowly but surely being supplanted by less self-assured approaches. Jesus in Disneyland might equally be seen, for example, as evidence of the transformation or restructuring of religion, or at least of its deregulation.[22] What if, given the tarnished status of several myths that make American life legitimate, the Crusade Christians at Disneyland were associating themselves with the somewhat more resilient myth of technology?[23] This would bolster Christian credibility by showing that believers can embrace high technology, and simultaneously counter any residual notion that Christians are obliged to be ascetically cut off from the real world. This interpretation would be in a venerable and plausible tradition.

Once religious activity is free of the secularization straitjacket, however, we discover all sorts of other ways to consider it sociologically. British sociologist James Beckford, for instance, concludes that religion is best thought of as a cultural resource.[24] In this way, religion can be seen to "convey symbols of newly-perceived social realities," whether to do with ethnicity, ecology, or the emancipation of women, and to be combined in flexible and unpredictable ways with all kinds of ideas and values. Jesus in Disneyland represents one such curious combination. Without its crippling conceptual tether to local community or to social institution, religion may be re-thought in fresh ways. Without the academic presumption that religion's social significance declines in the modern world, its actual social significance may be gauged appropriately.

The self-assured secularization story has little space for spiritual and supra-rational quests, whether formally religious or not. They tend to be seen as socially insignificant. Although Max Weber foresaw what he expected would be attempts to escape from the iron cage of bureaucratic rationality into a world of gods and spirits,[25] it was the iron cage itself that preoccupied sociologists for the longest time. So the later twentieth century's sacralization of the Self – as a means of finding some continuity for multiple identities – comes as a surprise. This is seen above all in the multifarious New Age movements – and their commercial parasites – but also in the "self-absorbed solipsism"[26] of the cybersurfer, creating a customized cosmos inside a virtual reality headset, or even, perhaps, constructing a personal website on the Internet. In this case, paradoxically, the cage offers the escape!

Of course, Disneyland is itself a classic mode of escape (and this is a common Disneyfication theme). There, one may find release from the humdrum world of everyday reality, as well as from the tensions and the conflicts, the violence and the degradation that characterize the real world. It is, on the one hand, a controlled release[27] into a fantasy world of childhood, but on the other, a means of organizing its subjects, and of moral regulation. It offers an attractive alternative reality while simultaneously ignoring the outside world of discrimination, disease, and death, and persuading its customers that the world beyond the park gates is really gray, monotonous, or boring. But it also portrays as normal a world in which good and evil are seldom ambiguous, in which right triumphs, where patriarchy rules – think of the *Lion King* – and which encourages robot-like passivity as a response.[28] As one critic said, sanitizing the stories renders them cute rather than acute, and with their cutting edge blunted they lose "the pulse of life under the skin of events."[29] This ordering of the world through media discourse is a theme that straddles the modern–postmodern debate.

To what extent is an event like Jesus in Disneyland a capitulation to consumerism, and to what extent does it represent a carefully controlled compromise with contemporary cultural realities? As we explore the worlds of the new media and of consumer identities in relation to expressions of faith and of religious commitment, we shall find, as in this event, that there are no simple answers. The demise of regulated, institutional religion seems to open space for all manner of alternatives, as varied as they are unpredictable. All we can comment on here is the contexts that increasingly constrain and enable those alternatives to appear. The taken-for-granted religious monopolies of yesterday have now lost much of their former power, and in Christian contexts this may as often be applauded as bemoaned, in the sense that religious commitment may now be unshackled from its less worthy cultural accoutrements. The question confronted by believers operating in those contexts now is, with which aspects of today's culture can contracts be made, and which – infantilism? consumerism? fun? nostalgia? – must be eschewed?

These, then, are the kinds of phenomena and the kinds of questions that cry out for renewed attention as sociology emerges from its secular space-warp. Part of the reason that such issues are on the agenda again is that radical questions are raised about the future of modernity itself. If modernity challenges religion, then what happens when modernity itself is challenged? Although the debate about postmodernity often generates more heat than light, the very existence of the debate enables us to take a critical look at time-honoured assumptions about both modernity and religion. Jesus in Disneyland may make more sense within some alternative frames, fashioned from fresh resources. Perhaps Jesus in Disneyland signals the arrival of the postmodern Christian?

Authority and identity, space and time

The Jesus in Disneyland event certainly seems postmodern. The Magic Kingdom is all about fantasy, illusion, slippery surfaces, revised realities, multiple meanings. It is also centered on play and the pleasure principle. These fit popular perceptions of the postmodern. Little wonder that Disneyland finds frequent references in postmodern literature. In the pastiche style that unblushingly mixes disparate images and experiences, Disneyland epitomizes the postmodern. The simulated nations of the world – Canadian Mounties, British Beefeaters, Japanese *samurai* – meet in one place. Like zapping with the remote, to visit Disneyland is to walk through a TV set. Different epochs and cultures jostle together, mocking the old distinctions of time and space.[30] In 1998 the classic bicycle race, the Tour de France, began a fresh leg at Main Street, Disneyland Paris, thus inserting the unreal further into the real. The relativity of reality is reinforced.

But the reality question has a number of facets. Let me comment on four themes that are present in Disneyland, prominent in debates about postmodernity, and which will structure the discussion that follows. They are authority, identity, time, and space. The postmodern places question marks over older, modern assumptions about authority, and it foregrounds questions of identity. It does so because at a profound social level, time and space, the very matrix of human social life, are undergoing radical restructuring. Each of them is at the same time central to the religious quest and central to religious ways of being. Conventionally, one might think of religious utterances and texts as authoritative, so that they help shape social realities; of identity as deriving from a sense of connection with the divine, and with fellow-believers; of space as a tension between the fixity of a monastery and the movement of a pilgrimage; and time as a means of holding in place a memory that unites believers within a common frame of commitment.[31] These four themes are woven into the account that follows.

If classical sociological accounts tried to see the influences on religion of science and technology, urbanism and the state, and industrial capitalism, we should enquire what, in the emerging conditions of postmodernity, are the shaping factors at work today. After all, industrialism had once disturbed traditional patterns of largely agrarian and rural life, with its natural rhythms and its stronger ties to place, and these had profound religious effects. During the twentieth century, as I argued above, two interrelated trends became central to an increasingly globalized world: the rise of consumerism and the development of new technologies (CITs). Whereas the modern world tended by then to be held together by the routines and rules of the industrial work world and the bureaucracy of the nation state, a sense of disintegration has set in as both time and space are in flux. Slow, steady, sequential time is displaced by the instant and the simultaneous, and fixed space gives way to flows – of information, of capital, of power. These are the major factors behind postmodernity – which, of course, are epitomized in, and diffused by, the Disney Corporation – and they have more than a minor bearing on the modes and meanings of contemporary religious phenomena.

Disneyland may be viewed as a concentrated form of consumerism. All attractions are alluringly on display; an *embarras de richesses*. Personal enjoyment is paramount; family FUN is the goal. Indeed, shopping malls the world over – from the West Edmonton Mall in Canada to the Toison d'Or in France – take their cues from Disney. Entire landscapes of consumption characterize the Disneyized world.[32] Consumer choice has, in turn, become the criterion for much more than shopping. Such skills are now required in education, health, and of course politics, where the slogan "free to choose" has achieved credal status. This is why choice has become such a potent political slogan; a market culture displaces citizenship with consumership.[33]

And on a personal level, identities are constructed through consuming. Forget the idea that who we are is given by God or achieved through hard work in a calling or a career; we shape our malleable image by what we buy – our clothing, our kitchens, and our cars tell the story of who we are (becoming). It is no accident that the world of fashion is seen as an "identity industry;" the idea is that self-esteem and our recognition by others may be purchased over the counter. The most anxious identity crises tend to occur in adolescence, but it is easy to see how this stage can be exploited by marketers. Artificially delaying the arrival of adulthood, and thus extending the period of identity exploration, is an obvious ploy, seen archetypically in Disneyland, but in many other contexts as well. "Playdium" in Mississauga, Ontario, for example, attracts more adults – often corporate groups – than children to its go-carts and video games.[34] They seem to have a hard time following St Paul's example of "putting away childish things"[35] on entering adulthood.

Communication technologies are the other aspect of contemporary culture also epitomized in Disneyland. The entertainment media available for local consumption in Anaheim, Paris, Tokyo, or Orlando are also globally available by electronic means. After all, movies made Disney's name in the first place. The growth of communication and information technologies (CITs) is one of the most striking and transformative changes of the twentieth century. They do not in themselves transform anything, but they contribute to the establishment of novel contexts of social interaction. They thus extend the process set in motion during earlier phases of modernity – especially through the telephone – of doing things at a distance.[36] They help to alter the significance of face-to-face relationships while simultaneously bringing all of us into daily contact with cultures once remote or strange.

Disneyland is a global phenomenon. Not merely in the sense that Disney World, Disneyland Paris, and so on, have spread themselves into international contexts, but in the sense that Disney culture is known worldwide, and that its mode of imagination and its practices have seeped into numerous fields, from politics to architecture. At the same time, Disney respresents just one of many global flows of entertainment, information, and wealth that pulsate around the planet. Once associated mainly with nation states, modernity itself is now a global phenomenon. Of course, modernity was for centuries predicated on international trade, but today's situation is different; hence the hints of a new *post*modern order. The nation state is no longer the central cockpit of action; old systems of government are in confused disarray. Transnational corporations not only cross borders without passports; they dissolve the borders. And Disney is part of this dissolving process.

CITs, along with vastly increased travel, tourism, and job mobility, also help bring into question all traditional modes of authority. There are ways of doing things that are different from those passed down from the previous generation, audible voices other than those which once held a monopoly on identifying the good, the true, and the beautiful. The increased culture contact between diverse and once separated groups produces the pluralism of today's world, which is either celebrated as part of a larger, global village – the portrayal offered by Disneyland's World Showcase – or feared as the raw visibility of incommensurate and conflicting beliefs characterizing the "clash of civilizations."[37] Either way, authority cannot in any sense be taken for granted in the emerging globalized environment.

At the same time, the local world of compact discs, cable TV, and computers is very different from that of song-in-the-pub, neighbourly gossip, and the printed book. Again, this is not to say that new techniques create a new world, or that they eliminate the old. Rather, in certain social contexts new media enable fresh forms of communication

– in a little over a hundred years the stage-coach mail has given way to e-mail – that may challenge convention or attenuate tradition. As greater physical mobility had consequences for religion in early modernity, so the shrinking of space by electronic means has further effects, both positive and negative, today. People are able to relate in more and more fragmentary ways, sidestepping the commitments that once more naturally accompanied social interaction. And they do so aware that others operate from within cultures very different from their own, which can easily relativize what was previously thought of as *the* right way of doing things.

Our turn-of-the-century, fluid, permeable, mobile (post)modern social experience has been described by Danièle Hervieu-Léger as the first post-traditional generation.[38] What she sees as a "situation of structural uncertainty, characterised by the mobility, reversibility and exchangeability of all reference points," is closely related to the relativizing tendency of CITs. Traditional religious outlooks, with their fixed points, transcendental anchors, and universal scope, seem out of kilter with the emerging spirit of the age. While Jesus in Disneyland may appear again as a metaphor for this disjuncture, it could also be the starting point for exploring the transformations of religion and the new modes of expressing religiosity that are flourishing as the third millennium gets under way.

Religion in or of theme parks?

The Jesus in Disneyland event described at the start of this chapter provokes new approaches in the sociology of religion and of culture. The inadequacy of sociologies dominated by secularization is highlighted when we try to grasp the significance of this phenomenon. Rather than cling to such a secularization framework, it makes much more sense to see Jesus in Disneyland in the light of globalized and (post)modern processes which, paradoxically, allow religious activities to be seen more in their own right than as mere reflections of something else. Older models of the sociology of religion also tend to assume that one type of practice excludes another, or that people are forced to make choices between alternative approaches. The thought that religious organizations might *both* resist *and* adapt to (post)modernity, or that, as in Alice's wonderland, it might be conceivable to "believe several impossible things before breakfast" is not prominent in these outlooks.

This is not for a moment to say that secularization is an entirely flawed way of examining events like Jesus in Disneyland. From the perspective of standard secularization theory, the event could be construed as evidence of inner secularization, a capitulation of the church to the world, an event that renders religion an innocuous and inconsequential pastime, pursued along with picnics or pinball machines to help take tired minds off the real world. Disneyland Christians would be revealed as religious dupes of consumerist seduction. This may well account appropriately for some of what goes on in such contexts. In this light, serious believers could be forgiven for taking a dim view of Disneyfication, especially where such collusion of Christianity with consumer culture diminishes the deity, downplays the divine, or denies that the non-consumer is our neighbour. The religiously musical may well find Disney discordant; deep believers may well deplore the shallowness of the saccharine sacred.

Christians colluding with Disneyfication does not sound very dignified. It also seems to deny certain things that Christians have, at their best, classically stood for, such as realism and concern for the Other. Disneyland is a powerful purveyor of practices and a popular resource for politics, architecture, education, and city planning, as well as a way of organizing entertainment. It also appears to affect religious imagination and process. Disneyfication so effectively transforms real life into a theme park that the difference becomes blurred. Eventually, suggests Jean Baudrillard, America catches up with the theme parks by succumbing entirely to the spectacular melodramatic form.[39] The parks in turn become just "one more sign of the unreality of everything."[40] The more successfully this occurs, however, the less the world of suffering, diversity, conflict, and power stuggles is conceived of as real. And the more attractive will appear the *Pleasantville* world of simple, homely verities, of "normal" relationships, and of childish fun. But this will also veil the extent to which, in order to participate, consumers conform to the expectations of the Disneyfied world.

In the epigram at the beginning of this chapter, Baudrillard distinguishes the hyper-real America of Disneyland from the "galleries, the churches, the culture." But when we find Jesus in Disneyland, those distinctions dissipate. It seems that Disneyland USA now incorporates even conventional religion into the hyper-real. There's a double irony here. Religion refers, by any definition, to that which transcends mundane reality, yet for Baudrillard churches can cheerfully be consigned to a cultural realm where "reality" questions remain unasked. At the same time, hyper-real phenomena abound in Disneyland. Simulated environments that attempt to persuade the participants that they are really in a spacecraft or a Chinese village confound and blur old – modern and, in some cases Christian – boundaries between the real and the rest.

Here lies a further paradox. While Disneyland, as an example of dependence on advanced CITs, contributes to the structural uncertainty (Hervieu-Léger's term) of our times, the stories told, especially in film, remain relatively coherent. Right triumphs! Technology is progress! It seems that the search for solutions to problems of structural uncertainty may be taken right into the milieu that produces them. In constructing their novel traditions of belief, the pilgrims in Disneyland stumble upon – or choose – values and suppositions that echo their own.[41] Disneyland is itself recognizably rooted in the soil of American Protestantism, even if many of its original nutrients have leached out, and it is thus unremarkable that some of the old flavour can still be detected.

This also means that such pilgrims may also, whether wittingly or not, dispense with some of their heritage as they make alliances with Disney. The reduction of history to nostalgia, for instance, compromises all futures, except, for Disney, technological progress. Obsessive atavism draws the eye away from present and future, leaving what is yet to come in the hands of technological destiny. Yet what happens when both the ethical traditions of the past and the hopeful good society of the future are jettisoned? Will all values be reduced to consumer demand in the long run? A Disney spokesperson comments unblushingly that at times they have to ignore their own views in order to keep up with the competition.[42] The critical cutting edge of Christianity, which produced in the USA and Canada the ambiguous but highly influential social gospel, could easily be lost if such alliances proliferate.

But what if the event at Disneyland was more than an epiphenomenal reflex of consumer capitalism? What if, rather than look simply through the Disneyfication lens, we use instead the lens of Disney-ization? In this case, the task would be to discern how far Disney principles affect religiosity. Do principles such as themes and stories, a seamless slipping between categories, the centrality of the image (seen in merchandising), or a concern with the self show themselves here? One might ask, in this frame, how those actually involved saw their activities. Recall that the organizers self-consciously commented that they ". . . wouldn't turn down the opportunity simply because other things take place there." With Jesus as their "example," they concluded that to refuse the chance to be on radio, on TV, or at Disneyland would restrict them "to the four walls of their churches – and that's not why we're here." At face value, this sounds more like a consumerism of resistance; in but not of Disneyland. If so, this is hardly different from the approach of believers for two millennia.

Could it be that the Crusade Christians in the theme park saw themselves as a kind of Trojan mouse, sneaking right inside the secular citadel of the Disney empire, to subvert (or convert) it from within? This approach could neither be condemned as capitulation nor read as refusal. Without our pursuing all the possibilities for such cultural guerilla tactics, grasping the chance for a religious revival in Disneyland could be seen as being quite in line with the apostle Paul's injunction to be "all things to all people" – a task he exemplified by his evangelistic discussions with guards while in jail in Rome or by his intervention as a visiting philosopher at the Athenian debating arena, the Areopagus.

At least from the point of view of the pilgrims at Disneyland, it was the context that was being co-opted for religious purposes, not vice versa. In a detraditionalized world of deregulated religion, it is hardly surprising that new alliances are formed, or that new combinations are sought from the fragments of older, once coherent cultural forms. These players in the plot – social actors[43] – deserve to be taken more seriously than they often were by secularization theorists. They seek credible ways of expressing faith in contemporary modes, but outside the walls of conventional churches. They work out ways of coming to terms with the world of circulating signs, and in this case choose to strike a deal with Disney. The social actors are still active.

Whether or not this could count as a valid explanation remains to be seen. It would certainly come as a welcome relief from the depressing studies that consistently indicate the co-optation of American evangelicals by consumerism. And it would fit well with what little empirical evidence has been garnered on the social effects of parks and fairs. Ley and Olds, for instance, in their analysis of world fairs, and especially the 1986 World Exposition,[44] conclude that fairgoers may be anything but "passive and deluded;" they may engage actively and critically with such simulated environments. In the case of the World Exposition, fairgoers often sought positively to learn modes of global citizenship. As for the sociology of religion, to countenance such an alternative approach takes one a long way from full-blooded secularization theory. This other perspective would consider not only the transformations of religion, but also the possibility that spheres of spirituality could become their own centers of intelligibility.

These reflections, though illustrated in this book by reference mainly to Christianity, also affect other faiths. How different religious groups grapple with the challenges thrown up by new media and consumerism will be looked at in later chapters, but one thing is clear: such responses are far from identical. Many Islamic groups, for example, denounce Western decadence and secular materialism, aspects of which seem to be embraced by Christian proponents of a "prosperity gospel" in the USA. As far as identity is concerned, Jews, especially since their civil emancipation following the French Revolution, have had to contend with the phenomenon of "conscious choice" to remain Jews, with the paradoxical result that one can choose religious identity without religious belief.[45]

Unlike these Jews, some Christians, at least in the UK[46] and Canada, may do the opposite; choose to believe but not identify with believers. In this latter case, however, there is little evidence of struggle. You choose which group, if any, to associate with, on the basis of common interests, musical tastes, liturgical preference, ecclesiastical orientation, spiritual inclination (to use a phrase from one of the popular "Moosewood" cookbooks). So far from Disneyland appearing foreign to such practices, one could be forgiven for imagining that confessional consumers would feel quite at home there. Dedifferentiation affects the relations between religion and leisure as well.

All this suggests that the Jesus in Disneyland event may represent part of a wider transformation of religion. The idea of making up your personal bricolage of beliefs, choosing what fits and what does not, appears to be a popular mode of religiosity or spirituality today, especially in North America. And what goes on in such mixed religious realms, or in the religious regions that lie well beyond the conventional, relates increasingly to religious identity. A careful sociological listening to contemporary voices reveals a trend towards the more general sacralization of the self.

The kinds of approaches encouraged in this book suggest we should be prepared to listen sympathetically to the accounts of believers[47] and to incorporate them into social explanation. The accounts could be mistaken or misguided, on their own terms, and a sociological interpretation could throw light on such apparent inconsistencies. But taking seriously insider accounts also helps us avoid the elitism of some secularization dominated stories. Nancy Ammerman relates how she once sat among several hundred academics earnestly discoursing on secularization and suddenly realized that they were nearly all men who had little sense of the practices of participants that "simply get them through everyday life."[48] "So what if," she asked, "instead of looking at the numbers in the establishment institutions, we looked at the practices that exist outside those institutions?" This book tries to do both, but accents the latter.

Disneyland serves as an apt trope for present times, especially but not exclusively in North America. This is because Disneyland faces in two directions, towards both modern and postmodern trends and tendencies. Religious groups, in coming to terms with this world, negotiate new conduits for commitment, fresh breakwaters for belief. At the same time, spirituality springs up on many sites, expected and unexpected. Religious life is not shrinking, collapsing, or evaporating, as predicted by modernistic secularization theorists. Rather, in deregulated and post-institutional forms, the religious life draws upon multifarious resources with consequences, for better or worse, that are hard to predict, but that cry out for understanding.

2 Faith's Fate

The retreating tidewater on Dover Beach in England sucked sand and stones out with it under a gray sky. As the Victorian gentleman stood watching wistfully on the wet shore, words of a poem formed in his mind:

> The Sea of Faith
> Was once, too, at the full, and round earth's shore
> Lay like the folds of a bright girdle furl'd.
> But now I only hear
> Its melancholy, long, withdrawing roar[1]

Thus Matthew Arnold lamented faith's fate in the modern world. But as a contemporary theologian, Alister McGrath, observes, this is a pathetic picture. For one thing, the cultural tide may never turn, and certainly not to carry Christendom back to shore. For another, the idea of faith being "full, and round earth's shore" was absurd when Christianity had hardly touched Africa, Asia, or even the North American west coast. The poem betrays a blithely blinkered Eurocentrism.

McGrath's alternative story comes from Australian Aboriginals, who tell of a mighty river that once flowed strongly across the land. Many generations living on its banks were sustained by the river, until gradually it ceased to flow. The people watched aghast as the symbol of their security dried and disappeared. Some waited for it to return while others went to find out what had happened. It turned out that the river still flowed, but had changed course upstream, creating a billabong on the curve where the Aboriginals still sat.[2] For

Arnold, the tide was out. In the Australian story, the river still ran, but elsewhere.

Many contemporary accounts of religion in the modern world are charmingly simple but profoundly misleading. This state of affairs can be traced to a single sociological one-idea-fits-all theory, called secularization. The theory suggests that the growth of science and technology, of urban industrial social patterns, and of the nation state, has deleterious effects on religious life. Modern society, so the story goes, runs on non-religious principles, churches lose social influence, and people stop attending them. Simplistic secularization theories all too frequently picture the resulting religion as a "shrunken, emasculated apparition at the periphery of modern society."[3]

Such secularization theories were the product of confidently rationalistic mid-twentieth-century European sociologies. They harked back to several crucial themes from classical sociology, sought confirmation in particular kinds of evidence, and assumed a generally linear progression towards a secularized world. Today, the difficulties with this view have multiplied. Re-reading the classical sociologists reveals more subtle analysis than was often credited to them. It has become harder and harder to squeeze the apparently contradictory evidence regarding both institutional fortunes and people's everyday beliefs and practices into the thoroughgoing secularization frame. And if long-term trends may still be discerned, simple secularization – as the fate of faith – does not seem to be among them.

One major difficulty arises from the fact that to modern eyes the most obvious religious phenomena are institutional ones; they are architecturally visible in churches, mosques, temples, and synagogues, or seen on the street in the habits or hijabs worn respectively by Catholic nuns and Muslim women. Secularization may be used to refer to the declining strength of some traditional religious group in a specific cultural milieu, but at the same time say nothing of the spiritualities or faiths that may be growing in popularity and influence. If we view religion in typically modern, institutional fashion, other religious realities may be missed.

But if "religion" constitutes one terminological trap, then "modernity" represents another. Just as there is no one way of conceptually capturing "religion," so it is misleading to think of modernity as monochrome. Many modernities exist, and they may be shown to have different ways of relating to the religious sphere. Many European modernities seem particularly prone to prise apart religious institutions from the rest of social life, whereas in the United States they seem cheerfully to coexist. In Latin America, Africa, and the Pacific Rim, still different patterns emerge. In addition, of course, these modernities never stand still. As modernities mutate, so their relations to religious life also alter.

In what follows, I shall first elaborate these introductory comments in relation to one or two examples of the misuse of secularization, not to set up straw figures so much as to show the dangers of one-dimensional approaches. Then I take a look at the themes of religion and secularization in classical sociological accounts, comment on the positive value of the concept of secularization for our understanding of some aspects of modernity, and, lastly, indicate how religious resurgence, re-enchantment, and restructuring also characterize the contemporary world.

Mistaking secularization

Originally, secularization could be described historically as the transfer to the state of properties once owned by organized religion, or the movement of a person out of a religious order into some other occupation. The resulting loss of religious influence was generalized into a theory that viewed societies as increasingly marked by a mutual exclusion of religion and modernity. This could be seen in the progressive splitting apart of church and state in many modern societies, and the parcelling out of social responsibilities into different jurisdictions. Such movements still offer a cogent sense for secularization. Nothing that I say by way of critique of secularization's magnified meanings should be heard as denying the basic usefulness of "secularization" in this context. But its metaphorical meaning has long since burst the bounds of that guarded definition to refer more generally to the fate of faith in the modern world. It is with this latter usage that I take issue.

Modernity, we are constantly and authoritatively assured, is inhospitable to faith, religion, and the sacred. Listen, for example, to leading British social theorist Anthony Giddens, explaining some of the *Consequences of Modernity*: "Secularization is no doubt a complex matter and does not seem to result in the complete disappearance of religious thought and activity – probably because of the purchase of religion on some existential questions . . . Yet most of the situations of modern social life are manifestly incompatible with religion as a pervasive influence on day-to-day life."[4] Giddens goes on to say that this is because "reflexively organized knowledge" supplants "religious cosmology" and that this undermines tradition even more than it does religion. Of course, Giddens is absolutely right to remind us that secularization is complex, but the way he deals with the question does less than full justice to that complexity.

On a statistical level, Giddens is correct to note that certain kinds of overtly religious activity, such as attending a place of worship on a week-by-week basis, are in decline, at least in Europe. The picture is varied even in Europe, and in the USA church-going rates are still relatively buoyant. They turn from buoyant to booming, however, in parts of Latin America, Africa, and the Pacific Rim. None the less, where attendance declines, one also finds a diminishing interest in rites of passage, and fewer people offering themselves for service as religious professionals. The exception to the latter is Scandinavia, where growing interest in occasional offices and ordinations defies lower attendance levels.[5] On the face of it, these facts appear to offer at least limited support to the secularization theorist.

Beyond this, however, in Giddens's account, religious "thought" is lumped together with religious activity. But while it may be true that everyday modern life runs on principles that are in some ways inimical to "religious cosmology" this does not seem to stop people believing in God. In Canada, for instance, more than 80 percent of the population claim to believe in God, and over 30 percent connect this with some very conventional Christian commitments to Jesus as "personal saviour." The point is this: religion can easily be mis-understood as merely customary behaviour (like church-going) or as cognitive activity (logical beliefs), whereas in fact it also – more pro-foundly – has to do with faith, identity, and non-cognitive aspects of life, such as emotion.[6] It also informs – sometimes *transforms* – very practical, everyday life activities. In contemporary Colombia, for instance, the Pentecostal revival is credited with resisting corruption and reducing domestic violence.[7] From this one might begin to draw counter-evidence that perhaps secularization is less systematic than some suppose.

On the other hand, this does not mean that religion occurs only in an individualized context, cut off from the rest of social and cultural life, as people seek private answers to the "existential questions" alluded to by Giddens. Contemporary studies of religion suggest that far more ambiguity and ambivalence attends belief and practice than meets the eyes of those who reduce those phenomena to cognitive and behavioural levels. Religion is a vital aspect of what Robert Bellah calls the "habits of the heart,"[8] those essential cultural elements of life that connect the abstract structural sphere with the motives and actions of human agents. Understood thus, it may be both public and private, collective and individual, emotional and intellectual, and so on. Indeed, this may be in line with the rather recent designation of "religion" as such. As Peter Beyer observes, religion as a differenti-ated category appeared only in the European seventeenth century.

Perhaps it is religion's return to non-differentiation that is witnessed today.[9]

The importance of this ambiguity and ambivalence cannot be over-stressed. Neither religion nor modernity is unidimensional or unidirectional in its development. Through its peculiar historical trajectory, some modern sociology may have ended up with some rather rigid and unrefined notions of religion and modernity. But while an openness to ambiguity and ambivalence certainly makes for more complexity, it is arguable that such complexity is closer to what is really occurring in the contemporary world.

Another way of looking at this would be to say that faith's fate in the modern world may turn out not so much to be lost in the every-day life-paths of ordinary people, but to be *lost from view* in academic accounts of the modern world. The secularization of scholarship thus precedes the scholarship of secularization. As Peter Berger now says, the secularization studies to which he himself contributed in the 1960s and 1970s were "essentially mistaken."[10] Yet his work in secularization studies was hugely important, perhaps more import-ant than that of any other single sociologist working in the field. And it is not as if Berger wished to deny the reality of the religious within modernity! He also wrote about "signals of transcendence" and "rumours of angels" within that same social world.[11] But one is hard-pressed to find accounts of religious activity, let alone vitality, in general sociological studies today, even in contexts, like Pacific Asian countries, where it is quite clear that secularity is not assumed, as it often is in the West, to be a condition of transition to a high-technology capitalist economy.[12]

So the question of definition of and, perhaps more so, of stance towards religion is important. Some secularization scholarship may well be tainted by anti-religious assumptions – Jeffery Hadden claims this,[13] and Steve Bruce,[14] for instance, is open about the lack of sym-pathy for the religious dimension that accompanies his research on the theme – but this would be to fall back on a merely theological critique of the field. The curious thing is that neither the religious tone deafness of Max Weber nor the avowed atheism of Karl Marx or Émile Durkheim precluded them from saying some significant things about religion-and-modernity and secularization. It was as-sumed in classical sociology that the religious life was an aspect of everyday social relations, as well as being inscribed in various social institutions. For a number of reasons, among which must figure the success of the overdone secularization thesis, religion has been rendered invisible in many sociological discussions of contemporary conditions.

Besides this, several other aspects of the debate about secularization are worth exploring. The view that modernity is inhospitable to religion has to be unraveled historically. Weber observed how certain elements of Calvinistic religion would serve to help generate crucial aspects of the capitalistic and scientific spirits that have imbued modernity, and that ironically the latter would undermine the former. Even this, of course, may be taken too far. The point is that some religiously informed discourses – such as Calvin's biblical assessment of usury – undergo transposition into a key discordant with the original in certain contexts, in this case early capitalism. Modernity continues to carry the apparently "religious values" long after their revelatory impulse has been abandoned or allowed to atrophy. None the less, the very intertwining of religion with modernity's beginnings should give pause to those who now assume that modernity's corrosive effects on religion will somehow, some day, be complete.

Furthermore, it is highly misleading to assume that either religion or modernity is a settled condition. The days of Christendom, with their rather tight church-state embrace, are undeniably, probably irrevocably, past, but there is no reason to assume that only ecclesiastical traditionalists or right-wing fundamentalists seek to reassert those conditions.[15] Also, modernity itself is constantly self-modifying; as Marx said, "Constant revolutionizing of production, uninterrupted disturbance of all social relations, everlasting uncertainty and agitation, distinguish the bourgeois epoch from all previous ones." And he continued, "all that is solid melts into air, all that is holy is profaned, and men are forced at last to face . . . the real conditions of their lives." The characteristic features of modernity, such as the growth of an urban working class, which may once have created some difficulties for organized religion, are now fading social realities in an information age. Needless to say, such comments project us straight into the central subject matter of the book, the putative shift into postmodern times, and its consequences for religion.

An ambiguous legacy

Marx, Weber, and Durkheim, often taken to be the founding fathers of modern sociology, each had interesting things to say about religion in their accounts of modernity. Weber lamented the irony that Protestantism, having unintentionally lent its power to the initial thrust of capitalism, would find its spirituality stifled by subsequent developments within the selfsame capitalism. But he left to the world a very pessimistic view of relentless rationalization that had little place for religious developments. Marx, on the other hand, was down-right antagonistic to organized religion on a number of counts. And Durkheim claimed that God, having once been at the center of all human relations, was now abandoning the world to humans and their disputes. Each theorist has now been rehabilitated as offering useful perspectives on contemporary religion.[16]

Whatever the specific contributions of these theorists to contemporary understandings of religion, it is still the case that their overriding influence may be seen in theories of secularization. For Marx, the issue was the illusory nature of religion but, unlike the philosophers, he did not regard this simply as an intellectual error. Rather, he viewed religion as a (flawed) means of making sense of intolerable social and economic conditions, and thus as one of those things that had to be not only understood but also changed. But capitalism, which gave rise to these conditions within modernity, could not survive in the long term, crippled, as it seemed to Marx, by its own contradictions. Thus religion, however well it managed to express the "heart of a heartless world," was destined to die when that heartlessness was transcended by the abolition of capitalism.

For all that Durkheim seemed to offer a theory showing how religion is constitutive of stable social life,[17] he also proposed that in modern times religion embraces a smaller and smaller portion of that social life. Little by little, he maintained, political, economic, and scientific features of life cut themselves free from their erstwhile religious moorings, taking on a more temporal character. This Durkheim saw as a steady, long-term process. That secularization is a long-term historical view was a perspective shared by Weber.

For Weber, religion is a vital means of making sense, not just of suffering or exploitative social conditions, but of the mysteries of human life itself. Religion produces meaning itself, and in so doing, relates to everyday human affairs in an influential way. For instance, believing that both hard work and self-denial are appropriate responses to God prompted modes of capital accumulation that led, under some specific and sometimes surprising circumstances, to the early initiatives of capitalism; or so Weber argued. However, the ensuing rationalization of more and more areas of social life would in the end have a boomerang effect, warned Weber, in what he termed the "disenchantment of the world." This essentially tragic vision has, arguably, become the abiding legacy of Weber's work.

The uses to which these classical theories were put, in sociology and history, tended to focus on the social rather than on the religious per se. Assuming that the movement described by these three and others was progressive, linear, and irreversible, the assumption stuck that religion was a phenomenon in demise, and that other social changes would ultimately be more significant. Thus what religion supposedly *does*, rather than what it *is*, in itself, became central within sociology, despite the fact that all three of these founders, at least, considered both kinds of question in their work. As Beckford observes,[18] most classical social theorists, apart from Alexis de Tocqueville, sought insights into the future of religion from some supposed master trends, or else suggested that religion illustrated some underlying trends.

The end result of this is that secularization, seen now merely as a handy catch-phrase referring to the decline of religion, is frequently taken for granted in academic and media accounts of the modern world. Thus, for example, British sociologist Bryan Wilson argues that in the debate about secularization, the insights of the classics are aligned with the commonsense knowledge of ordinary people.[19] This may well be true, but the question is, where did the "commonsense knowledge" come from? While some of it no doubt originates in everyday observation, such conclusions are usually informed by wider comparison. It would be unremarkable if that wider comparison were pieced together in part from popularized academic accounts emanating from the classical sociologists.

For Wilson, the crucial sociological question surrounding secularization is how far religion has lost its social influence. But because he sees religion as rooted in community, a form of association that he takes to have been lost in the modern, *societal* world, it is hard to see how religion could ever make a comeback. Bruce takes a similar view, although he adds a "religion-as-intellectual-error" dimension to his account.[20] In these dominant accounts of secularization it is large religious organizations that are in focus, in relation to modern nation states. But while secularization may well make sense of some aspects of this distinctively modern relationship, the issue for the twenty-first century is that neither side of the secularization equation has remained constant. It is now dangerous to assume without qualification that either large religious organizations are the chief habitat of faith or that the nation state is the main focus of political power. This can best be seen by distinguishing different aspects of secularization.

Dismantling secularization

A classic strong account of secularization was produced by Karel Dobbelaere.[21] To his credit he at least did not assume general irreversible religious decline. He proposed, helpfully, that secularization is a multidimensional concept, involving at least three levels: the institutional, the organizational, and the personal. By looking at each of these, we can see how, whatever the original merits of the secularization scheme, its salience is limited today. I suggest that, when carefully circumscribed with qualifications – and distinguishing between levels is one such – secularization is a useful sociological and historical tool. But remove those qualifications, and secularization becomes perilously misleading.

At the institutional level, the basic cleavage is between religious organizations and the modern administrative state. This Dobbelaere refers to as *laïcization*, and it can be illustrated with reference to fields such as health and welfare. Where once, in Europe and North America, providing poor relief and health care were mainly religious initiatives, under the aegis of the churches, a gradual shift of control occurred, which placed these firmly within government bureaucracies, with their corresponding specialized bearers of expertise. The churches, which were once the hub of many activities – in relation to education, work, health and welfare, and leisure – thus find their role whittled down to some rather narrow concerns about worship, parish and pastoral work, and so on. Of course, this process may occur at different rates in different countries – slow and almost imperceptible in Britain; late and cataclysmic in Quebec, for example – but the differentiating process of *laïcization* is readily recognizable in many countries none the less.

Several questions may be posed regarding this, however. One, raised by José Casanova, concerns the manifestly "public religions" that in Spain, Poland, Brazil, and the USA had huge and lasting political impact from the 1980s onwards. "Solidarity" in Poland is a clearly religious political movement, as is the New Christian Right in the USA. Casanova points out that this came as a surprise to secularization theorists because of a basic mistake – conflating different aspects of the process into one master trend. In particular, it was all too often assumed that the privatization of religion would be an inevitable concomitant of differentiation. However, Casanova argues, some religions are today (re)entering the public sphere, not just to "defend their traditional turf" but also to "participate in the very struggles to define and set the modern boundaries between public and private . . . between family, civil society, and state" and so on.[22]

Of course, it must also be remembered that part of this re-entry process is made possible by changes and even crises within the public sphere itself. It is by no means clear that the central role of the sovereign nation state is assured. Indeed, there are many signs that, especially under pressure from globalizing forces, the future of the state – particularly the welfare state – is in radical doubt. As Manuel Castells says, "Bypassed by global networks of wealth, power, and information, the modern nation-state has lost much of its sovereignty."[23] It is losing its grip on the organization of space and time that gave it its modern power. Among other things, deregulation is the order of the day, and in some circumstances this can mean the remobilization of religious resources for educational or welfare purposes.

But even without such remobilization, in the later twentieth century religious controversy became increasingly visible within state-controlled agencies. The language used for matters relating to life and the body – such as abortion, euthanasia, and same-sex relations – has been a point of conflict. Richard Fenn argues that this is precisely because, for many, the clinical language of bureaucratic expertise is simply inadequate for the situations in which it is invoked.[24] Thus the supposedly "secular" situation actually generates religious responses that contest its now dominant position. Secularization, in this view, is a dynamic process of boundary disputes, without any easily predictable outcome.

On its own, modern terms, then, one might ask, with Beckford, "whether the separation of religion from the apparatus of social control and legitimation necessarily means that religion's significance is in decline."[25] Even if laïcization has demonstrably occurred in most modern societies, can we assume either that it will continue to happen in the same way, or that it will not generate responses that lead one to doubt the wisdom of restricting religious influence only to the activities of large, overtly religious organizations? But beyond this, one might also ask, if religion continues to exist in contemporary societies, what forms it will take after establishments such as Christendom have finally disappeared, or after mainline denominations have met their bureaucratic nemesis.

Dobbelaere's second dimension of secularization is organizational change. The focus moves from the large-scale splitting apart of church and state to alterations within religious organization. One could, for instance, invoke Weber's classic and resonant phrase, the "routinization of charisma" to sum this up. In this case, religious agencies themselves succumb to secularization from within. Thus, again following classical analyses of Weber and his colleague Ernst Troeltsch, one might argue that a form of secularization takes place as the initial effervescence of a sectarian breakaway group calms down, and as the resulting group becomes more church-like than sect-like. In Canada, for instance, the bubbling enthusiasms of mid-Victorian camp-meeting Methodists took a more staid form towards the end of the century, and were subject to further bureaucratic absorption when Methodists merged with others to form the only Canadian indigenous denomination, the United Church, in 1925.

Organizational change often means that religious groups conform more and more to the modern world. To take on characteristics of bureaucratic organization – a defining feature of the denomination – would be one obvious way in which this would happen. Peter Berger and others[26] argue (or rather, they once did) that this places religious groups in a dreadful dilemma: accommodate to modernity and risk practical and doctrinal dilution of the faith, or resist modernity and risk marginalization as an irrelevance. While there may be something to this, it downplays a third option, that religious groups frequently face both ways at once. Danièle Hervieu-Léger argues that successful churches use both strategies, accepting and resisting modernity.[27] Such ambivalence may be the norm for successful religious groups.

On the other hand, organizational change may be understood in broader terms. It may take forms other than bureaucratization. For instance, while the old mainline Christian denominations fell on hard times in the second half of the twentieth century, networks of Christian groups, often geared to particular, limited objectives such as Third World relief programs or educational alternatives, became increasingly important, at least in North America.[28] Again, unless there is some good reason for seeing big organizations as the main social habitat for religion, it may be worth heeding Robert Wuthnow's advice that religion may better be sought in what he calls "moral communities" or "networks of mutual obligation and shared belief."[29]

Nancy Ammerman has provided plenty of concrete evidence for such communities related to American congregational life in the 1990s. And she observes that many male white sociologists failed to find this vitality because they had limited their studies to numbers in establishment institutions rather than exploring the margins, the so-called private sphere, which, it is assumed, has a negligible effect on "public" life. On the contrary, she argues, it is just here that vital tools for navigating through all kinds of everyday life situations are developed, tools that sometimes produce modes of resistance or social innovation. The sacred and profane, the public and the private, the religious and the secular may be "mixed up" (that is from the viewpoint of those who expect neat categories), but "when we begin to read the history of religion from the bottom up, we may see a constant 'both-and,' rather than a decline from all to nothing."[30]

The third aspect of secularization isolated by Dobbelaere is personal – what might be called the secularization of consciousness. In a haunting phrase of Berger, Berger, and Kellner, moderns have "home-less minds."[31] Among other things this is seen in a "technological con-sciousness" that considers life to be things that fit together like machine components, and explains events as "natural" occurrences, explicable in the language of weather forecasts or stock-market reports. Facing life's issues without the benefit of religious interpretations, people turn instead to other sources of explanation, justification, or hope. It must be said, however, that these "other sources" often include some that are not exactly "technological" in origin, such as horoscopes or self-improving techniques such as meditation. Increasingly, however, while there may be some evidence of a "technological conscious-ness," many people do not see this as incompatible with other kinds of belief. Today's world, after all, is one increasingly characterized by the dedifferentiated bricolage of Disneyland.

It is difficult to gauge just how far the secularization of conscious-ness may have proceeded in any given context, but for many it is just this process that has inspired what Daniel Bell once dubbed the "return of the sacred."[32] He foresaw a time when the "core questions," such as love, tragedy, obligation, and death – Giddens' "existential questions," in other words – would find a response in the rise of new religions. If not new religions *per se*, it is certainly the case that many countries touched by modernity have witnessed the rapid rise of the New Age Movement in the last decades of the twentieth century.[33]

One could argue that this aspect of secularization is becoming more marked at the start of the Third Millennium, although one must quickly add that, once again, the picture is ambiguous. The cultural changes towards postmodern situations exacerbate the ten-dency towards forms of individualism, but these are by no means necessarily irreligious forms of individualism. The story is more com-plex. To be sure, some traditional religious emphases on the long-term, the established, the canonical, the communal are under pressure in a world of instantaneous communication, theme-park history, and point-and-click information. Yet it does seem that many still work to patch together the shreds and shards of spirituality and faith, many do seek homespun and *ad hoc* means of coping with the apparently anomalous tragic moment, and many also evince a wistful quest of the communal, even if that, too, involves fleeting encounters. Indeed, the greater the felt fragmentation, it seems, the greater the quest for compensatory communities. These two are not contradictory, but mutually informing.

The possibility that in contemporary societies there may be a more individualistic approach to the religious does not necessarily spell a flight from faith – as the thoroughgoing secularization perspective might imply – so much as the fragmentation of faith. The massive outpouring of grief at the death of Princess Diana in 1997, with its multiple and idiosyncratic religious auras, illustrates just this situation.[34] Such fragmentation reflects at least two aspects of today's individualism. On the one hand, it addresses expressive individualism, in which the self is central, and where needs are met through experiences, especially bodily ones. On the other, it touches on acquisitive individualism, in which consuming is central. It may lead to the actual accumulation of things (and to a quasi-religious justification of this in terms, say, of American "prosperity gospels") but, more significantly, it may be associated with consumerist attitudes and lifestyles, in which choice is paramount.

Of course, Bruce sees consumer religion as a part of secularization, because these private beliefs – he claims – have less and less direct impact on the way society runs, and as part of a grand downturn in religion, as he puts it, "from cathedrals to cults." The "sovereign consuming individual of late modernity" leads inexorably, but in diverse ways, to the "cultic milieu," whose relativism will "prevent any of these innovations acquiring the power and influence of previous religious innovations."[35] But what if, as I argue in chapters 3 and 5, consumption plays an increasingly significant role in the way society runs? This would mean, on Bruce's own argument, that openings for religious activity would lie right here. They would not have to acquire the *same kinds* of power and influence to be socially significant. Others, who also perceive the growth of faith fragmentation, see new possibilities not unrelated to consumption. Reginald Bibby, discussing the Canadian situation, argues that many still choose at least partial commitments of conventional – in this case Christian – kinds. The thrust of his case is that religious groups capable of good marketing may still succeed in the new environment.[36]

But one need not go so far. David Martin, commenting on the mushrooming growth of global Pentecostalism (and, to an extent, a broader Evangelicalism), suggests that in response to present trends particularly expressive individualism may be incorporated and contained.[37] So while the relativistic individualism of what is "right for me" may be manifest in some quarters, in others the attractive fragments of faith, if compatible with a shared religious outlook, may be recycled for use in more conventional containers. The point is that religion, in this view, would no longer be seen as some faltering force whose erstwhile institutional supports have crumbled, but rather as a dynamic cultural resource.

Revival, re-enchantment, restructuring

To see religion as a cultural resource immediately restores it as a phenomenon worthy of serious study, rather than as a failing feature of a bygone era. While the limited secularization thesis unquestionably tells us a lot about the particular trajectories for religion and society relations within modern societies, it tells us all too little about the fate of faith in general. We should not expect to find ever diminishing dried up pools of religiosity in the late- or postmodern world, but rather conceive of religion as a cultural resource, and discover ways in which it is expressed, utilized, and forged, even in its interactions with those worlds.

Of course, it may well be that, paradoxically, secularization is in part the stimulus for religious growth. If secularization properly refers to the process of differentiation, which breaks up old religious monopolies – such as Christendom – then the resulting competing fragments, now compelled to reassess their vision, mission, and strategies, may well find new vigor in a pluralistic situation of competition.[38] If religious groups capitalize (deliberately or otherwise) on, say, expressive individualism, but are able to connect – or reconnect – this with aspects of ancient traditions, and to curb potential excesses of individualism with reference to communal loyalties, as suggested above, then the growth of major movements such as Evangelicalism or Fundamentalism, or minor ones, such as Catholic communities or Celtic Christianity, becomes somewhat less surprising.

Certain kinds of late- or postmodern conditions may act as impulses for particular kinds of religious development. Hervieu-Léger suggests that, far from being incompatible with religious life, late modernity may actually generate certain kinds of religious response.[39] This is because modernity's forward-thrusting dynamic has utopian aspects (themselves, one might add, an aspect of Western modernity's reliance on secularized religious – read Christian – philosophies of history), but by definition those aspirations can never fully be fulfilled. The space thus created is in a sense a natural one for religious activity, a structural location where this religious-secular drama is played out. Although Hervieu-Léger rejects a notion of postmodernity, her argument would fit this case as well. For if, as argued here, postmodernity is a social condition in which certain aspects of modernity are inflated to the extent that the old modernity is hard to recognize, then at just those points new opportunities may open themselves for religious activity. Having brought beliefs and practices of explicitly religious provenance into late modern conditions, though without the faith that formed them, postmodern conditions now demand a reassessment.

Firstly, while some conventional religious organizations and movements do indeed seem to be past their peak, in many parts of the world religious revival and resurgence is the order of the day (and some of these may also reinforce older organizations). The growth of Islam, particularly in North Africa and in the Middle East, has been striking. Besides the situations on which the media focus – armed fundamentalism – there is a huge upsurge of what Gilles Kepel calls "re-Islamization from below,"[40] which affects the everyday lives of a large proportion of the populations of several Muslim societies. At the same time, the massive rise of Pentecostalism, particularly in Latin America, but also in other parts of the world, has put Evangelicalism (of which it is an offshoot) on a par with Catholicism as one of two truly global religions in today's world.[41] The majority of Pentecostal growth is "from below." Combined with the fact that violence is not associated with Pentecostalism, and the lack of Western influence in non-English-speaking countries, this means that such growth is often more hidden from (media and, all too often, academic) view.

Secondly, one can argue that the later twentieth century witnessed widespread re-enchantment, in ways that might well have surprised Weber. So far from the secularization of consciousness producing a situation in which technoscience offers satisfactory solutions to the recurring riddles of life, plenty of evidence exists for interest and involvement in many kinds of unconventional beliefs, practices, and spiritualities. Globalizing Eastern influences, along with some thoroughly modern emphases on technique, have encouraged movements such as New Age; the (re)feminization of religion has prompted quests for women-friendly religiosities such as Wicca;[42] and attention to horoscopes and other means of seeking guidance and wisdom shows no signs of abating. It could be, of course, that the disenchantment thesis was itself somewhat overblown, and that what Martin once called "subterranean theologies" have never ceased to appeal. Today, the deregulation and deinstitutionalization of religion, plus, perhaps, millennial fervor, are simply offering them a new lease of more public life.

Thirdly, one can point to the more mundane evidence for the restructuring of religion. Secularization correctly highlights the deregulation of religion (as monopolies crumble) and the deinstitutionalization of religion (as organizational foci become less significant for spirituality), but this is just part of a larger picture, in which questions must be asked about the relocation of the religious and the restructuring of those patterns within postmodernizing situations. How exactly are fragments of belief re-woven into the lives of those for whom religious choice is central, and who seek the faith-means of coming to terms with contemporary realities? Significant populations may well believe without belonging, in a conventional sense, but what are the new elements of belief, how do they affect daily practice, and what sorts of attachment and connection do persist, after formal membership or attendance in religious institutions is left on one side? In other words, the real focus of interest in religion today is in how the "symbolic boundaries" are shifting.[43]

Although numerous efforts have been made to oust secularization as a master narrative from its dominant position, it was not until the mid-1990s that alternative formulations began to offer sufficient space for sociologists to do their work unhampered by the clinging legacy from the past. Arguably, this came about not because sociologists suddenly saw the light regarding religious resilience, but because this was the period in which modernity itself came more radically to be questioned. The combined and interacting effects of religious change and changes within the structures and cultures of modernity may be highlighted by examining the principal features of the postmodernizing world.

3 Postmodern Premonitions

Men, in their thousands, holding hands, singing, praying, marching. This is the scene in Washington DC one Sunday in October 1997. The Promise Keepers are on the move. A mass movement that has grown from nothing to a $90 million organization in less than half a decade, that sponsors rallies in sports stadiums, now hits the American capital. But what is it?

This Promise Keepers demonstration has all the trappings of religious revivalism (but without a Billy Graham figure at its center) and personal spiritual response is central. Yet it is patently political in thrust, otherwise why stage it in Washington DC? And it is for men only, which makes the issue of gender crucial. Highly controversial, much debate centers on whether this movement represents a positive or a negative response to feminism. The fact that there is a debate reveals something else about Promise Keepers – no clear, unequivocal statements exist on these matters, which allows for adherents to hold together apparently contradictory views. If one were to seek such statements, the quickest access to them is via the Internet.

In several respects, events such as the Promise Keepers demonstration offer premonitions of the postmodern in religion. Classic, mainline religious organizations are not involved, yet it is hardly a spontaneous happening. It is a coordinated, carefully orchestrated occurrence, dependent on networking and new media. It appears – because of its apparent tendency to reject abortion and gay rights – to lean to the (New) Right, and to make a political point by meeting where it does, but few voices admit to party affiliation. Indeed, there seems to be more than politics at work here, where family responsibility and racial reconciliation top the agenda. Although the majority are white, and have above-average incomes, strenuous efforts are made to include men of colour and from the working classes. It is gendered by definition, yet these are in some ways more like 1990s "New Men" than supporters of an older patriarchy. Women's opinions of the movement are mixed.

If events and movements such as those encountered in Promise Keepers are puzzling, it is in part because they are a product of new circumstances. Here we find men in a celebratory context, experiencing communal solidarity, and expressing their feelings through touching and through tears. The occasion is manifestly religious, but includes no references to religious organization, refers to no long-term memory and only lightly refers to canonical texts. While the focus of major rallies is local, the membership is networked over a broad geographical area using the Internet and the telephone. It is a social movement, whose history is brief and whose future is uncertain, and whose relation to other movements (feminism, the "secular" men's movement) is ambiguous. And it seems to refer to an identity as yet under construction – the non-chauvinist, non-racist religious male.

Postmodern reconnaissance

These new circumstances are postmodern ones. The condition of postmodernity is best thought of as a social-cultural configuration, whose contours became increasingly clear from the 1980s, and whose effects are felt in many parts of the world. Postmodernity results from the expansion of some aspects of modernity, at the expense of others, that serves to render modernity less recognizable as such. Above all, the postmodern relates to the development and diffusion of communication and information technologies, and to the growth of consumerism. These in turn both depend upon and stimulate global flows of information, cultural codes, wealth, and power. Other features of postmodernity include the reorganization of cities, the deregulation of financial markets and public utilities, the bypassing of nation-state power, leading to its partial obsolescence, global travel and tourism, experimentation with traditional life courses, and the sense of growing social and environmental risk.

The account of postmodernity offered here derives in part at least from a number of analyses, not all of which – paradoxically – accept the term "postmodernity" as the best way to describe contemporary conditions. Anthony Giddens, for instance, uses a number of terms, such as "high" or "reflexive" modernity, but stops short of "postmodernity."[1] Danièle Hervieu-Léger follows his use of "high" modernity. But they both discuss phenomena that can equally well be thought of as "postmodern."[2] At any rate, the work of a further two authors in particular is significant for what follows: Manuel Castells and Zygmunt Bauman. They are what might be called critical theorists, respectively, of the new technology and consumer aspects of contemporary conditions. I should add quickly that I refer to their work in so far as it illuminates contemporary conditions. This does not necessarily include religious and spiritual aspects of those conditions. Indeed, it is in part because fine authors such as these acknowledge the need to theorize the religious in fresh ways, but either do not go on to do so or do so in ways that leave some important gaps, that this present book was first conceived.

Castells, who encapsulates present conditions in the phrase "the information age,"[3] makes a persuasive case for a new sociology, for new times. The information technology revolution, starting in the 1970s, marks the beginnings of this development, and underpins all else. The social structure corresponding to this is the "network society," which is open and dynamic, highly appropriate to the innovative, globalized, decentralized capitalism to which it relates. What flows within the networks is crucial; indeed, for Castells flows are more significant than spaces and lead to restructuring and realignments of economy, polity, and culture. Who holds the switches in the network society holds power, but the switches are multiple and the flows of power unpredictable. On the ground, all this is experienced as, for instance, the appearance of a new production plant, owned multinationally, that briefly provides jobs for the local economy, before disappearing again, to be relocated where labour or taxation conditions are more favorable. Or it may be felt as financial fluctuations, when a butterfly wing-flap in an Asian economy reduces the capacity of a European country to buy exotic fruits from Central America.

The sense of living in a world where the unpredictable power of flows controls destinies, far beyond the political grasp of the nation state, let alone of the local community or the individual person, creates a tension, which Castells identifies as the new axis of social change. The network society cannot provide stable meanings and sources of identity, which once were related to associations (including churches), political parties, nation states, or local communities. So personal and communal identities become centrally important as sources of meaning, either – in Castells' account – proactively pulling towards a better future – feminism, environmentalism – or reactively harking back to a preferred past, related to God, family, ethnicity, family, locality.

The new creative tension point lies between the "net" and the "self." In the desire to find a sense of direction and purpose in a world of anonymously flowing power, identity construction becomes a central preoccupation, whether as resistance to exclusion outside the net, or as a project expressing a desire for a better future. What Castells views as reactive movements are often religiously informed quests for communal identity, whether in the Christian Right in the USA, in the Aum Shinrikyo cult in Japan, or in Islamic fundamentalism in, say, Pakistan. Whether Castells is right to see only as reactive the movements that refer explicitly to religious roots, and whether his own wistful comments about spiritual experimentation in the Third Millennium could be interpreted as an aspect of social theorizing, are questions that will be addressed later.

The network society and the power of identity are two central items within postmodernity, as I see it, and each relates to the influences traceable to the diffusion of communication and information technologies. But where Castells is strong on these, he makes less comment about the other feature that also permeates the postmodern: consumerism. This, however, is very much the centerpiece of Zygmunt Bauman's account of postmodernity.[4] While Castells still sees the work process as the center of social structure,[5] Bauman insists that in fact wage labor is being displaced by consumer freedom as the driving force of the social cultural system. It is pleasure in consuming that holds today's affluent societies together, not struggles for control between labor and capital. As Bauman puts it, consumption is moving "steadily into the position of, simultaneously, the cognitive and moral focus of life, the integrative bond of society, and the focus of systemic management."[6] Capitalism continues, but now working through consumer seduction.

In this world, political legitimation, central values, and dominant ideologies are no longer needed (according to Castells, they have in any case been bypassed by global flows). Unlimited consumer choice and a variety of tastes integrate everyone into a spending utopia. It is these factors that are behind the decline of certainty, and of authority, and the rise of what some call neo-tribalism. So life is increasingly experienced as pastiche, ambiguity, polyvalence, and, of course, uncertainty. At this point Bauman and Castells explain in different ways why fundamentalisms might be an authentic product of the postmodern. Observing that one – now discredited – source of moral guidance was religion, Bauman suggests that hyperconsumerism might be a cause of religious revival. In everyday life people are obliged more and more to choose between alternatives, political and moral as well as between commodities in the mall. Yet at the same time they are deprived of the universal guidance that modern self-confidence once promised. Bauman sees possibilities of religious returns in the attractions of expertise in moral guidance. In particular, fundamentalism is seen by Bauman not as an atavistic throwback but as a postmodern response to choice overload.

By connecting religious activity with consumerism, Bauman is onto something significant. But it must also be remembered that questions of choice have become increasingly important in modern times, especially since the Second World War, and have been discussed classically by philosophers such as Jean-Paul Sartre, who sensed acutely the "vertigo" of infinite possibilities. Consumer choices are perhaps less angst-filled than Bauman argues. We are guided into them by the niche marketers, and we are often offered pre-set packages that dull any pain of decision. On the other hand, as we shall see, religious responses may offer respite from such Disneyfied trivialization of choice, rather than the supposed agonies of choice themselves. Or again, it may be the confrontation with new existential choices for which consumerism ill prepares us that sparks interest in the sacred and the spiritual.[7]

Bauman's is similar to Giddens' argument about fundamentalism as a solid set of answers to moral questions thrown up by high modernity. Yet Bauman, like Giddens, thus limits his understanding of religion to issues of moral choice by individuals. Nothing is said of a Durkheimian collective "effervescence" (as might be seen in Promise Keepers or the mourning for Princess Diana, or in the Toronto Blessing), or of creative returns to a public role for conventional religion, or of the numerous new religious movements available today, both those relating to conventional religions and those taking a more deviant path. And when Bauman discusses religion more fully,[8] like Giddens and Castells, he leans heavily on analysts – such as Gilles Kepel[9] – whose studies are flawed through not taking religious activities seriously in their own right, or through assuming that what is true of one religious outlook is also true of another. On the other hand, it is refreshing to find that authors such as these acknowledge that the questions raised by fundamentalism demand answers – because they reveal and highlight society's ills.

The most significant current analyses of cultural shifts and social trends rightly focus more attention on the conditions they discuss than on whether or not it is possible to encapsulate them under one heading. My use of the word "postmodernity" to refer to the cluster of changes that relate particularly to the diffusion of CITs and to the rise of what might be called hyperconsumerism is a form of conceptual shorthand. It points on the one hand to the material sources of the key dynamics of transformations in the present, and on the other to its connections with the more intellectual and aesthetic dimensions of the same set of transformations. The latter I refer to, again as shorthand, as "postmodernism."

Postmodern*ity* relates to postmodern*ism* in that the social, economic, and political conditions discussed above encourage a sense of cultural fragmentation and diversity. Contact with other cultures raises on the one hand questions of authority, when the time-honoured homogeneity of national cultures is gradually broken down, and questions of cultural and personal identity, when beliefs and practices come under reflexive scrutiny within the fusing and mixing of cultures characteristic of globalizing situations. Travel, migration, and communications enable such culture contact, but at the same time everyday, local life is also affected by consumerism (and also by the inability of some to consume). Now that everyday life is part of a globalized system of commodity exchange, faith and commitment become more problematic, and less easily influenced by political, religious, and intellectual leaders. What is unsurprising in these contexts is to run across nostalgic quests to rediscover lost pasts and a search for anchor points within the swirling sea of opinion, lifestyles, and viewpoints. Social routines of time and space, disturbed once again by the postmodern, also pose cultural questions of some magnitude.

Split canopy to floating signs

Assuming, then, that it makes sense to speak of the postmodern, what differences do these conditions make to religious practices and activities? If once the contexts for understanding religion in the modern world included reliance on science and technology, the presence of industrial development, and the growth of urbanism, of the nation state, and of bureaucratic organization, along with an outlook generally framed by the notion of progress, then what has changed? Well, the key issues now have to do with CITs, with consumerism, with changing experiences of time and space, with new social movements, with a focus on the body and on identity, with a sense of fragmentation and of multi-directional development, and with a much more radically doubted authority. This is the global information age, expressed as postmodernity.

The modern world split apart the medieval sacred canopy that once sheltered much of Europe, and even extended to North America and elsewhere in more limited forms. Christendom stood little chance of survival after Protestantism created a rift between it and Roman

Catholicism, and then acted as midwife in the birth of modernity. The old alliances of church-and-state on both sides of the Atlantic were more and less radically questioned (depending on where you were), and a fault line appeared between the representatives of earthly and heavenly powers. Religion and society seemed to be parting company. At the same time, the modern world gradually became a taken-for-granted reality thoughout much of the world during the twentieth century, even if its supposed benefits were not exactly distributed evenly. Ideas such as "progress through democracy and science and technology," often derived in part from Christian religious sources, acted as generalized belief systems that at least gave the powers that be a sense of direction.

In the end, even the overarching ideals of modernity became tarnished and torn, with the result that French philosopher Jean-François Lyotard could eventually proclaim – perhaps prematurely – that the postmodern had arrived, seen as "incredulity towards all metanarratives."[10] Each little cultural and social segment could now exist in its own right, and refer to its own logic, without an apparent need for overall coherence. Even if Lyotard overstated his case, the significant thing is that as less and less can be taken as given, so more and more responsibility is placed on the individual to account for, and act in, the world. As Zygmunt Bauman puts it, this is "life in fragments,"[11] relating only to the floating signs that seem to merge and mix without any overarching meaning.

In terms of religion, the differentiation process that produced modern splits and specialization finally undermines religious organization, leaving the religious realm to develop in much more autonomous ways. Not just the grand sacred canopy of an old Christendom, but all religious metanarratives now start to look somewhat threadbare. Many commentators see this as a cultural crisis, from W. B. Yeats and T. S. Eliot earlier in the century to Alan Bloom, Neil Postman, Alasdair MacIntyre, and Charles Taylor today. This has also been echoed in explicitly Christian contexts in the later twentieth century; it may been felt, for instance, in the pages of the Catholic periodical *First Things*, and in the evangelical L'Abri Fellowship, which from the 1970s warned in numerous publications of the "death of culture," as Christianity seemed to be being squeezed out of artistic and intellectual life.

Looked at another way, within postmodern contexts the religious realm is increasingly deregulated, and the focus shifts from state-buttressing bureaucratic organization to clusters of networks without the necessary connection to older organizations, and individuals who seek their own meaning-routes[12] through the postmodern maze. This allows plenty of scope for what Mike Featherstone calls cultural "cross-overs" in the religious sphere. Beliefs and practices that once were sealed within an institutional form now flow freely over formerly policed boundaries. Syncretism, previously a problem peculiar to certain intellectual and theological settings, is now generalized and popularized, in practice as in belief. New possibilities emerge, creating liturgical smorgasbords, doctrinal potlucks. As the sacred canopy recedes and the floating signs multiply, the problem becomes less "how do I conform?" and more "how do I choose?" Peter Berger stresses this shift in his neat book subtitle "faith in an age of credulity."[13]

Danièle Hervieu-Léger suggests that, although traditional forms of religion may have lost some of their strength in modern conditions, those conditions also help to create space for religious expression. Rather like Durkheim, she sees modernity as built on certain utopian longings which, when unfulfilled, give rise to the religious in a variety of manifestations. So while older "lines of memory"[14] may become disturbed or broken, this does not mean that modern societies are incapable of repairing or replacing them. New meaning systems are being generated all the time, with more or less connection with traditional groups. Hervieu-Léger's examples from the French context include small "emotional" groups, ethno-religious groupings, and the Pope's European re-evangelization campaign involving, especially, young people. One could easily see other formations, such as Promise Keepers, in such categories.

Such observations need not be seen as a new phase of history, so much as prompting a fresh way of thinking about modernity, in which religion and culture are released from the grip of older elites and form new alliances and patterns, the outlines of which are, perhaps chronically, unclear. Postwar cultures, says Mike Featherstone,[15] have been de-monopolized. Tight control has weakened, and a range of "outsider" cultural goods is available. The fact that signs float does not necessarily mean that they float free, however. Religious commitments and activities, along with culture in general, retain their connections with the economy and polity, even while they return towards centre stage. Cultural fragmentation and the collapse of symbolic hierarchies have to do with a shift in value of symbolic power and cultural capital.

Beyond church and state

The splitting of the sacred canopy had political and administrative implications, best seen in the prising apart of church and state. But this was very much a modern move; mainstream religious organizations became bureaucratic in structure, and could respond to the similarly bureaucratic state. By the end of the twentieth century, however, it had become clear that whatever *entente* had been built between church and state, other factors were also at work. In the modern world, inequalities of class and status had stretched the capacity of any overarching, religiously rooted ideals to offer conditions of communication between unequals. And the state and the church as large-scale organizations found their power eroded and circumvented in the emerging conditions of postmodernity; and other kinds of relationships appear and other conflicts occur.

The boundaries also become more fuzzy, the more differentiation occurs, such that some argue that "dedifferentiation" starts to set in after a certain point. This is clearly seen in Disneyized consumer contexts such as airports, where all manner of business is transacted in addition to boarding planes. The proliferation of distinctions, in popular music for instance, can produce situations in which differences become less significant, and in which supposed contradictions between different spheres start to disappear. At this point the cultural reservoir can be drawn on increasingly at will. Dedifferentiated categories such as "world music" and "fusion" illustrate this tendency. Such shifts can be seen in various other contexts too: the ways in which the courts may be used to settle "religious" disputes, the growing importance of "body" issues, and the so-called "culture wars," seen especially strongly in the USA.

Whereas in early modern times the USA could look to religion as a sacred canopy that provided a means of communication between those divided by region, race, or family (even though women and blacks would have to wait some while for this to be fully worked out), today no such canopy exists, and in its place are *ad hoc*, managerial strategies. These latter are pursued by the courts, and depend upon a Disneyesque foreshortening of history. As Richard Fenn puts it, "A cultural lobotomy of sorts has allowed the Supreme Court to invent history, to misconstrue the intentions of Madison, and to create a series of legal fictions that allow the State to manage religion and the Church while appearing to adopt a hands-off or neutral policy under the rubric of a 'wall of separation' between Church and State."[16] The courts, lacking any picture of a whole society, still less of transcendent religion, simply play with the pieces in order to keep the maximum options of stakeholders open.

Fenn gives some marvellous examples of the inconsistencies that result from this. In an effort to "accommodate" all faiths while "advancing" none, as required by the American Constitution, one

Chief Justice Burger concluded that a Christmas manger scene in Pawtucket, Rhode Island, was permissible on the grounds that even the Supreme Court contains symbols of Moses and the Ten Commandments. The whole display in question – also Disneyesque – included a Santa Claus house, candy-striped poles, a Christmas tree, a cut-out clown, elephant, and teddy bear, a "Season's Greetings" banner and the crèche in question. If the inner logic of these items is hard to discern, so also is the logic of the judge's further jump to include as justification for his position the existence of government-supported masterpieces in the National Gallery, depicting the birth of Christ, the Last Supper, and the crucifixion.

Such amnesiac judgments deny what the framers of the American Constitution intended, observes Fenn, which was to "permit religion to inform the public sphere without threat of division caused by enthusiasm, bigotry and outright monopoly."[17] The effect of this and similar decisions is to confine the religious to the so-called private sphere of the individual, the family, and the institutions of private choice. In John O'Neill's words, this eliminates any notion of "gift, sacrifice, community" from informing the public sphere, leaving in their place "narcissistic consumerism."[18] In the end, concludes Fenn, "In place of critical theory, religion offers at best a consumer-basket of items for the consumption of the religious. . . ."[19]

Similar processes, in which background history is ignored for the sake of a permanent present, may have different effects in other countries. In France and Germany, for instance, (melo)dramatic media reports of cultic activities, such as those of the Branch Davidians at Waco, Texas, or the Solar Temple in Quebec and Switzerland, have led to measures with draconian implications being taken against certain religious groups. In Germany some charismatic and pentecostal groups – such as Full Gospel Business Fellowship – have been proscribed, and in France the activities of so-called *sectes* are monitored by a special government body set up for the purpose. Indeed, innocuous so-called sects and cults have become the objects of renewed moral panics, following all-too-real abuses or violence in specific deviant cases, such as the Solar Temple.[20] These panics may be read as a form of reaction to postmodern religious developments that occur outside both established secularity (Europe) and mainstream churches.[21]

When one considers the kinds of political struggle occurring in today's advanced societies it becomes clear that conventional church and state terminology does not describe them well. On the other hand, many such struggles clearly involve a clash between views that are religiously rooted and others that are not. The battle-lines are

drawn in ways that defy older logics of party political and denominational affiliation, yet the arenas of contest are much more public than
such older battles often were. They are in the public eye just because
of the proliferation of media coverage, which suggests that the very
meaning of "public" is changing. These battles and skirmishes are,
moreover, fought over terrain that usually has tremendous emotion-
laden stakes – James Davison Hunter describes the "culture wars" in
the USA as "the struggle to define America."[22]

Hunter describes in detail recent major cultural clashes over homosexuality, abortion, and the content of education, arguing that these
draw not on mere differences of opinion, but on "fundamentally
different conceptions of moral authority, over different ideas and
beliefs about truth, the good, obligation to one another, the nature of
community, and so on."[23] Thus, in the USA, where national identity
is for many a cherished item, this deep cultural conflict is seen as a
battle to (re)define the nation. It also touches many individual lives
and institutions. The conflict relates to the family, in so far as it is
about reproduction, abortion, sexuality, women and men, childraising,
and family definition. It affects what happens in public education
and in the media. Because it is often cast in the language of rights, it
is a legal debate, and one that often gives managerial responsibilities
to the courts. And it has an impact on politics, not only on which
become hot-button issues that may affect the politicians' electoral
chances, but also in the way that public discussions are handled.

Hunter concludes that these opposing moral visions become political chasms that threaten to further fragment the "common culture"
of the USA as they are taken up by single-issue pressure groups, and
as they are filtered by the various media of communication. It becomes less and less possible to take ambivalent or mediating stances,
because the logic of the culture wars pushes participants to take sides
as if there were clear binary oppositions. It was to test where public
opinions really lay that a later (1995) survey was carried out under
the auspices of the "Post-Modernity Project" to check the "state of
disunion" in America. It reveals that there are indeed a number of
competing moral languages for talking about politics, along with a
growing disaffection with conventional political process. On the other
hand, identity politics does not necessarily prevail across the population, except for a significant minority. It is noteworthy, however, that
that minority is mainly black and religiously liberal.[24]

It is not without interest that a central focus of the culture wars is
the body. Whereas once religious involvement was associated with
so-called bar-room vices, such as smoking and drinking, the body
itself is now at the forefront of debate, whether in relation to genetic

engineering, abortion, pornography, or the rights of gays and lesbians. While it is true that sharp divisions over these issues are most highly pronounced in the USA, they are also significant in other countries as well.[25]

Several reasons may be adduced for this foregrounding of the body, some of which again relate to a Christian legacy within many Western cultures. Technologically, it has become increasingly possible to intervene in and alter the body, and this coincides with the consumer emphasis on constructing the ideal body and the sense that little can be done about external influences upon the body. Self-identity is thus closely connected with the body, which raises the stakes when some body-related matter – from condoms to cloning – achieves controversial status. Modernity made a lot of the mind, especially as a means of controlling and regulating the body, but in a postmodernizing world, the body itself becomes a site of consumption, of controversy, and of conflict. Roman Catholic and Protestant theologies have placed different emphases on the body in modern times, with a lasting cultural effect of producing tensions between discipline and desire that may only now be working themselves out.[26]

The connection of body politics with the religious sphere points not only to questions of legitimacy and identity in postmodern contexts, but also to other boundaries, now made less salient. If the rending of the sacred canopy reduced some religious options for operating in the so-called public sphere, it is not a little ironic that "private" sphere issues, to which some religious activities were supposedly confined, have become politically volatile as the modern distinctions dissolve. This irony makes more sense, however, if we return to the basic distinction made by Castells, between the net and the self.

The net and the self

Castells' case is that, in a world increasingly dominated by the flows of power, wealth, and information within the network society, modes of resistance coalesce around the "power of identity." As people find in everyday life that power and experience part company, they try to find new ways of exerting some influence over their situations. For Castells, the mainstream churches, which once were linked with "legitimating identities," are now drained of their dynamic and compromised by residual associations with the state or the market.[27] But as legitimating identities are dispersed, what he calls resistance identities come into being, partly in reaction against those identities that once were felt to constrain and control. In the religious field Castells thinks of fundamentalisms as resistance identities. They form, he says, partly to compensate for the dissolution of older shared identities, and partly to counter the new demands and constraints of the network society. Beyond resistance identities, moreover, are other communal identities, structured around projects that aim positively to engender new social realities. Castells has nothing to say about how faith and spirituality might contribute to these. We shall see later how religious activity today is related to forward- as well as to backward-looking movements.

It is important to note that Castells also argues that this is a cultural turn, representing a qualitative change in human experience. If once human life was a struggle for survival against the forces of nature, which have then been increasingly "tamed" by culture in modern times, the information age – or, I suggest, postmodernity – human life is experienced more and more as a realm of culture. This is why, he says, "information is the key ingredient of our social organization and why flows of messages and images between networks constitute the basic thread of our social structure."[28] Now, Castells is probably right to note the demise of conventional religious organization, but it may turn out that religious activities have more resilience *across the whole spectrum of net-and-self* than he currently gives credence to. Religious activities may be associated with both net and self, in varied permutations, and indeed, may echo some significant structural changes taking place within postmodernizing situations.

During the twentieth century the dominant mode of church life was the denomination. These bureaucratic organizations, sometimes with links to business and cultural groups, which claimed no monopoly on the truth but worked within a framework of religious competition, were used by social scientists and opinion pollsters as a means of gauging the strength of religion. They were also a guide to ethnic composition and class location. Thus, in Canada, for example, Anglicans, usually English speaking, could be expected to vote Tory, United Church people for the New Democratic Party, and Catholics, often French speaking, for the Liberal Party. But at the turn of the twenty-first century, denominations are failing to maintain their erstwhile strength, some people switch at will between denominations, forsaking old family loyalties and theological preferences, while others may claim denominational ties but effectively ignore them, because they have ceased to attend services or church actitivies.

But new kinds of religious connectedness are emerging, even as the traditional hierarchies fade and fall. Some work with and through older containers; others leave them behind entirely. In his study of Canadian evangelicalism, for instance, John Stackhouse concludes that this Christian tendency exists more within loose affiliations and networks than in some specific identifiable settings. It may be found within mainstream denominations, but also within newer charismatic groups and fellowships. Even so, he points out, the old categories do not work any more; some *mentalités* are best thought of as "sectish" or "churchish" but not as "churches" or "sects" in the style of Ernst Troeltsch or S. D. Clark. But evangelicalism also exists, beyond formal local congregational structures, in para-church organizations, such as those involved with student campus activities (Inter-Varsity Christian Fellowship), high school or university-level educational institutions (such as Trinity Western University in British Columbia or St Paul's University in Ottawa), the mass media (such as Crossroads TV studios), or global relief programs (such as World Vision Canada).

The quest for some kind of antidote to the power of flows may well be sought in nostalgic forms of religion, but this need not take the forms of fundamentalism. Some traditional forms of religiosity are flourishing, especially in the more richly symbolic currents of Orthodoxy, Catholicism, and Anglicanism. At the same time, these may sometimes be merged with New Age ideas and ideals, such as happens at St James's Church, Piccadilly, in London, UK, and elsewhere. Easter, already reduced to a mere rite of spring, becomes less and less distinguishable from Earth Day celebrations. In other contexts the iconic and the communal may be sought within non-traditional settings, for instance in the churches meeting in pubs, particularly, again, in London. The culturally mainstream revival of "Celtic" music and art may also be combined with serious spiritual quests, which may also be found in new intentional communities.

Again, some interesting contrasts exist – as they probably always have existed – within the world of Bible believers and Jesus followers. Evangelicalism seems more elastic than it once was. One feature of this is groups growing out of grass roots and urban churches that deplore the parallel universe created by older evangelical subcultures. Often referred to as "post-evangelicals," they tend to embrace elements of the postmodern, and to accept aspects of contemporary culture that would once have been anathema. Dave Tomlinson, for example, working in London, UK, argues for a fresh hermeneutic for biblical interpretation, a renewed spirituality, one that learns from Roman Catholic and Orthodox traditions and shies away from the absolutism that he says characterizes some evangelical attitudes, especially to sexuality.[29]

The postmodern is viewed positively by Tomlinson, who associates it with the dignity of emotion and intuition, communication through symbol as well as words, an affinity with the environment, and a sense of global unity. It is suspicious of bureaucracy and hierarchy, and stresses the spiritual dimension of everyday life. Such sentiments are echoed in the antipodes by Mike Riddell, who also argues for an affirming postmodern stance.[30] Within the urban, plural, culturally juxtaposed, community-questing, high-tech, even apocalyptic and despairing world of the postmodern, Riddell argues that the church has a chance for a new beginning. Eschewing the safety of fundamentalism, Riddell prefers the risks of involvement and cultural engagement.

At the same time, some religious tendencies within evangelicalism seem to mirror the world of power flows. The 16,000-strong Willow Creek Community Church in Chicago, with its 1995 revenue in excess of US$22 million and the Crystal Cathedral in California are high-technology, megachurches which, like Disneyland, reflect some dominant tendencies within American culture. Willow Creek holds four weekend services to accommodate its large community, plus a midweek service for 6,000. The average age of those attending is 40, well below the American average church-attending age of 55. Despite attacks from denigrators that this is "religion lite,"[31] the Willow Creek Association now holds seminars to teach other churches how to market themselves. The challenge for all wealthy religious organizations, as we shall see, is how to transcend their cultural settings despite their extensive collusion with them.

Interestingly enough, it may again be religious groups outside Europe and North America that are able to recognize such collusion, and perhaps to find ways of extricating themselves, more quickly than those for whom the American way may be confused with the Christian way. Korean megachurches, for example, some of whom developed "prosperity gospels" not dissimilar from those in the USA, responded with "repentance" to the economic downtown affecting Asian economies in 1998. It seems that they took currency devaluation and growing unemployment as a cue for some internal spiritual stocktaking and for attempts to disentangle themselves from the competitive affluence that had started to characterize their activities.[32]

Postmodern pilgrims

If modernity produced what Peter Berger called "homeless minds," then postmodernity may be producing "homeless hearts." The postmodern mood is not merely cognitive, but affective too. The mobility of which Berger wrote has become even more marked. Hence the importance of being in touch, and of touching. A number of theorists have commented on ways in which the individual subject has become important in social structuring. Alain Touraine[33] and Manuel Castells suggest that subjects assert themselves in a world where autonomous self-definition has become difficult. New identities are sought that appeal to life, personal freedom, and creativity, and that seek emancipation, says Touraine, from transcendent principles and community rules.

This echoes, of course, the Romantically inspired expressive individualism of the 1960s, which came home to roost in the 1990s. As Charles Taylor says, this general cultural trend is premised on the view that "everyone has a right to develop their own form of life, grounded on their own sense of what is important or of value."[34] And it is unsurprising, especially given the now ironic contribution of some forms of Protestantism to that expressive individualism, that religious varieties of such postmodern self-construction may readily be observed. Spirituality comes to be seen as an aspect of the autonomous subject, in which, in Robert Wuthnow's words, "religious expression is becoming increasingly the product of individual biographies."[35]

Tracing individual paths of biographical identity-construction may be done by looking at the practices that are adopted to make sense of life, and this is the particular focus of Pierre Bourdieu's work. He argues that contemporary subjects choose their daily life-paths or "practices" within a "habitus."[36] The practices are both structured and fluid, while the habitus is the cumulative ensemble of cultural and personal experiences that accompanies each human being. Habitus has an impact on how one is perceived – identity – but also on patterns of interaction, and on the frames that guide social outcomes. These life-paths are also what Raymond Lemieux calls the "meaning routes" that people follow from day to day. In everyday practices people bring together their ethnic and religious backgrounds, but also the larger world and its choices and constraints that have brought them to each moment.

How can such practices be made visible? In the USA, Nancy Ammerman[37] finds evidence that Christian believers may use the services of a number of churches and religious organizations, without necessarily offering primary allegiance to any. One family she encountered in her research, the Penners, were United Methodists by denomination, but attended "Grief Relief" sessions at a Baptist church and had their children in day-care at yet another church. Religious actors tend to choose to construct religious identity in an ongoing, dynamic way, from the different offerings of religious groups. So, argues Ammerman, it is not a question of who is religious, or how religious they are, but "how religious rhetorics and practices are enacted and how they are situated in various organizational contexts."[38] Looked at this way, we may *expect* what from a modernist viewpoint would be called contradictions of belief and practice. Sociology should focus, then, on how people *make a life* rather than just on how they make sense.

Needless to say, those who think of themselves as autonomous spiritual subjects who construct their own religious identity through peculiar patterns of practices not only create new questions for social analysis but also for ongoing religious activity itself. In conventional religious organizations, attention is always paid to the matter of transmission, how particular beliefs are inculcated, traditions taught, and outsiders initiated into the faith. Danièle Hervieu-Léger[39] argues that, while the processes of restructuring religious identification multiply, lines of collective belief may yet be forming as the communal, emotional, ethical, and cultural dimensions of religious practice are recombined in fresh ways.

Within these processes, questions of gender loom large in postmodernizing contexts. The growing feminization of the clergy, male responses to feminization (of which Promise Keepers is an instance), and gay Christian movements are all significant aspects of this. In modern situations it became increasingly the case that women outnumbered men in church, even though men have tended to remain in power. In so far as the tasks of the church have forsaken the public for the personal realm, the closeness of women to birth and death has reinforced the women–religion link. Also, the general feminization of the professions has often led religious women to seek equality in (generally liberal) feminist ways.

Sympathies towards feminism have been reinforced in churches by the obvious lack of difference between churchgoers and the general population in levels of family violence,[40] and by the anxious protection of patriarchy within some religious communities and teachings. In addition, shifting boundaries have raised questions about the gender of God (seen strikingly in an early 1990s Minneapolis conference on re-imaging God) and about whether more mutable understandings of sexuality – to include gay and lesbian liaisons – are compatible with Christian or other traditionally religious teaching.

Situating the postmodern

It is worth pausing at this point to comment on the perspective adopted in the analyses that follow. For many, especially within religious folds, the appearance of postmodern conditions is threatening. Indeed, such responses are part of what is examined here. This is perfectly understandable. For example, on his twentieth anniversary in the Vatican,

Pope John Paul II issued an encyclical entitled *Fides et Ratio*, in which he made a plea for an end to the "fateful separation" of faith and reason. He attacked twentieth-century philosophies of post-Enlightenment rationalism, Marxism, *and* "postmodern nihilism." This may be seen, explained Archbishop Zycinski,[41] in the reduction of grand philosophical questions to "naive faith in UFOs, astrology and the New Age," but also, said the Pope, in "the widespread mentality which claims that a definitive commitment should no longer be made, because everything is fleeting and provisional."

This account is paralleled, for example, in the work of social theologian John Milbank, who claims that while the "secular reason" of modernity was insidious enough, its pernicious effects are amplified in the postmodern. Taking Nietzsche as his primary foil, Milbank insists that "postmodern suspicion is more drastic, more all-encompassing than that of modernism."[42] It is founded, he continues, on a dangerously destructive "ontology of violence" seen in ubiquitous, unavoidable power – the power of management, of expertise, of pure power against pure power. Even the church can be co-opted within this, argues Milbank, to become a "hellish anti-Church [that] confines Christianity like everything else, within the cycle of the ceaseless exhaustion and return of violence."[43] In this view, although for a brief moment the postmodern can unmask modern violence, in the end it too has to be refused. Milbank sees his task as opposing the postmodern with the "ontology of peace," expressed above all in the power-refusing cross of Christ.

These two examples of negativity towards the postmodern may easily be multiplied. Many such views exist, and many are as cogent and compelling. However, I suggest that other perspectives are permissible, but my hesitation regarding these accounts should be made clear. It is true that each tends to overplay the intellectual card and neglects the everyday influences of new media and consumerism. But they are not entirely unsociological; these comments do speak to social structural conditions. It is also evident that they speak from an explicitly religious standpoint, but this does not invalidate their work either – there is a significant sense in which all thought has some kind of religious roots, whether acknowledged or suppressed. Rather, my hesitation stems from two sources. First, the postmodern relates to social and cultural conditions, and thus is worthy of analysis as a way of structuring and influencing relationships. That analysis does not have to be carried out in what may be thought of as a postmodern*ist* fashion. This leads to the second point: there are in any case positive as well as negative stances within what is often called postmodern*ism*.

Pauline Rosenau suggests that postmodernisms should be thought of as positive as well as negative or, in her words, "affirming" as well as "skeptical." The popular preconception of postmodernism is of the skeptical variety. In this, the postmodern age is one of "fragmentation, disintegration, meaninglessness, malaise, a vagueness or even absence of moral parameters and societal chaos."[44] Grim, dark, apocalyptic despair about modernity is lightened only by the empty laughter of those who have shaken off illusions and drift in the play of words and meanings. This is the postmodernism of which the Pope and many other religious leaders take such a dim view. But there is another approach, perhaps better known in North America than in Europe, "affirmative postmodernism."

Affirmative postmodernists, while they may share some of the skeptics' critique of modernity, do not "shy away from affirming an ethic, making normative choices, and striving to build issue-specific political coalitions."[45] Indeed, they can also be heard arguing that certain value choices are superior to others. This is a helpful proposal, not least because it is difficult to see how "skeptical postmodernism" could ever make headway. Along with all other radical skepticisms, it is immediately defeated by its own logic. In terms of *perspectives* on the postmodern, then, a spectrum of positions is possible, and it is not necessary to take sides. Indeed, Rosenau points out that her scheme is not at all a mutually exclusive set of categories but, rather, a means of alerting us to the varieties of postmodernisms that are available today.

The postmodern may be situated, located, placed. While it is increasingly the context of contemporary life, it is not all-encompassing, even though its influence is felt everywhere. As far as the religious dimension is concerned, postmodernity contributes to the further fragmentation of institutional structures and intellectual belief systems, but the religious practices of believers and seekers reunite such fragments in fresh forms. Indeed, this may be seen in concerns with the body, and with the relation of the spiritual to everyday life, which is evident not only in some aspects of the New Age movement but also in the development of community building or earthkeeping emphases of more conventional religiosity. What will happen as religion, like the rest of life, is caught in the tension between the net and the self is unclear. As always, all social and cultural contexts offer positive and negative opportunities for both conventional and deregulated religion. The precarious path is one of discerning the essential and weighing the risks of radicalism. In what follows, postmodern premonitions are explored further, as we look at CITs and authority, consumerism and identity, space and globalization, and time and memory.

4 Signs of the Times

Father Ray, an inner-city priest whose parish lacks both congregation and cash, rolls out of bed, and puts on the coffee and a blues CD to help him wake up, before saying mass in front of one other soul – a fellow priest. Thus began a controversial TV show, "Nothing Sacred," networked by ABC, which was launched in North America in the fall of 1997. Father Ray employs Sidney, an atheist business manager, and is associated with Sister Maureen, who resents the depiction of God as male. He advises that conscience be a guide in matters – on which the Roman Catholic church itself is unequivocal – such as abortion and homosexuality; and he is not entirely clear about the extent of his personal faith.

The show was roundly condemned by the (American) Catholic League for Religious and Civil Rights – an "outrage" – and its appearance intensified the religious boycott campaign against the Walt Disney Company, owners of ABC television. The boycott, which started in the mid-1990s, by 1997 involved almost thirty major religious groups, including Focus on the Family, Morality in Media, and the Jewish Action Alliance. The American Family Association declared that the show was "not only blasphemous, but it is an insulting portrayal of the Catholic clergy and orthodox Christian teaching," and urged members to use their website list of advertising companies to complain about their sponsorship of the show.[1]

What is going on here? This controversy clearly counts as an episode in the continuing conflict between some religious groups and the media. From the earliest days of film and photography, charges of, among other things, blasphemy have been laid against portrayals of religious themes and persons. The earliest British Film Censorship rules prohibited the presenting of a "materialist Christ."[2] But equally, in the USA and in many other countries, Christian uses were made of the new media, primarily but not exclusively as a vehicle for evangelism. Now, following the partial withdrawal of the state from direct involvement in such wrangles, the blasphemy charges are made by churches against companies, for the courts to sort out.

However, the episode is revealing in a number of other respects as well. Indeed, several key features of the relations between the media and religion in postmodernizing situations are highlighted by this case, and I catalogue them in the first part of the chapter. This larger frame includes questions about the power of the media in network societies, and in particular about its relation to cultural authority and the construction of identity. This connects closely with the religious sphere, not least because the ways in which religious messages are delivered depend more and more upon conformity to new kinds of media. Thus the focus of this chapter is on religious communication, or even on religion *as* communication.

The relative decline of conventional religious organizations in the advanced societies has been accompanied by the growth of various kinds of religious association of a "parachurch" kind that express the increasing individualism of contemporary religious activities and quests and, at the same time, do so in a more specialized manner than was typical of more traditional churches. This means that religiously significant symbols are available in what is in effect a single market-place, dominated by the cultural commodification practices of the media industries.[3] At the same time, that market-place is extremely deregulated, so that signs circulate freely, and personal choice rather than traditional authority determines how they are appropriated.

Media power

What is the supposed influence of a show like "Nothing Sacred," such that its message is taken so seriously? Does TV really have the power to shape social relations, moral conduct, and belief? And, if so, in what ways? The Disney Company, like any other profit-seeking corporation, clearly has an eye to the ratings, and may well see controversy as furthering this end. The Catholic Church, on the other hand, equally clearly believes that the show has potential for serious harm. Moral guidance, already at a low premium, will probably be eroded even further by this depiction of an irresolute priest. Each of these positions is contested, and it could be argued that what is in fact sacred will be determined by negotiation over just this boundary.[4]

While the media may correctly be thought of as purveying messages, religious or otherwise, this is to limit our understanding to a conventional, substantive definition of religion (and, for that matter, of the media). It takes little account of the negotiation that occurs between media and audience in producing "effects." People construct religious meanings from the raw materials provided by the media, repositioning and patterning the elements according to logics both local and global, both innovative and traditional. In this sense, "Nothing Sacred" may be seen as but one item in a late-twentieth-century process in which the Disney Corporation has figured prominently – the proliferation of images and symbols within electronic media of all kinds, which are consumed in a variety of ways.

This is one of the defining features of postmodern times. Looked at this way, television shows are but one instance of the reproduction and multiplication of data and symbols that bring multifarious effects in their wake. Image and reality become blurred, leading to general cultural destabilization. Symbols are overproduced, and the resulting glut generates doubt for the receivers of and participants in communication. So far from the modern notion of knowledge yielding reassurance and predictability, this seems to create risk and provide the most obvious direct cause of structural uncertainty. The media are thus deeply implicated in the perturbation of conventional cultural configurations, which has become a principal feature of our times.

The point, almost too obvious to mention, is that the media mediate. They act as conduits for communication, and at the turn of the twenty-first century electronic media operate increasingly as the dominant context for cultural practices of communication. Thus, if one considers the American culture wars for instance, while some battles may be about media, all battles are fought on mediated terrain. As Hunter observes, this also helps to account for the polarization on issues that occur. Middle ground is eclipsed, he argues, not only because the discourse occurs among elites, or because the issues tend to be highly charged, or even because of the growing politics of suspicion. Polarization, he argues, "is intensified by and institutionalized through the very media by which the discussion takes place."[5] At the same time, TV soundbites and direct mail appeals tend towards shallowness, with the effect that, says Hunter, "we are left with a language and a moral reasoning that are as extreme as they are superficial."[6]

The fact that cultural practices of communciation are increasingly mediated electronically means more than the polarization of public debate, however. As far as religious communication is concerned, the integrated communication system based in electronic production weakens the symbolic power of senders who think they can "use" the system, just because the messages have to be recoded for the medium. Having to compete with soap operas and melodrama newscasts on TV, and chat-lines and niche-market commercials on the Internet, electronically mediated religious activity alters its character. Soundbites affect attention spans and the exaggerated polarization of positions may constrain the capacity to deal with complex issues of faith and life. The "televangelist" or the serious religious broadcaster or the interactive fundamentalist network may each be successful in this context, but only at a price. Each offers one message among many, and the competitive imperative is central. The final step, suggests Castells, is a paradoxical "conspicuous consumption of religion, under all kinds of generic and brand names . . . all wonders are on-line and can be combined into self-constructed image-worlds."[7]

And indeed, various kinds of evidence point to the role of these data, these symbols and images, in the construction of identities. Shows such as "Nothing Sacred" touch on this in two ways. First, by providing models of how people assemble religious identities by choosing elements that are "right for them," the conventional authority of the church, mosque, synagogue, or temple, along with its role in religious formation, is bypassed. Second, by simply parading the various religious and social options across the screen, this show, along with many others of course, itself provides resources that are thus available for appropriation and recombination as "new myths." Thus it is worth examining not just the portrayal of a Catholic priest whose doubts and desires are out in the open – the centerpiece of the heresy charge – but the subtler ways in which the media contribute to the processes of meaning and identity construction.

At every point, both "Nothing Sacred" and the broad debates over the new media of information and their associated communication practices are shot through with paradox and ambiguity. Media effects are not one-way only. Although in general they tend to contribute to structural uncertainty, they may also offer modes of reconfiguring the self and the body. While controversies may appear to have features of old debates – blasphemy versus opportunity, right versus left – the self-construction aspect may point to a fresh feature, a modern–postmodern tension.

In what follows, we explore these themes further, starting with the question of religion and communication, and contrasting older and newer communicative contexts: liturgy, the mass media, and cyberspace. The paradoxes and ambiguities of the emergence of a sign-saturated world are considered in terms of their relevance to religion. Both structural uncertainty, generated by new media, and the quest of new modes of social identity, resourced by the same media, are touched on, to be examined more fully in the next chapter.

Religious communication

A very promising way of overcoming traditional disciplinary divisions, such that a more integrated understanding of media and religion is made possible, is to focus on religion as communication. Peter Beyer argues for this approach as a means of discussing sociologically the dynamics of religion, seeing the basic dichotomy of the latter as immanence/transcendence.[8] The transcendent – the realm beyond observable reality – is communicated in immanent terms, and yet to deal with the immanent – that is, all observable reality – the transcendent must be posited as its partner. The sacred symbols of religion point beyond themselves to the transcendent realm, in order to give meaning to the immanent realm, with all its ambiguity, contingency, mortality, and suffering. The transcendent is beyond the immanent human world, but it is accessible through special means of communication.

In what follows I wish to follow this approach, in part at least, to look at the ways in which communicative contexts change. I begin by examining traditional modes of religious communication in liturgy, and move through other media to the most recent of communicative contexts, cyberspace. The mood and the method of these two ripple out well beyond cloisters and computers. I refer to the extremes of liturgy and cyberspace as signs that signify discourses and practices that characterize a culture. While liturgy speaks of a realm of authority, continuity, community, wholeness, and purpose, cyberspace hints at an exuberant anarchy and at the instantaneous, individualized, fragmentary, and inconsequential. The older mass media, between the two, follow from print culture and prepare the way for today's cyberspatial virtuality. My aim in what follows immediately is to explore the features of each rather than to argue for one over the other as a preferable or superior context.

While searching in Queen's University library for a different book I stumbled across *Liturgy and Society* by Gabriel Herbert, published in 1935. Herbert deplored the disintegration of modern life, the confusion of belief, and the falling into ruins of the towers of Babel that human idealism tries to build. Yet he hoped that in the sacred symbolism of liturgy his readers would find "an expression of reality, of the things that cannot be shaken, of the City that hath foundations, whose builder and Maker is God."[9] Apart from the very contemporary ring of his more-than-half-century-old cultural analysis, it is striking that for Herbert liturgy is a context in which a common life, a common conflict against evil, and help in the conflict can be expressed. As a way of avoiding what he saw as the shallowness of appeals for individual conversion or the rationalistic defence of propositional beliefs, he turns instead to the ancient authority of the church.

Time was, of course, when much of everyday life in medieval Europe found its touchstones of transcendent meaning in liturgical utterance. That ancient authority could solemnize a marriage, welcome an infant into this world, or dignify the corridor leading to the next. What few choices there were in premodern times often sought significance in the symbolic language of liturgy. Intentions and consequences were quite clear. In marriage, for instance, a binding declaration of mutual commitment – "I do," "I will" – was made, which only death could dissolve. Participants in the ceremony were also participants in the marriage, in that they entered a covenant to nurture the new relationship and to discourage any others from meddling with the marriage.

Other vestiges of the liturgical past besides marriage still find their place in ceremonies today. Prayer precedes the business of the Canadian House of Commons, as it does the British, as a reminder of the seriousness of what is said there, and oaths to speak the truth – all of it and only it – are taken on the Bible (or another religious book) in courts of law. As Richard Fenn notes, the seriousness of these kinds of words, often promises, depends partly on the context and partly on the relationship of speaker and hearer.[10] Words can always be slippery, but what renders them solid is the relationship of trust between the parties between whom they are exchanged. This trust, liturgically speaking, is ultimately between God and human beings. In Eden, the wedge of mistrust was driven in with the words "has God said?"

Liturgy as a communicative context and as a source of sacred symbolism has some interesting social characteristics. Authority is evident, not least from the fact that only certain people are authorized – often ordained – to lead liturgical events, but also that only certain statements are permitted. Changing the wording of a wedding service does not have infinite possibilities. (It is interesting, however, that precisely within new communicative contexts of the present the cry has arisen in some countries for the inclusion of same-sex relations within the marriage rubric.) Continuity is another feature of liturgy, connecting with similar settings several hundred – or in the case of the Orthodox churches and Judaism well over a thousand – years ago.

Similarly, liturgy presupposes community. It is fundamentally shared and deflects decisively away from personal opinion and private practice. Even the first person "I believe in God . . ." is meant to be said in unison with others, emphasizing only each believer's responsibility for the affirmation. Community in turn suggests wholeness; liturgy links participants with that which is beyond and bigger than us, but it also reminds them of their relation to the rest of creation. Then, lastly, liturgy points to purpose. While placing believers within a tried and tested tradition, liturgy also has a forward thrust. The Christian communion service, after all, is only "until He comes."

In all these respects, liturgy points beyond itself, to the transcendent. It refers to a reality outside, yet one that impinges on our human experience. In Christian liturgy, the word made flesh – incarnated – is discovered, and shares in human life so that humans might share in the divine. Daily, bodily life is hinged to a larger reality through words and through the Word. And because people experience each other as bodily presence, in face-to-face relationships, the word made flesh is mirrored in the everyday lives of participants.

As Kieran Flanagan rightly observes, however, "It cannot be said that liturgies operate at the centre of modern consciousness. To the secular mind, these Christian rites belong to a pre-modern age, relics of past anxieties which technology and modernity have assuaged."[11] Contemporaries are more likely to listen to the weather forecast than to pray for rain, and to heed opinion polls than to hold tenaciously to pre-set principles. By and large, we live in a communicative context quite different than that provided by liturgy. Where that earlier time was dominated by the written word and print, ours is increasingly an electronically mediated context. But does this mean that all religious communication somehow shrivels away (as Flanagan might be heard hinting), or might we find restructured or revised religious communication within altered communicative contexts?

Trials of televangelism

Central to the cultural story of the twentieth century is the rapid rise of the all-pervasive media of electrical and then electronic communication. Although the telephone was originally touted as a means of piping music into homes, the notion of mass media started with radio broadcasts, and by the postwar period became increasingly associated with television. Although many other media have joined TV, such as video games, compact disks, and, now, computer-based communications such as the Internet, TV is still dominant. TV is watched both for longer periods of time in a given day – second only to sleeping[12] – and over more of the globe than any other medium. By the early 1980s, for instance, *Dallas* was reaching a global audience of over a billion people. Above all it is this medium that theorists such as Marshall McLuhan, and after him Neil Postman, believe reconfigure the content of communications.

TV is also part of what Jürgen Habermas calls the public sphere, characteristic of modern societies, in which opinions are formed and attitudes shaped. TV helps to frame modes of interpretation and response to the social world by organizing experience in particular ways. Thus it has the effect of contributing to a sense of what the real world is all about. Paradoxically, however, there is more to this story than Habermas tells. Jean Baudrillard argues that in fact the mass media also blur the boundaries of reality by creating a continuum from the self-confessedly fictional to the supposedly documentary. The media today are highly commodified, and both create and reflect culture, in an ongoing, complex, dialogical fashion.

Religious organizations, led by Christian churches in the USA, were not slow to use new media during the twentieth century. Billy Graham and others pioneered the use of the mass media as a means of extending the evangelistic scope of their activities – that is, preaching to larger audiences – from the 1950s and 1960s. By the 1990s, the same Billy Graham was experimenting very successfully with satellite-linked MTV-style broadcasts to reach a postmodern "Generation X." Between the two periods, a religious industry had arisen in the USA, the "electronic church," which, contrary to the efforts of Graham, served to shift the communicative center of gravity out of church pews and into living-room couches. Despite being widely discredited through the scandals that became synonymous with the "prime time evangelists" in the 1980s, the electronic churches still flourish, and the idea has been exported to certain other religious markets, not least in Central and Latin America.[13] As we shall see, they have also diversified their product into newer media, such as the Internet.

The scandals, of course, made news headlines. Jim and Tammy Bakker, for instance, made fine footage for televangelism's detractors when their empire collapsed in disgrace in 1987. They had built an "Inspirational Network" worth US$3 million a week in donations, including those from "lifetime partners," who would receive the right to three nights lodging per year in their "ecclesiastic Disneyland"[14] called "Heritage USA" in South Carolina. This Christian theme park was a visible expression of the "prosperity doctrine" promoted by the Bakkers. Jim Bakker's undoing was a brief extramarital affair, but the disturbance brought to light activities for which he would be charged with mail fraud, wire fraud, and conspiracy, for which he was initially sentenced for 45 years. (This was reduced to 18 and then to eight, of which he actually served less than five.) Hence the stereotype of greedy and disingenuous televangelists, parasitic on a gullible public.

As Quentin Schultze rightly argues,[15] however, the stereotypes seriously mislead. Behind these stories, Schultze argues, are some basic social realities that seem to have eluded scandal-seeking journalists. Televangelists are a diverse group, representing different religious orientations; few are reactionary fundamentalists, though they are often politically conservative; and not all practice ecstatic utterance and divine healing. Graham, for instance, is clearly not a fundamentalist, is politically to the left of most well-known televangelists, and distances himself from the spectacular and the sentimental. Schultze shows that televangelism, or the electronic church, has a number of common characteristics. It is audience-supported, in the manner of commercial television, of which it is an outgrowth. It followed earlier models of "sawdust trail" and radio preachers, being supported though donations. Not surprisingly, televangelism is personality-led, modeled on Hollywood-style stars and celebrities, who rely on entertainment and are primarily performers. This is another way in which the medium recodes the message.

A further feature identified by Schultze is the experiential validation of televangelism. The American Dream, rather than reference to conventional Christian creeds and confessions, is its popular epistemological touchstone. This is conveyed, however, within highly sophisticated state-of-the-art technological systems, belying again the stereotype of TV preachers as premodern backwoodsmen. The electronic church also aims to expand, constantly, which is why, in order to compete, it tends to diversify into hunger relief and "family values" programs. Schultze concludes that the scandals besetting the electronic church are unlikely to slow it, primarily because, like Disneyland itself, the medium is an American product that also reflects dominant aspects of the culture whence it comes – materialist, hedonist, consumerist, and ethnocentric.[16]

The electronic church aims to promote specific forms of religiosity, using TV as its carrier. Religion appears in other guises on TV, however, such as in the *Nothing Sacred* series with which this chapter began. In this case, using the same medium, the show both questions received religious authority and offers models for self-identification. It is the former, primarily, that kindled the ire of the protesters, because the institutional church is exposed in its – fictional but not far-fetched – contradictions and compromises. Still, the latter role, of offering potential for self-identification, may be an equally powerful process. TV, and particularly shows such as this one, with its earthy realism, can be a source of plausibility, a structure for supporting the emergent self.

At the same time, to limit discussion of the social and cultural meaning of the mass media – thinking primarily, of course, of TV – to its religious uses, or its portrayals of religion, would be to miss some of the main points of current media analysis. Questions about the disintegration of authority and about the – sometimes religious – reintegration of the self through identity-construction are central to such analysis, whether or not the religious is explicitly in view. Issues of pluralism and the postmodern touch directly on the matter of authority, and are highlighted, for instance, in the work of Italian philosopher Gianni Vattimo. In addition, questions of reality are raised by media analysis, most provocatively, perhaps, by Baudrillard.

Vattimo argues that there are two crucial contributors to the break-down of a single, western, authoritative, Christianly coded, scientific-ally warranted voice in the postmodernizing world. One is the collapse of colonialism, and the other is the rise of communication and information technologies to make what he calls the "society of communication."[17] Modern history, according to Vattimo, recounted the story of those in power, but the demise of imperialism and colonialism also undermines the intellectual superiority of the West, and produces "no single history, only images from the past projected from different points of view."[18] The possibility of hearing other voices is vastly amplified by contemporary media.

Vattimo sees the profusion of tongues, the diversity of dialects, enabled by the media, as a new emancipatory Babel. The resulting disorientation, he insists, reminds each person that his or her language is not the only one, and propels people into a process of hearing, understanding, and interpreting between themselves and others. (He has obviously not spent much time watching televangelists!) The multiplicity of local rationalities, of ethnic, sexual, religious, cultural, and aesthetic minorities, may finally be heard in their own right. No longer cowed into silence by the need to conform to a fixed reality, each discovers its own voice, its own dignity. The old idea, that out of the perfect knowledge produced by the Enlightenment would grow freedom, is a pernicious myth, whose falsity is made clear only within the society of communication.

There is something to the Vattimo thesis, even if he has exaggerated the liberatory potential of CITs in his enthusiasm for the dissolution of the Enlightenment grand narratives. But by connecting it with the Enlightenment, Vattimo betrays his intellectual approach, which finally fails to touch down firmly on the everyday experience of the new media (and of consumerism, the topic of the next chapter). The cultural pluralism enabled by the CITs, and above all by TV, does contribute to their more generally relativizing effect. Again, Vattimo is probably right about the unravelling of single-thread histories in postcolonial accounts of the world, but TV, MTV, video, and CDs are likely to have an even more corrosive effect. As Akbar Ahmed says, the threat to Islam today is not so much Jesus as Madonna.[19]

The most controversial but also in some respects one of the most insightful analysts of the mass media is Parisian sociologist Jean Baudrillard. For him reality itself is revised by the media. Although symbolic exchanges were once primarily face-to-face, and then latterly used print media, it is images from electronic media that are culturally dominant at the end of the twentieth century, argues Baudrillard. Today's hyper-real world dissolves the distinctions between objects and their representations, leaving only simulacra, which refer to nothing but themselves. Although this may be seen *par excellence* in TV advertising, the process is a general one according to Baudrillard. Signs lose contact with the things signified, and meaning vanishes. In any case, insisted Baudrillard in the early phase of his work, in this world the masses no longer want meaning; they seek spectacle instead.

For Baudrillard, the world of media is entirely fragmented, ironic, constructed, and simulated, which is indeed a far cry from the authoritative world of high culture that it replaces. But this world is not merely the one in which audiences consume images, but also the supposedly real one in which money is made and things produced. As he notes, millions of dollars can now be made on the stock market without anything being produced or a worker meeting an employer. Earlier, he analyzed the consumer world, where the utility of goods and services is absorbed into the images and signs associated with them. More recently he has argued that a fractal stage has been reached, in which value circulates without any reference to people, things, or any driving logic save that of its own momentum.[20] Symbolic exchanges in the world of embodied people seem to have dropped out of the picture.

One could argue that, just as telecommuting facilities allow employees to work without going to the office, or telematics permit managers to control production without being on site, so a phenomenon like the electronic church – now also in on-line form – enables believers to participate in acts of worship and religious devotion without attending a place of worship. But what are the implications of this for a human sense of what is real? Is the (joyful) disorientation of which Vattimo speaks to be extended to this sphere? The sense of disorientation, let me repeat, is not merely cognitive. Baudrillard's hyper-real world is one that goes beyond the intellectual realm of Vattimo into the sensual realm of bodies, experiences and emotions.[21] Perhaps this partly explains the popularity of physical healing and of remote touch within the repertoire of televangelists. At any rate, these questions cannot fully be addressed without looking at the most recent forms of electronic media(tion), cyberspace, and virtual reality.

Going to cyberchurch

The very idea of "going" to cyberchurch involves a fiction. In cyber-speak the virtual spaces of the Internet are "visited" by their users even though literal geography and movement are not involved. This is a postmodern aspect of cyberspace, superimposed on the very modern high technology that enables it and the commercial impulse that now drives it. That aside, is it even possible to characterize cyber-religion sociologically? Very little work has been done in this area, although, given the ease of researching at least the more obvious on-line aspects of the phenomenon, it is becoming a popular field of study. In what follows, while other aspects of the relations between the postmodern and cyberspace are explored, the particular focus of this section is the religious connection.

On the one hand, some so-called cybernauts find God in the medium itself: "people see the Net as a new metaphor for God" declares sociologist Sherry Turkle. "God *is* the distributed, decentralized system."[22] A little – but not much – more guardedly than such "info-mystics," William Gibson suggests that the Net "may regard itself as God. And it may be God on its own terms." At a 1997 Massachusetts Institute of Technology conference Charles Henderson proposed that in the 1930s Teilhard de Chardin had predicted the arrival of cyberspace spirituality in his concept of the "noosphere," a realm beyond the biosphere, towards which humans are evolving.[23] On the other, rather more sociological hand, Lorne Dawson and Jenna Hennebry ask, "Is the 'disembedded' social reality of life in cyberspace contributing to the transformation of religion into a 'cultural resource' in a postmodern society?"[24]

In the 1980s cyberspace was just a new word in a sci-fi novel, William Gibson's *Neuromancer*.[25] Today cyberspace is used freely to describe a world mediated by computer networks, a world of direct access to a digital realm of information and communication technology. In a kind of realized prophecy, fiction becomes fact (at least for the minority who can afford it). Jean-François Lyotard argued that this is a key to the emerging new social and cultural reality, and he traces the way that computerization leads to a loss of meaning. "Narrative knowledge is replaced by a plurality of language games, universalism by localism."[26] Baudrillard also points to this new situation, arguing that new forms of technology and information are central to a shift from a productive to a reproductive order, where simulations and models constitute the world so that the distinction between reality and image is erased.

Cyberspace is inhabited both by total devotees – as Gibson's *Neuromancer* has it, "wrapped in media . . . excluding daily life" – and by ordinary souls like me who simply rely on a handy means of quick, cheap, worldwide communication, e-mail. Cyberspace is used here as a metaphor for electronically mediated communication. In this communicative context, people are literally absent from each other as bodies, however literarily close they might be, courtesy of telephone lines, e-mail text, video image, or electronic impulse. When Gibson says "wrapped in media," then, several meanings are possible. People could be preoccupied, absorbed with their digital companions – as kids with Nintendo or computer buffs with their keyboards – but there is also a sense in which they are available to others only *through* these media.

The blurring of fact and fiction is not new, but the context, arguably, is. Cyberspace is in some senses both child and parent of the postmodern, which complicates matters. One aspect of this is that doubt is entertained about the taken-for-granted verities of the Enlightenment, such as confidence in science and technology to promote progress. Another aspect is that information and communication technologies themselves are helping to hasten the breakdown of conventional, modern ways. *Neuromancer* is rightly described as a postmodern novel, and it epitomizes the cultural dimensions of the technological shifts it portrays. In this world, fluidity, not fixity, is the norm. New technologies are marked by their capacity to bend and melt rather than to structure and solidify reality. Three aspects of this may be distinguished.

Firstly, cyberspace is a relatively open medium. In cyberspace, it is often said, anything goes (or, at least, almost anything). In contrast with a world in which authoritative statements are made and heeded – like liturgy, royal command, or legal summons – cyberspace knows no priorities, respects no precedents, promotes no principles. But there are limits to this. Unlike the telephone, it is less than a common carrier. Some of its conduits are blocked at family level (for instance, using "netnanny"), organizational level (where employers permit access only to certain specific sites), or state level (where providers are regulated). There are indeed many voices, but often the messages are a *mélange*, untraceable to any single source. The medium can indeed be used for almost anything; but it cannot simply be "used." The medium also creates new problems in each sphere.

What is happening is the topic of much debate. It is not a clash between word and image, although in the process the word does get devalued. It is not a switch to the society of the spectacle either. Although passive consumption is a large part of the story, cyberspace also stimulates more interactive participation than TV does. Indeed, cyberspace is already being used as a communicative context for weddings: people marry electronically. In its virtual reality aspect, cybersex is also available, as seen for instance in the film *Lawnmower Man*, surely the safest of safe sex yet. A new narrative, a new story line for sex, is here inscribed on the body. In cyberspace, it seems, flesh becomes word, which lives among us, malleable and pointing only to itself. Is this deincarnation?

Secondly, reality slips out of focus. Some have claimed that *Neuromancer*'s cyberspace inspired the developers of virtual reality (although Gibson himself says many miss layers of irony in his novel). In any case, virtual reality, the electronic simulation of environments, is more and more widely used. Queen's University, where I work, boasts an advanced VR lab. Research subjects can mount and control a bike and experience many sights and sensations of riding through vastly differing landscapes and conditions without ever moving in physical space beyond the lab. Televirtuality, the capacity to share such three-dimensional environments over a telecommunications network, is believed by some pundits to be a next step, with great entertainment, work, and educational potential. Mercifully, technical potential is not social destiny.

All this challenges the conventional notion, common to many moderns and to followers of the Abrahamic faiths, that a single universe exists out there, independent of our perception. Reality is not what it used to be, and now electronics, not just drugs, offer entry into virtuality. Life itself appears to be a more fluid category; Stephen Hawking is the latest to lend his name to the view that computer viruses constitute (albeit parasitic) life-forms.[27] Does this amount to artificial life? As French new-technology theorist Paul Virilio says, "The true problem with virtual reality is that orientation is no longer possible. We have lost our points of reference. . . ."[28] But he continues, "the ironic outcome of this technoscientific development is a renewed need for the idea of God. Many people question their religious identity today. . . ."[29]

Lastly, then, consider the virtual self. Once again, nothing is straightforward, because the self is both central and fragmented. Cybernauts recognize that identity is in question on-line. One says that "we who populate cyberspaces deliberately experiment with fracturing traditional notions of identity by living as multiple simultaneous personae in different virtual neighbourhoods."[30] It is important to note that data about as well as from or for us also circulate freely in cyberspace. Virtual selves are created in part by marketing companies and government departments whose composite but partial pictures of us pass as our data image, to be supplemented by every remote transaction we make, wittingly – at the bank machine – or unwittingly – when caught in the photo-radar speed trap.

At the same time, the self is believed to be at the core of the information universe of cyberspace, choosing, communicating, controlling. Young people in the electronic arcade find themselves in charge of powerful machines to fight or race, on earth or in space. This is an exhilarating contrast to the meaning-drained routines of school, street, or home. As Benjamin Woolley rightly observes, "the sight of someone wearing a virtual reality headset is the ultimate image of solipsistic self-absorption."[31] God-like control is bestowed upon mortals by the power of computers and the grace of VR.

Postmodern selves are constructed in different but complementary ways. For some, especially but not only younger people, as we shall see, self is the outcome of consumer choices, in which symbols such as brand names and Disneyesque merchandising logos feature strongly. For others, self is part of therapeutic regimes or a quest for intimacy. For cybernauts, self is construed as the digital personae developed within electronic communication. Either way, identity is not so much given – by family name or as the image of God – or ascribed, as produced, the result of a continuing process of discovery. Selfhood becomes a postmodern project. Modern style control is still sought, but meaning is less than apparent.

Earlier I suggested that, in contrast with liturgy's world of authority, continuity, community, wholeness, and purpose, cyberspace offers anarchy, the instant, the individualistic, the fragmented, and the inconsequential. The anarchic dimension is seen in the relative lack of law or governance in cyberspace. It remains an undefined, largely unregulated realm where authority is inherently dubitable. For one thing, multiple authorship by electronic accretion is common, on bulletin boards for example; and for another, the lack of supplementary signals such as body language or tone inflection has contributed to a blurring of conventional communicative boundaries and thus a breaking of hierarchy. A sense of limitlessness, of ecstasy, is available in cyberspace. Whether illusory or not in more conventional terms, its devotees undoubtedly find it desirable.

If authority is questionable, so are categories like time. Distinctions have to be made between "real time" and the asynchronous dimension within which messages are passed to and fro. E-mail users enjoy what the medium offers by way of speed and ease of communication. Because messages are stored it matters little when users log on. Until this capacity became available, instant communication depended on two parties being on the ends of a telephone line or on a TV company broadcasting and audiences switching on their sets at the right moment. Lives once regulated by rhythms of season and light gave way to ones coordinated by timetable and schedule. Electronic media, represented by cyberspace, break the connection between time, space, and communication. But they tend to have more impact on space than on time. Reach and flexibility are favored over permanence.[32] This general question of religion in cyberspace is tremendously important and connects with the issue of time discussed more broadly in chapter 7. The question of community in cyberspace, on the other hand, is particular and practical.

While great debates occur about the creation of new communities in cyberspace, the reality is rather mundane. One is tempted to wonder if cyberspace is more than merely a handy distraction from the real world.[33] Just as a peculiar kind of individualism prevails in automobile use, so much evidence suggests that a similar trend is observable with computers. The electronic mediation of communication does not necessarily enhance community. At best, the Internet may be used, like any other relevant medium, for adding another dimension to already existing communal networks.[34] Because this medium "attenuates presence by enabling only disembodied and abstract connections between persons" argues Holmes, "and the number of means of recognizing another person declines . . . commitment to co-operative or collective projects become one-dimensional, or, at best, self-referential."[35]

There is promise, so some claim, of educative, democratic, and emancipatory potential in cyberspace. British Telecom's electronic university idea and various electronic town hall projects – such as "Iperbole" in Bologna, Italy – are cases in point. Many social movements make use of the Internet to promote their positions, or to network with others of like mind. Unsurprisingly churches, too, are realizing the potential of cyberspace for explaining their views, proselytizing, and networking. Religions old and new use the Internet in fairly conventional ways, for promotion and publicity purposes.[36] On an academic level theological groups find the opportunities for discussions with distant people especially useful, not only in the far-flung geography of Canada or Australia, but worldwide.

The capacities ushered in by new technologies probably offer as many opportunities for fragmentation as for harmonious interaction. There is little evidence as yet of cyberspace creating a world of organic wholeness, whereas there is plenty to suggest an explosive multiplication of minor interests and specialized tastes using this medium. If the communicative context does not appeal, a fresh network can always start up. As in Disneyland, another attraction always awaits the media nomad. But it may well be that countervailing tendencies develop. On the one hand, religious hybrids and idiosyncratic theologies are likely to continue appearing on the web. Moreover, conflict between different groups may produce doctrinal skirmishes in cyberspace. But on the other hand, given the growing sophistication and expense of using the web, religious institutions and movements with money may be the ones that reassert their presence.[37]

More soberly, both rabid bigotry and electronic ecumenism may be found on the Internet. In so far as it is a common carrier, it acts as a crucible for sometimes explosive exchanges in the chat rooms, offering space for views forbidden elsewhere, and for direct confrontations between religious groups at loggerheads with one another, particularly over the issue of conversion from one major faith to another. The Nation of Islam was probably the first quasi-religious site to be sabotaged by an angry hacker, who left a message, claiming responsibility. The American Family Foundation offers a counter-cult site, but also links to the official sites of New Religious Movements. Other sites run by eccentric individuals may be less circumspect. One of them accuses Jehovah's Witnesses of resorting to subliminal messages to aid their cause.[38] At the same time, by clicking on linked sites more erudite users can also explore the possibilities of "hypertheology," connecting, for instance, texts in the Qur'ān with those in the Bible. Enthusiasts for this approach believe that it provides a crucial tool for mutual understanding and for isolating real as distinct from prejudicial differences between religious ways.

Those using the new media for religious purposes range from the local church setting up a website – a vital step for any religious group that does not wish to appear unconnected with the present generation – to any crank, charlatan, controversialist, or comic who seizes the chance of widespread publicity for his splinter-sect. There are groups such as the Starseed Schools of Melchizedek and the Aquarian Concepts Community Divine New Order Government alongside the rather better known Wicca, Gaia, Druidism, and Pantheism. The Universal Life Church offers ordination for a mere double-click. One may also visit the First Cyberchurch of the Scientific God or – perhaps with some relief – attend the Virtual Perfect Church. No doubt, like cybersex, participating in this will be safe, risk-free (they boast an animated vision of Jesus walking on the water, although the waves are rather tame). At the Alpha and Omega Almighty Wind Holy Ghost Fire Church you will meet Messianic Jews, and at the Internet Church a 17-year-old pastor. So it goes.

In a deregulated marketplace, where cultural commodification practices proliferate, the sacred symbols of religious communication circulate unpredictably, promiscuously. In the expanding public sphere numerous opportunities present themselves for what a *Time* magazine article, in its lyrical closing moments, described as the chance that ordinary people "working as one, can create on this World Wide Web that binds all of us, Christian and Jew, Muslim and Buddhist, together. Interconnected, we may be able to find God in places we never imagined."[39] But, as we have seen, cyberspace is not by any stretch of the imagination a kind of pure public sphere as in Habermasian theory. It is also the locus of the hyper-real, where reality itself is destabilized, and authority is grasped by any who can. More likely, authority itself is demoted, to be supplanted by identity, or the quest of identity, where the religious self is constructed and flourishes on terms chosen individually.

How far the electronic church, and now cyberchurches, will grow is impossible to predict. However, in the post-denominational world of parachurch organizational networks and proliferating new religious movements, where believing without belonging is an increasingly popular religious position, these options appear to correspond least with felt needs and aspirations. According to some theorists, the sheer mass of available alternatives may produce divergent effects. The cyber-religious may prefer to keep their options open, of course, with limited involvement in several religious groups. At the same time, the plethora of choices may also encourage the development of truly different, exclusive religious options. This would be paradoxical, given the apparent bias of the medium to openness and inclusivity.[40]

Evidence suggests that those who "participate" in the electronic church are likely already to be believers who share the basic outlook of the programs.[41] It may turn out that devotees of cyber-religiosity have comparable predilections. And if what we know about other spheres is anything to go by, on-line connections with the off-line world will be vital to any continuity that cyberchurches are capable of ensuring. Further research is thus required into what Castells calls the "self-constructed image-worlds" within today's "conspicuous consumption of religion."[42] As these phrases remind us, communications and consumerism must be understood in relation to each other.

5 Shopping for a Self

In 1999 a winter week in Britain was dominated by the news that Glenn Hoddle, coach of the England soccer team, had lost his job. The point of recalling this is not that soccer has religious status in Europe, or that the prime minister was involved in the controversy, or even that the media were particularly starved for newsworthy items that week. Rather, the significance of the apparently trivial *brouhaha* was this: Hoddle was obliged to forsake his elevated occupation because of a religious statement: "You and I have been physically given two hands and two legs and half-decent brains. Some people have not been born like that for a reason. The karma is working from another lifetime. I have nothing to hide about that. It is not only people with disabilities. What you sow, you have to reap."[1] This is no ordinary religious statement. The perceived problem in Britain was the offence thus given to people with disabilities, because Hoddle seemed to be suggesting that their condition is their fault. Little was said, at the time, about the possible problems that the firing could have for others in Britain who might believe in karma.

But is the statement so extraordinary? To claim that it is is to betray a position: it is to say that religious beliefs ought to be coherent, internally consistent, plus, perhaps, private. In today's world, such claims are losing credibility. Statements of mixed religious belief are actually becoming more ordinary, more commonplace. Hoddle's apparent Hinduism is hitched to a biblical phrase about reaping what you sow. Indeed, for the first few days of the storm, Hoddle's supposedly "born-again" beliefs were in the foreground. But how did that square with his consulting a New Age faith healer, Eileen Drewery ("the woman taken in credulity" as one newspaper put it[2])? The answer, it transpired, was that Hoddle's apparent evangelicalism ("born again" beliefs) was more than a little tenuous. So what exactly did he believe?

Owing to his prominent position, Hoddle had in fact explained his beliefs to more than one interviewer and biographer. Their main three elements were an admiration for Christ and a knowledge of some scattered Bible verses; Hinduism and, particularly, reincarnation; and Romanticism. The latter is of the kind that stresses personal spiritual authority beyond the reach of churches, and a sense of destiny which in his case included the belief that he would manage the England team.[3] This kind of mixture is not particularly unusual. In North America and (even more) in Europe, many liberal Christians combine their faith with a belief in reincarnation.[4] This mixture, now including Romanticism as well, is often thought of as being part of the New Age. In this outlook, emotion and intuition often rank higher in value than mere intellect, thus downplaying coherence. And as the self is the reference point, external authority, or a community of faith, counts for little. As Hoddle explained, ". . . my faith in God is at spirit level . . . a very individual situation."[5]

So Hoddle's destructively public mistake, allowing these "very individual" beliefs to be expressed in a leading newspaper, cost him his job. But it also brought into the limelight the constellation of beliefs that are held by many in the globalizing world today. The evidence referred to above shows that more and more people can both claim some fairly conventional religious position and cheerfully add on other elements, Feng Shui, yoga, mysticism, astrology, Shiatsu, Reiki, and the rest. It has been likened to souvenir hunting, bringing back exotic cultural items to adorn one's personal pantheon, or to cocktail creation, mixing divine drinks to individual taste.[6] Many also make the connection with consumer culture, in which one develops a pick'n'mix approach within the spiritual supermarket. Consuming has become central to social life in new ways. There is more to these tropes than just colorful description. Hoddle's sense of identity was completely bound up with his particular set of beliefs, in a way that both directed and then destroyed his career.

Consumerism has become central to the social and cultural life of the technologically advanced societies in the later twentieth century. Meaning is sought as a "redemptive gospel" in consumption.[7] And cultural identities are formed through processes of selective consumption. As Robert Bocock says, "Consumption now affects the ways in which people build up, and maintain, a sense of who they are, of who they wish to be."[8] If the new media yield fragments of former systems as images and symbols, then consumer processes are implicated in reassembling these fragments into a constantly shifting pattern, customized by and for the individual. This kind of process is also at work in religious identity-construction: how people make sense – or, rather, make a life – religiously, at the ordinary, mundane, everyday level.

The process is a challenge to religious institutions, on several levels. It may be seen – with qualification – in terms of an economic model, in which cultural and religious monopolies are being dismantled, and a deregulated cultural market-place is emerging. So the old institutions lose business, and are unable to compete. Believing subjects show no particular loss of interest in matters that once were the concern of religious institutions (indeed, in many countries religious interest indices show an upswing), but seek to satisfy that interest in ways that sideline the old institutions. Patterns of belief are discernible, and these seem to combine elements from the old with a streak of self-determination in religious choices. Who needs the authority of religious specialists when the autonomous individual can choose for herself? Such patterns also raise questions about time, space, authority, and truth. This may be seen in conventional religious options and also in the New Age, which again offers a means of combining old and new features of the religious quest.

The same processes may also help to generate other forms of religious practice, not least fundamentalisms, which could be viewed as negative responses, both to the disintegration of authority and to the relatively autonomous ways in which fresh religious identities are put together. A number of factors – the vulnerability of the choosing subject to charismatic figures, the choice-overload from consumerism (with its lack of guidelines and reference points), and unease with the trivialization of choice – offer a chance for retrenchment and trust in new authority figures, absolute truths, and fixed certainties. Structural uncertainty, generated by floating symbols and other voices and institutionalized in apparently infinite consumer choice, finds an antidote in fundamentalisms, which may turn out to have particular importance as a postmodern religious form.

This chapter aims to explore two areas that have mainly been considered separately. On the one hand, many who discuss the putative postmodern condition argue that several things are occurring here. Consumption moves to centre stage, it democratizes culture – Disneyland is paradigmatic of this – as choices are made between a range of circulating signs, it becomes increasingly dedifferentiated, thus breaking down old boundaries, and it displaces at least some aspects of culture that may once have been more related to work. In particular, the sense of personal and cultural identity may fragment, under bombardment from signs and images, with the result that self-construction is carried out in an ongoing, piecemeal fashion, and multiple or serial identities may result. As Daniel Bell put it, the emerging situation may be seen in the paradox of the person who is a puritan in the daytime and a playboy at night.[9]

On the other hand, it has become a truism that religious activity is, increasingly, subject to personal choice, or voluntarism, and that, increasingly, for many in the advanced societies, religious identities are assembled to create a bricolage of beliefs and practices. From an early suggestion of Peter Berger[10] that the contemporary religious world resembles a supermarket, in which customers are shopping for suitable commodities that are right for them, to today's rational choice theories of religious behaviour,[11] consumption has become central to many sociologies of religion. Thus Reginald Bibby can talk of "religion as a consumer item" that is available "à la carte" at least in turn-of-the-century Canada.[12] He even sees the current difficulties of religious suppliers as being "product, promotion, and distribution problems."[13] While the economic model has some merit, however, it also has limitations, some of which are examined briefly below.

Despite the fact that much of the literature on identity, certainly since Max Weber, has focussed on how identities might be formed in a time of religious disenchantment, only a few authors discussing postmodern self-construction examine the religious aspects of the process. And, although analyses of consumer religion are coincident with explorations of the postmodern, not much from the latter debate has been permitted to inform the former. Bringing the two together, at least in a tentative and programmatic way, offers great benefits to each area. The quest for elements of religious identities is, I propose, part of a more general response to identity fragmentation character-istic of postmodern times. And the ways in which beliefs and prac-tices are incorporated into the habitus has much to do with the pervasiveness of consumer conduct.

However, before going further, a few caveats must be made. To discuss postmodern times in terms of a social and cultural tilt towards the effects of communication and information technologies along with the increasing centrality of consumerism is not to say that we have entered a new era. These are, as I stressed earlier, postmodern *premonitions*, hints and harbingers of modes of life as yet far from fully developed. Indeed, the very idea that they may thus develop is to assume that some sort of stable order, as was once evident in at least the accounts of modernity if not in modernity itself, will emerge again. To the contrary, the very character of what I describe here is mobile, mutable, fluid, flexible. Consumer culture, dependent as it is on the electronically mediated signs and images that restlessly circle the globe, is in constant flux. More like a screen-saver than a movie, it is always altering into new configurations. Thus consumer culture, while it may be pervasive and influential, resembles in only some discrete and specific ways older sign systems or means of orientation that could (however mistakenly) be thought of as dominant ideologies.

As far as the construction of religious identity goes, the notion of consumer attitudes may be the cause of some disquiet among the guardians and devotees of the sacred, and this is understandable. What I shall show here, however, is that more than one perspective on this is possible. In Berger's view, for instance, the spiritual super-market prefigured a situation of increasing pluralism, which would irreversibly undermine conventional forms of religiosity, centred on institutions, and accelerate secularization. However, today's religious choices may reflect a seriousness of faith that did not figure in the lives of those involved in organized religion from the cradle. Again, while much in consumer culture may well be transient, ephemeral, inconsequential, this does not necessarily mean that those qualities feature prominently, let alone exclusively, in the religious decisions confronted in the course of accomplishing individual self-identities. For instance, evidence from the USA suggests that some "switchers" who move from one denomination to another do so on the basis of spiritual and moral choice rather than for more cynical reasons; it is religious change, sometimes conversion, that prompts such moves.[14]

Postmodern consumption

Consumerism, that is lifestyles and cultures structured around con-sumption, is a defining feature of the postmodern. Consumerism works in tandem with new media as one of two crucial characteristics and carriers of postmodernity. Direct mail, computer-generated niche marketing, expresses this marriage perfectly. Strolling and shopping have become an important part of life for many people in the affluent societies. Leisure consumption is displacing work as the source of identity. Disneyland draws all this together in one symbolic place, epitomizing the postmodern focus on consumption and the self, on desire and choice.

Mickey Mouse is one of the globally best-known symbols of the American corporate culture that promotes consumerism. None the less, the Disney empire is still that culture's prophet, priest, and king. In the realm of Disney, with its multitude of lookalike theme parks and shopping-as-amusement malls, the consumer is sovereign. The variegated culture of serial seductive sideshows is designed for desire, planned for pleasure. "Born to shop" is a deceptively trivial-sounding bumper sticker. In Britain, the huge supermarket chain Tesco provides the perfect pun: "tesco ergo sum." But what is behind these reflexive comments on contemporary culture? How has shopping – even designer grocery shopping! – achieved such lofty status?

Another important consumer symbol is McDonald's, the acme of fast food production and marketing. At McDonald's we see modern and postmodern overlapping in the person of the automated consumer. McDonald's must take credit for turning the restaurant into a factory system in which customers are processed as they walk or drive through, to be churned out, refueled, at the other end. That is modern rationalization, without a doubt. But note that it is the consumer who has been automated, not now the worker. Moreover, customers are being automated the world over, indicating the global aspect of McDonaldization. McDonald's is part of the accelerated compression of time and space which is characteristic of the postmodern. The universal menu is hyper-modern, as is global employee training.

Mike Featherstone offers some now classic reflections on consumer culture and postmodernism.[15] He distinguishes three perspectives on consumer culture. First, there is the view that it arises from the expansion of capitalist commodity production with its vast accumulation of material culture, both in goods for purchase and sites – above all the mall – for consuming. Many exponents of this view treat consumer culture negatively. It is Disneyfied, in that leisure and consumption can be ways of seducing and manipulating consumers so that they miss a better life. In addition, such theorists tend to read consumption off production rather than see it in its own right.

The second perspective concentrates on how people consume, and what this says about their ways of creating social bonds or distinctions. In this case, satisfaction and status depend upon how goods and even images can be used to display and sustain differences between people.

A third way of thinking about consumption is to look at the pleasures it brings, and at the dreams and desires celebrated within consumer cultural imagery. Why do people consume? What do they get out of it? These questions offer ways of seeing consumption that neither denigrate it as a capitalist cage nor celebrate it as a cornucopia.

Such consumer culture is an important aspect of the postmodern in that "social groups seek to classify and order their social circumstances and use cultural goods as a means of demarcation, as communicators which establish boundaries between some people and build bridges with others."[16] How people in everyday life make sense of consumer symbols, how they construct their identities, how they assemble their realities – these become the crucial questions. Zygmunt Bauman takes this further, arguing that in consumerism the shape of the postmodern social circumstance is already dimly visible. As noted earlier, consumer conduct is at once the "cognitive and moral focus of life, the integrative bond of society, and the focus of systemic management."[17]

As far as the first of Bauman's items is concerned, contemporary life is increasingly structured around consumption. It becomes a way of seeing the world, and of responding to its challenges. Consumer skills are required for survival in the advanced market economy, and such skills start to be applied across different spheres. For the individual consumer, consuming is a "pleasurable fulfillment of social duties."[18] So shopping skills rise to great prominence in consumer culture. They are central to market dependency. People who know the best deals, who have scrutinized their catalogs, they are truly store-wise. The broader result is that postmodern consumers constantly "try on" not only new clothes, new perfumes, but new identities, fresh personalities, different partners. This cognitive and moral cast of consumer conduct also holds good, at least to some extent, in the religious sphere.

Secondly, consumer conduct increasingly holds things together, culturally and socially. This relates directly to Featherstone's point, mentioned above, that people establish significant boundaries and build bridges through consuming. In this view the satisfaction that derives from CDs or computers or cars relates to how far people have access to them, which in turn is largely determined by social structural factors such as socio-economic position. This is part of a system of symbolic rivalry, in which people construct their selves through acquiring commodities that make them distinct from others, and seek approval through lifestyle and symbolic membership.[19] This is perhaps most clearly seen in teenage concerns with image and style, with hair color or piercing, with being seen to be cool. But it is also visible in preferences for yogurt over ice-cream, four-wheel-drive jeeps over family sedans, and attending live music over listening to the radio. In the emerging situation people find their niches in society, their means of social integration, and their identities, through consuming.

Thirdly, consumer conduct is the focus of systemic management. The consumer society needs consumers. Pressure comes from companies who monopolize the definition of the good life, of what our needs are, and how they are to be satisfied. This process works alongside and is reinforced by marketing companies, who constantly seek more data to put us in their very precise consumption niches. Marketers use zipcodes and postcodes to classify us into types, "bohemian mix," "shotguns and pickups," "pools and patios," "young influentials," and so on. They know not to send yoghurt and granola coupons to "shotguns and pickups," or diaper deals to "bohemian mix." The "city guides" available on the Internet also serve to channel desire and collect further consumer data, suggesting where to eat after the show you plan to attend, where to shop after the game.[20]

These pressures are not experienced as oppressive, however. They are the pressures to surrender to something bigger than ourselves and are experienced as pleasure. They are part of social management, or of social orchestration.[21] As Pierre Bourdieu suggests, they are the pressures not of coercion but above all of seduction. But there are some who cannot even be seduced. What Bauman calls flawed or failed consumers (as companies and governments in fact think of them) are outside this arrangement. They do not have the will or the capacity to consume, and they act as a warning to all whose lives are geared to ensuring they stay within the consuming majority. As Bauman warns, "In a society of consumers, it is above all the inadequacy of the person as a consumer that leads to social degradation and 'internal exile'."[22]

This is the postmodern consumer society. Its effects are felt well beyond the store and the market, as more and more institutions – schools, hospitals, museums, government departments, universities, libraries, and so on – see their users as consumers, and their members and users respond as such. "Will it sell?" and "Can I buy it?" have become metaphors commonly used in all sectors of life, including religion. Nothing is non-marketable. In hospitals, well-insured clients take up beds and exercise choice in menus, medications, and doctors. Hospitals, schools, and even prisons now talk of "delivering products and services" of promotion, marketing, and competition. In universities, excellence is increasingly defined in terms of success, success in terms of competition, and competition in terms of dollars. Official questionnaires ask for our "religious preferences." Just as the impact of McDonaldization is felt throughout the world, and in diverse contexts, so that of which it is a sign, consumerism, leaves no area of life untouched. As Philip Sampson cautions, "Once established, such a culture of consumption is quite undiscriminating and everything becomes a consumer item, including meaning, truth and knowledge."[23] The old metanarratives of modernity look rather jaded against the flashy new criteria of image, style, fashion, and presentation. But while nothing is untouched by consumerism, how transformative is that touch?

Religious consumers

Max Weber once commented that one effect of the rise of Protestantism was that religion strode confidently into the public square of
worldly affairs, slamming shut the monastery door behind it. As
modernity developed further, however, one might say that religion
kept moving. It may now be found in the consumer market-place, the
shopping mall, the TV screen, and the website – even in Disneyland.
In a very suggestive chapter Mike Featherstone[24] has argued that this
is highly significant for the postmodern. Religion expands into spheres
less visible than the institutional and public ones it occupied in Weber's
day. Thus it takes its place alongside other meaning clusters available
in the so-called private sphere. There, people are free to choose on
their own what to do with their time, their homes, their bodies, and
their gods.

What happens to the religious dimension under these conditions?
Does it tend to be reduced to a leisure pursuit, in reality as well as in
the advertising sections of the Saturday newspapers? Or does the
increasing economic and cultural importance of leisure time mean
that the religious is just relocating to an equally significant sphere?
Do other meaning clusters compete more successfully in the free-
market setting, reducing religion's market-share? What sorts of item
are offered, and which make a practical difference, when religion is
found within this consumer sphere? Does national or regional context make any difference to the extent to which religion can thus be
commodified? And how far does the consumer market-place encourage an interchange of beliefs and practices, so that elements from one
meaning cluster flow into another? All these questions are important,
although not all of them can fully be addressed here.

Of course, the privatizing of religion antedates the consumer society. It was a response to the withdrawal of institutional religion from
many segments of modern social life. Agencies born in religious contexts – law, education, health, welfare – would eventually loosen ties
with their origins, claiming independence. There are limits to this
process; the public sphere has never been anything like entirely evacuated of the religious, and some religions have gone decidedly public
in recent times.[25] Moreover, the very distinction between public and
private has less salience in postmodern times. As the institutional
steeple's shadow shrank, so private life – that is, beyond the institution – appeared increasingly as the natural locus of religiosity. Simultaneously, however, non-institutional areas became more significant
for social relations and for the way societies as a whole function. The
so-called privatizing process is certainly not arrested and in some

ways is accelerated by consumerism. The acquisitive quest and the growth of consumption for its own sake, along with religious privatization, are often seen as destructive of religion. But how far privatism is the best term, and what exactly its effects on contemporary religiosity are, remain to be seen.

In terms of conventional, Christian-based religion in the West, the trend towards present pleasures, egoistic lifestyles, and freedom from obligation represents a radical departure. The frequently caricatured puritan ideals of asceticism, self-denial, fixed boundaries that would lead to delayed enjoyment, saving for a rainy day, and marriage for life are clearly out of kilter with the culture of the so-called "me generation" that "does its own thing" and where "anything goes." The Protestant ethic does seem to have been supplanted in its entirety by a consumer culture, but the overproduction of signs and a loss of referents within contemporary culture are not without effects. Consuming is no longer about utilities that address fixed needs, but about constructing an expressive lifestyle in which "individuals are encouraged to adopt a non-utilitarian attitude towards commodities and carefully choose, arrange, adapt, and display goods – whether furnishings, house, car, clothing, the body or leisure pursuits" to make a unique personal statement.[26]

Some, like Daniel Bell,[27] view this shift negatively, arguing that unless the modern void of belief is refilled by a religious revival, all sense of order in the cosmos, of humility, and of caring will be lost. Similarly, Robert Bellah and his associates lament these individualistic tendencies, seeing them only in relation to "lifestyle enclaves" that connote shallowness and mutual narcissism.[28] This Disneyfication stance may also be heard in Paul Heelas's comment that "So long as there is a consumer market to cater for, especially in its postmodern cultural form, spiritual Disneylands will thrive. Ignoring tradition-based limits to consumption, they cannot operate as religion. The payoff, however, lies in what can therefore be offered – provisions for those intent on 'narcissistically pleasing themselves'."[29]

But as was hinted above, some apparently consumer choices in the religious realm seem to be made in sober seriousness. Switching denominations at a certain time, for instance, may reflect moral and spiritual commitment. There may be a place for religious tension and ambiguity beyond what modernist intellectuals may be prepared to tolerate. As Featherstone says, "When religion is defined as providing the most coherent set of answers to . . . core existential questions, a decline in religion must necessarily be seen as providing a threat to social integration and the social bond."[30] But what if different questions were asked?

Featherstone shows how since the eighteenth century a separate cultural sphere has developed, paralleling the overturning of church authority. He enquires about how within this sphere people's everyday cultural practices function. For instance, so far from magazines, tabloids, and TV shows encouraging protest or the breakdown of traditional values, many actually stress respectability, cleanliness, good food, law and order, and individual success. Consuming itself may be more dutiful than it appears. In any case, Featherstone goes on, it may be a mistake to imagine that there was once a time when a general agreement existed about basic beliefs. Puritan preachers worried about the complacency of their flocks, and were themselves the targets of mockery at the popular carnivals and fairs at least of early modern England. Alternative, deviant, and transgressive activities and symbols may not be recent innovations at all. Perhaps just the scale and "normality" of deviance has changed.

For Featherstone, a Durkheimian perspective would lead one to see the sacred in many layers of consumer culture and postmodern life. If, as Durkheim insisted, anything can become sacred, then this could include commodities. Although they are seen by some as mere utilities, they have a symbolic charge that bestows meaning beyond use or price. The symbolic charge of Levi jeans or Doc Martens, the Super Bowl or the Stanley Cup may, in this view, actually heighten the sense of the sacred. So also may some very special event that breaks into the normal routines of symbolic appropriation. The death of and global mourning process for Princess Diana in 1997 could be read as an instance of what Durkheim dubbed "collective effervescence." If the realm of religion is restricted to institutional churches and their social reach, then consumerism could be seen as an erosive force. Featherstone's proposal is counter-intuitive; more consuming does not necessarily mean less sacred: "the sacred is able to sustain itself outside of organized religion within consumer culture."[31]

While from a Durkheimian perspective the sacred might find itself in consumer culture, how it does so is still open to question. The intuitive may still operate appropriately and be a reliable guide. Durkheim's own position was notoriously ambiguous. In his effort to be scientific he did not demand that the sacred should refer to a transcendent realm in the way that religion as communication – discussed in the previous chapter – does. So while some religious life may well be relocated outside the bailiwick of religious institutions, it may also have to be redefined to do so. To say that consumer items or lifestyles could become sacred is one thing. They may even be marked by the kinds of devotion that others accord only to a transcendent deity. Saying that, however, is not to equate the life of faith, once associated primarily with religious institutions, with the "religious" attitudes or attachments that consumers may exhibit towards their commodities.

One important new factor in the latter part of the twentieth century was that a far larger proportion of people than ever before became involved in producing and marketing symbolic goods.

Whether employed in the mass media, so-called knowledge industries, education, or artistic fields, this area is expanding. So the one-time domains of intellectuals and cultural elites are invaded, specialties are popularized and old class barriers to cultural consumption come down. Continuing education courses, international news packaged as soundbites, and science and technology as EPCOT style entertainment illustrate this well. The cultural intermediaries – as Bourdieu calls the producers of images, information, and symbolic goods – who meet the escalating demand for these within consumer cultures include very prominently religious entrepreneurs. These people run book clubs, produce TV shows, set up websites, distribute religious music, and so on. Although theirs is frequently a parallel universe, their products – from a literary supplement lookalike *Books and Culture* to comic-strip Bibles – compete easily with their secular counterparts.

The postmodern thrives in the consumerist climate. In such an environment it bears the assumptions that the aesthetic life of experience and pleasure is the good life, that no such thing as "human nature" exists, and that life's goal is endlessly to pursue "new experiences, values and vocabularies."[32] Meanings are no longer stable. Signs are cut off from their original referents and acquire significance of their own. But there is good reason for skepticism about taking this as far as someone like Jean Baudrillard does. He thinks this will lead to a kind of information overload in which only the flow of images is left. It may be true of some people, of course. But many, practically speaking, seem to put images and signs into their own interpretive schemes – preserving the earth for our grandchildren or fulfilling self without hurting others – to make sense of them within their own stories.

So more consumption may mean less puritan-style religion but not less Durkheimian sacred. The new symbols that excite, inspire, or give a sense of connection with others may actually be cultural commodities, available in the mall, on TV, or on CD. In this light, the sacred may in one sense be reduced, in another relocated, in a third redefined. These processes have huge implications for understanding both the postmodern and its relation to contemporary religious life. The grand narratives of modernity or of the so-called Christian West may in some respects be fading. But does this really mean that no narratives, no stories are available any longer, or that what remains has no sacred aspects? I think not. Rather, the available stories are much more fluid, malleable, and personalized.

If this is so, then the question of where consumer religion might be found must be answered circumspectly. While Berger's initial ideas about conventional religion having to market itself are suggestive, the spiritual supermarket now contains many commodities, many brands. Thus the quest for anything like a full account has to go both to the older, local corner-store religious outlet and to the globalized direct-mail distributors, as well as to the more specialized, customized, and craft-oriented producers. Not only is there variety, however; it is also necessary to consider the historical background of the changing market-places.

A historical perspective always acts as a salutary lesson for those enamored with the idea that contemporary conditions are novel. The connections between Protestantism and popular theatre, for instance, go back at least to Shakespearean times in Britain.[33] And it comes as no surprise that in the USA, where consumer religion is more evident and more advanced than anywhere else in the world, such connections have been around for a long time. As historian R. Laurence Moore demonstrates, American religion, and especially Protestantism, grew up with a commercial bias. It learned early to make strategic concessions to cultural developments, such as the use of drama or music hall tunes. Indeed, Moore credits religious functionaries with pioneering aspects of contemporary consumer culture. In *Selling God*, he observes that "religion, with the various ways it has entered the cultural marketplace, has been more inventive that its detractors imagined. As an independent influence, it won some important victories. And as a commodity, it satisfied many buyers."[34]

Moore argues that, having no legal privilege, American religion was obliged to compete, not only in the competitive church market, but also in the general market for cultural commodities. "Like American politics," he says, "religion stayed lively and relevant to national life by reflecting popular taste and commanding media coverage."[35] Moore's only hesitation about all this – and it is a far from trivial matter – is that religion loses its critical cutting edge thereby. Can there be any real prophets "in a country whose self-image rests on fast, friendly, and guiltless consumption?" Here's the irony; "Would-be religious prophets have to learn the ways of Disneyland in order to find their audience, but even that popular touch cannot give them the capacity to reach many Americans who would feel perfectly comfortable at a prayer breakfast held under McDonald's generous golden arches."[36]

In Canada, Reginald Bibby describes an increasing movement "from religious commitment to religious consumption."[37] John Webster Grant proposes that consumer attitudes became prominent on the Canadian religious landscape only from the 1950s.[38] Churches display their wares, compete in the field of advertising and marketing, and allow their potential customers to browse among an ever more exotic array of religious possibilities. These range from the razzmatazz of TV faith-healers to the nostalgia of liturgical traditionalists. Religion à la carte is how Bibby terms it. According to his surveys, Canadians have fairly conventional beliefs about God, Jesus, and the afterlife, but display a wide variety of beliefs about such themes. Actual reference to a sacred text, the Bible, and concern about religious knowledge – unless you count ESP or horoscopes – or for prayer are way down the list. Selected religious fragments gathered by Bibby include an Anglican housewife in New Brunswick: "I believe in God but not the divinity of Jesus." An Alberta science administrator said, "I believe in Jesus Christ but have doubts about immortality."[39]

Of the 75 percent of the Canadian people who do not attend services regularly, 80 percent agree that they draw selectively on beliefs and practices, still identify with a religious tradition, and turn to religion for rites of passage. From all this Bibby concludes that Canadians are selective consumers.[40] They show great interest in mystery, the supernatural, the meaning of life, and rites of passage in church, and continue to identify positively with religious traditions, and their biographies have religious memory. But religious organizations are failing, claims Bibby, because of structural weakness, a lack of clarity about aims, an inability to identify potential markets, the non-delivery of products. No mention of Moore's rather more damning indictment of American religion, that it no longer offers social critique. It would not be stretching things to suggest that here again is a point at which the message is recoded, this time for the consumer context.

That the coming of consumer religion in Canada may be somewhat later than its coming in the USA is a reminder that national and regional differences may well be significant here too. It it clear that in Canada people want what churches offer, but not on the terms of commitment and participation that might once have been taken for granted. As Peter Beyer puts it, "most religious consumers, with a relatively modest demand for purely religious product, will consume eclectically, with perhaps a fair degree of 'brand' loyalty, but more often than not without membership and the sort of commitment that produced regular participation and communal incorporation in an organized body."[41] But if the Canadian situation is different from the American, the British case is different again.

In European societies, where the secularization thesis makes somewhat more sense of changing religious situations than it does in North
America, immense changes are also under way. Britain has a very
long history of intimate attachment to clearly definable Christian
traditions, many of which entailed complex church–state relations.
But today considerable heterogeneity of belief and practice is in evidence. Grace Davie describes the "ordinary gods" of British society
under the heading "common religion."[42] Preferable to the term "privat-
ized religion," common religion stresses how religion has become a
matter of personal or private choice, but without our overlooking the
fact that "Belief is not self-generated, nor does it exist in a vacuum; it
has both form and content – albeit unorthodox form and content –
which are shaped as much by the surrounding culture as by the individual believer."[43]

Davie makes much of the mutating nature of religious life in (pos-
sibly) postmodern conditions in Britain, while not ignoring the con-
tinuities of conventional religion that do still exist, if not flourish. She
comments on David Harvey's suggestion that Christian theological
emphasis shifts in postmodern times. Firstly, there is a fresh acknow-
ledgement of God the Holy Spirit, paralleling cultural decenteredness,
discontinuity, and fragmentation. Then further along the same continuum comes a New Age orientation, with its penchant for self-
selection and self-fulfillment. All this, says Davie, is quite consonant
with believing without belonging, as it "enables the believer to select
at will from the religious goods on offer and to mould these into a
variety of packages that suit a variety of lifestyles and subcultures."[44]
At the same time, negative reactions to this felt fragmentation may
also be seen in Britain, in the growth of conservative religiosity, sometimes coming very close to fundamentalism.[45]

One conclusion that might be reached from this is that the extent
of consumer religion varies by country or by region. Over recent
years a prominent debate in the sociology of religion has centered on
the question of how far the European-originating secularization paradigm can be made to fit North American and other situations. One
does not have to go along entirely with the somewhat reductionistic
rational choice theories which claim that in countries with numerous
churches religious belief and church attendence are greater than in
countries with a dominant, monopolistic church. Those rational choice
theories are limited both by their emphasis on the cognitive aspects
of faith and by the economic metaphor on which they rest.[46] But it
does make sense to see that the combination of disestablishment with
an open market for religion would make a difference to the levels of
religious mobilization.[47] However, while this may help explain the

early and pervasive influence of consumer attitudes in American religion, in a globalizing consumer world such trends are likely to make themselves felt even in contexts that previously enjoyed some degree of historical insulation from them.

In each case, moreover, it also makes sense to think of religion today more as a cultural resource than as a social institution. Hence, Beckford: "As such [religion] is characterised by a greater degree of flexibility and unpredictability. For the decline of the great religious monopolies in the West has been accompanied by the sporadic deployment of religion for a great variety of new purposes. Religion can be combined with virtually any other set of ideas or values."[48] One of those purposes, in postmodern times, is the construction of religious identities – not all of which are readily recognizable in terms of conventional religiosities. As Beckford notes, the deregulation of religion is one of the hidden ironies of secularization.

Thus, not only in North America, but in several European countries, a vague, inchoate, but seemingly serious religious quest is in evidence. In the USA, Wade Clark Roof dubs the actors in this religious resurgence "seekers." As he puts it, "Many within the baby-boomers generation who dropped out of churches and synagogues years ago are now shopping around for a congregation. They move freely in and out, across religious boundaries, many combine elements from various traditions to create their own personal tailor-made meaning systems."[49] More recently, Robert Wuthnow has documented a shift from religious life as "dwelling" to "seeking." As one of his respondents summed it up, "I'm not religious, but I'm very spiritual."[50]

Constructing identities

Let us return to the argument about postmodernity and consumer conduct in order to find some orientation for thinking about constructing religious identities. We noted earlier that the quest for new elements of religious identities is an outcome of broader processes of identity fragmentation in postmodern times. Those broader processes once had work close to their core. Today, in some ways, the consumer seems to be stepping into the cultural space once occupied by the worker. The world of work is slipping from its once central place as the organizing frame for daily life, giving way to consumerism as a form of social organization in its own right. The focus of social interaction and cultural meaning is displaced into the sphere of consumption.

Consumer goods and household patterns of consumption have become far more significant than they were in earlier times, in which work cultures were more accented. As Bocock says, "For many young people, for instance, the question of who they think they are, or how they would like to live, is as likely to be answered in terms of the kind of consumer life-style they aim for as the kind of occupation they seek."[51] No one with teenage children will be unaware of the importance of having the right kind of clothing, body piercings, music, electronic equipment, sporting goods, and other items. Peer pressure makes the lack of such things seem a real deprivation. But the same parents might do well to check their own aspirations, because they – we! – too are affected by the same consumer cultures. As Bocock wryly observes, "Not being able to consume, in the postmodern sense, becomes a source of deep discontent."[52]

Why is this happening? For one thing, paid employment has undergone some radical changes during the postwar period. Old expectations have crumbled, at least in Europe and North America; for most people paid employment would have been a relatively secure feature of life, for which preparation was made by way of specialized education or training, and which would remain fairly constant until retirement. Casualization, multiple careers, unemployment, and the unprecedented incorporation of women into the labor force have led to our seeing work as a source of fragmentation, insecurity, and uncertainty. The old scripts, which could clearly be played by men or women, which related to roots in place or kinship, or which worked steadily through a lifelong occupation or career are far less readily available. As Ray Pahl says, "many labels, scripts, and narratives that served as boundary markers for identity construction in the past have come to the end of their useful lives."[53] Conventional religious ways of making sense, although Pahl hardly mentions them, are among those discarded scripts.

Knowing who we are is pretty basic to the human condition, and, as Pahl continues, "If we cannot be sure of our gender identities, our jobs, our life-course pattern, and how enduring our present set of relationships may be, then evidently we are alone in constructing our self-identity in our own way."[54] For Anthony Giddens, "Self identity is a reflexive achievement" and a narrative of self-identity "provides the means of giving coherence to the finite life-span, given changing external circumstances."[55] The narrative approach is vital, and fits with what follows in the present chapter. One may be forgiven for asking, however, whether some nuance should be introduced into Giddens' description, one which seems to hint at a sense of regained personal control through narrative. It may well be there for some, of

course, but it must be a minority of people who enjoy a confident
sense of going through life, creating a coherent story as they go.
Many others feel constraint, oppression, limitations, or just a sense
of arbitrariness and caprice, on their capacity freely to forge a future
for themselves.

Manuel Castells suggests another approach, which follows from
Giddens, but also takes into account the sense of narrower passages
and limited options that many people experience in day-to-day life.
Legitimating identities, he proposes, are less significant today, attenu-
ated as they are by the global flows of power, information, and influence, which have undermined the social importance of the locations
and organizations that once framed them.[56] Conventional, organized
religion would be among these. However, two other kinds of identity
may be distinguished. Both are narrative ways of establishing social
identity in situations where the social narratives seem beyond our
control.[57] The first is resistance identity, which expresses a challenge
to the invisible powers – in the space of flows in the global network
– beyond the control of persons in everyday existence, and which yet
are felt as inhibiting life-chances. Forms of fundamentalism that tend
to be backward-looking and retrenching are prominent among the
modes of resistance identity documented by Castells. Bauman also
suggests that fundamentalisms are a response to choice-overload within
consumer societies.[58] The final form of identity Castells calls "project
identity." This is forward-looking and refers to the immanent tendencies of the present, among which Castells indicates environmental and
feminist – or sexual freedom – movements as typical carriers.

As with all such ideal types, these three can be misleading when it
comes to considering religious identity construction, but Castells'
scheme does offer helpful clues. One could look at any contemporary
cultural context and find people whose sense of self resonates most
closely with the outlook of traditional organizations, such as mainstream denominations. But in postmodern times even these are likely
to be tinged with traces of one of the other two types. Both resistance
identities – in which people feel threatened by shifts towards more
liberal or worldly approaches – and project identities – in which people
find ways of combining their faith commitment with emancipatory
or aesthetic concerns may be found within and beyond institutions
associated with legitimating identities. Moreover, as we shall see in
the next chapter, just as resistance identities need not necessarily be
limited to nostalgic and reactionary fundamentalisms, so project identities are not inevitably severed from older sources of legitimation. As
Castells and others observe, ethical seriousness is in no way absent
from current identity construction.

How does all this square with the postmodern? As I observed before, many authors whom I respect and on whom I rely do not use the term postmodernity, preferring to stick with "late" or "high" modernity. However, because I do not assume that postmodernity has by any means supplanted modernity, I believe that their analyses are quite consonant with mine. Moreover, it seems to me that by examining postmodernity as a socio-cultural formation, we can avoid the trivializing of analysis that characterizes some treatments of the postmodern. There is a certain hedonistic playfulness in the post-modern, and sometimes a depthless superficiality as well. But this is by no means the whole story, and to trace some of the processes of identity construction in postmodern times is to take the rest of the story seriously.

To recapitulate: where once we might have identified ourselves in terms of the villages or clans we came from, and located ourselves within a social hierarchy stretching down from prince or president to pauper, now nothing is fixed. International processes like migration, trade, and communications mean that our local lives are connected with the global, and signs circulate freely, producing an effect of cultural disorientation. The realm of choice has opened up tremendously for most people in the affluent societies, giving us unprecedented opportunities to choose lifestyles and beliefs from a range of options. At the same time, the older religious institutions that were once the conduits of meaning have drifted into decline, with the result that they are often little more than containers for cultural conservation. So how is identity formed under these conditions, and, in particular, what provides the resources for individual narratives of identity construction?

Religious identities are being reconstructed today to overcome the felt dysjuncture between the legacy of conventional identities, with their traditional, linear progression, and the diverse experiences cobbled together under the sign of mobility.[59] Rather than try to make sense merely of the residues of meaning provided by declining religious forms, or the more ephemeral markers of ever changing new religious tendencies, we should try to chart the actual "meaning routes" that individuals take in everyday life. Referring to Bibby's notion of à la carte religion, Quebec sociologist Raymond Lemieux notes that one has to choose between *haute cuisine* and McDonaldization.[60] These are meant as polar extremes, so no doubt there are positions in between. The *haute cuisine* folk – conventional religionists – are increasingly in a minority, at least in Quebec and the rest of Canada. Identity construction among the majority now has new markers, through which individuals trace new paths, their meaning routes, to make sense of the world. This is diffuse and implicit religion, subterranean religiosity, which determines actions without questioning them too carefully.

The playful postmodern account offers one story, which is highly consumerist. The popular image of the postmodern is of people flitting like butterflies from store to store and from symbol to symbol, constantly constructing themselves, trying on this fashion, that lifestyle. A sort of pastiche persona results, so the self – and life itself – becomes transient, ephemeral, episodic, and apparently insignificant. This is what we might call the "plastic self," flexible, amenable to infinite reshaping according to mood, whim, desire, and imagination. This self is most at home in Disneyland, where pleasures may be consumed continuously and personae donned like so many outfits. But while this may describe some, most interactions with the Disneyesque are more complex. For one thing, the quick-change persona may be felt as a necessary response to the demands for flexibility in mobile and asynchronous social situations. For another, it must be remembered that children seldom seem to lose their selfhood just because they play role games.

One might object, of course, that wearing masks, exchanging guises is a process as old as humanity, and this is quite right. But whereas once this was reserved for theatrical productions – "the play's the thing!" – now everyone is drawn in, and self-consciously so. Even the 1960s west coast "Society for Creative Anachronisms," which allowed people to make their own medieval characters (and attracted the jibe of being mere "legalized schizophrenia"), still sought fixed values such as chivalry as a gesture against the "false fronts" worn within modern society. Today, popular participation is heralded by the Germasian brothers' hotel in the West Edmonton Mall, where one can flirt lightly with any persona one chooses, from a toga'd Roman reclining at a floor level dinner to a Star Trek sleep in an Enterprise bunk (and, of course, similar but slightly more downmarket "fantasy suites" are now available in most hotel chains).

No doubt in some consumerist religiosities the holy hedonist is visible, moving from church to church, denomination to denomination, seeking new experiences, new stimuli. In this stained-glass window-shopping, the plastic self consumes sermons (where they are still available), new or old liturgical forms, and choir or folk-band music without ever stopping long enough to be seriously involved in any of them. Even more so in a tendency like New Age, choices galore are on offer. Staying at a New Age bed-and-breakfast a few years ago I was offered, as part of the service, spirit guidance, crystals, advice about ley-lines, vegan cuisine, and massage. But I was also assured that I was under no obligation to follow any particular path except that of maximizing experience.

But even as the plastic self appears to rule, paradoxically much is also invested in the self. Significance is still sought. Being authentic, expressing oneself, is raised to a high status. The virtues of *personality*, rather than those of *character* become significant.[61] The voice within assumes a new authority at just the time when other, traditional authorities are being more and more radically questioned. The process is obvious within contemporary therapeutic approaches in which a "manipulable sense of well-being" is central.[62] This is the reverse of the postmodern consumerist approach, an internalized narrative that persists despite the poor standing accorded to public metanarratives. At the same time, freedom *from* those metanarratives, including truth and morality, could be the occasion of freedom *for* the self. This we could call the "expressive self."[63]

This second self finds its roots in an older Romanticism, but more recently in the "expressive revolution" of the 1960s. In so far as the sixties movements were counter-cultural, they were loosening the ties of tradition and the mass-produced, mechanical ways of modernity. Both conventional religion and modern metanarratives were abandoned, but not necessarily in a nihilist way. Rather, the authentic self was sought, often in relation to some new metanarrative. The therapeutic would be one manifestation. The connection between personal and political in feminism and that between person and planet in green movements would be others. The expressive self, then, retains some sense of its own story, its own narrative, even though it is found in the same detraditionalized milieu as the "properly" postmodern plastic self.

One point of intersection between post-1960s movements and religious movements is sexual identity. Ironically, modernity introduced forms of autobiography – the narrative of self as an individual – that grew out of the Reformation's stress on "self-accreditation" rather than on "church accreditation."[64] Such texts validated particular identities as well as offering assurance of salvation. But the double irony is that, whereas the Protestant narratives were relatively "disembodied," the idea that a narrative may be used to accredit identity has today expanded to embrace "other" sexualities, bringing back a focus on the corporeal body. And this has been echoed within religious communities. At the Anglican Lambeth Conference of 1998, one group of bishops produced a document entitled *Seeking Gender Identity*, which argued for Christian acceptance of same-sex unions. As an Australian church leader observed, "this issue symbolises a watershed in the life of the Uniting Church."[65]

But believers construct their identities from various resources, depending upon the availability of symbols, and they tend to be able to hold together in fresh combination ideas and beliefs once thought of as unlikely companions. This of course is also characteristic of broader cultural trends, in which Disneyized sense can be made of "contradiction" through the creation of new narratives.[66] But not only Disneyized. On an explicitly religious front, the late twentieth century saw a confluence in Canada of traditional religious antagonists, Protestants and Catholics. Whereas once, in local situations, religious difference could be used as the means of exclusion and inclusion, strategic alliances against common external foes has drawn these groups into common causes. This may require new vocabularies (for example the pollsters' term "Catho-evangelicals") to cope conceptually with the change. Or it may produce some curious coalitions, such as those between feminists and Roman Catholics, together opposing intrusive medical technologies and fostering more natural means of contraception.

At this point one self blurs into the other. The New Age quest for experience also accents the inner life, the voice within. Religion in this case is less merely consumed, more internalized. The voice of ancient tradition or of divine revelation is muted or ignored altogether, but the inner voice is taken to be thoroughly authoritative. Needless to say, it takes little imagination to see that similar motifs are present within conventional church religion. Belief is demoted, experience promoted. Divisive doctrine diminished, a unifying stress on spirituality magnified. The feminization of church leadership reflects and fosters some aspects of this, a process that may in some respects be connected with the shift from stereotypically male-oriented production to female-oriented consumption.

Within New Age proper, if we take Shirley MacLaine as its prophet, self religion is central. "God is within . . . everyone is god." In certain respects, New Age represents a shaking off of the institutions of modernity: adherents no longer feel at home in them. The reality within is reality itself. At the same time, New Age has now been harnessed by modernity's classic institution, the business corporation. When IBM and Pacific Bell turn to self religions for help in management and marketing, something curious is afoot. "Zen and the art of telephoning," "Creative visualization to tap inner resources," "dissolving your limitations" – courses such as these are now on offer within mainstream corporate life.

All this is, of course, quite unappealing to some, for whom the postmodern, with its removal of old signposts and its rampant individualism, is negative and destructive. Neither the plastic self, nor the expressive self will do; the personal narrative needs to be subsumed in something greater than itself. The felt losses galvanize a quest for new overarching modes of organizing life that speaks at once to the fraying social bond, to the precariousness of life as a constant series of choices, and to the lack of established institutional anchor-points. For Bauman, fundamentalisms are a postmodern product, "born of the internal contradictions of postmodern life,"[67] the postmodern form in which human insufficiency is revealed. Fundamentalisms embrace rationalization and the technological developments of modernity but without accepting their price-tag.

Fundamentalisms reveal the ills of society – as Gilles Kepel also suggests[68] – but Bauman argues that they are new ills, the agonies of freedom, of risky choices. Fundamentalism completes postmodern quests for specialist guidance and counseling. A new, authoritative, alternative rationality offers certainties that are in such short supply in postmodern times. Curiously, this kind of offer is also available within some other aspects of contemporary culture. Relief from postmodernity's aporias and aleatory anxieties may also be found in Disneyland, where a "childlike trust that everything will be handled for you" is encouraged.[69]

Here, then, are three possible meaning-routes through the postmodern: the plastic self, the expressive self, and the subsumed self. They are selves that may or may not have an explicitly religious dimension, but the first two relate positively, while the last relates negatively, to the choices thrown up by an advanced consumer culture characteristic of postmodern times. Consumer choices are made, using skills acquired in the general consumer market-place, but the nature of these can vary from the shallow and superficial to the seriously considered. Fun and fundamentalism appear as points on a continuum of such choices, thus producing the possibility of new extremes of opinion and conduct far less frequently encountered in modern, let alone premodern, varieties of religious expression.

That such a variety of selves may be available in a range of combinations today is not in itself surprising. They reflect a cultural variety enabled and encouraged above all by new media and globalization. And the way they are constructed relates increasingly to consumer choices, whether playful or serious. The case of Glenn Hoddle is a reminder that when such choices are made they not only reveal the diverse sources of belief (Christianity, Hinduism, Romanticism, and so on) but also have real effects on the life-chances of individuals and groups. The conventional guardians of the sacred often respond to such situations by restating traditional sources of given or bestowed identity. But in so far as they limit themselves to this tactic they are unlikely to meet the challenge of today's construals of selfhood, some of which emanate, after all, from conventional religious sources.[70]

The meaning-routes through the postmodern are characterized by consumer choice in identity construction. The fragments used are drawn from, among other things, new media, but these may also refer to older sacred stories. The meaning-routes and varied selves help us understand the novel contexts within which faith is forged and spirituality explored in the new millennium. It would be a mistake, however, to allow the term meaning-routes to suggest anything too closely resembling the clearly defined highways or the precisely timetabled railways and flight corridors of modernity. Recall that Disneyland is both a highly regimented experience, and a place of fantasy and escape. And as we shall see in the next two chapters, time and space are themselves contracting and expanding, modulating and mutating, in postmodern times.

It would also be a mistake to imagine that the meaning-routes and alternative self-constructions I have described exhaust the possibilities. It is easy to be trapped by one's tropes, conned by one's concepts. Plenty of conventional religion will no doubt persist throughout the twenty-first century, even though it is hard to imagine how it could remain entirely untouched by the trends described here. Also, the same postmodern consumerism could generate opposition as well as conformity to it. After all, it was the excesses of expectation within capitalist work-oriented cultures of modernity that inspired religiously based as well as other forms of resistance to exploitation. Consumer groups are already involved in questioning unrestrained and unregulated consumption, so it is unsurprising to find spiritually minded project identities emerging in this area. The lead may be taken by those in non-Western countries, as suggested by the example of Korean churches rejecting the "prosperity gospels" mentioned in chapter 3.

As Bocock suggests, appropriately, "Religious critiques of the ideology of consumerism . . . may be more important for the future of planet earth than has been realised so far."[71] But for members of different religious groups to offer "caring orientations towards nature" and a "critique of capitalist consumption patterns," warns Bocock, they will also have to be "disengaged from ethnic groups' rivalries for territory."[72] Why this is so cannot be grasped without considering contemporary globalization.

6 A Global Spirit

On January 20, 1994, religious revival broke out under the flight path of aircraft taking off and landing at Lester B. Pearson International Airport, Toronto. This was no local, indigenous, self-contained event, but a "blessing" that flowed into, and then out of, Toronto, involving countries worldwide. John Arnott, pastor of the (California-based) Vineyard Fellowship at the airport, acknowledges the contribution of at least two intermediaries of the blessing. In November 1993, during a visit to Argentina, Arnott was prayed for by Assemblies of God minister Claudio Friedzon. The other channel of influence was Rodney Howard Browne, who had experienced "laughing revival" in South Africa. Browne imparted the blessing to Randy Clark in Rhena Bible Church, Tulsa, Oklahoma, and Clark, in turn, was the invited preacher at the Airport Vineyard on that decisive night in January 1994, when the blessing touched down at Toronto.

Within a few months, the blessing had not only spread far and wide from Toronto, but, because of its apparently unique features, it had also hit the headlines, first in the UK. Unusual behaviours, such as uncontrolled laughter and falling to the floor, are easily sensationalized. They make good media copy. Although South Africa and Argentina did not figure prominently in the visitor roster, Canadians, Americans, and Britons came in large numbers, plus many from non-English-speaking Asian countries, such as Japan. The American connection was weakened to some extent when the Vineyard movement parted company with the airport people (now known as the Airport Christian Fellowship). The blessing crosses religious boundaries, involving Pentecostals and Anglicans, although about one-third of the visitors come from independent and non-denominational churches.[1] But it also arouses controversy and has been accused of divisiveness.

The Toronto Blessing offers opportunities for considering some of the relations between globalization – as the most significant space shift of the postmodern – and religion. It has manifestly global connections, and evidences diversity. Whether the latter will be embraced in new alliances or will splinter the movement remains to be seen. It raises questions about class, ethnicity, and gender in globalized contexts. But it also raises questions of media effects. Do such events as the Toronto Blessing attract a disproportionate amount of media attention, not only because of the supposedly strange phenomena, but also because, despite glossalalia, the predominant language of interaction is English, and because a major North American city is its hub? Could this northern variant of Pentecostalism distract attention from other, perhaps more truly global manifestations of the same religious tendency?

Of course, other religious events and processes could also be used as a focus for this debate. The mass suicide in March 1997 in the Heaven's Gate cult, for instance, became instant world news through newspapers, television, and the Internet. Indeed, the local event in the San Diego area was much more successful in drawing attention to the cult than the evangelistic efforts undertaken by Heaven's Gate in 1995, when hostility and ridicule was the main response.[2] Are events like this and the Toronto Blessing primarily local – Heaven's Gate devotees resided in a Californian mansion – or global – in the sense that the events have a worldwide life of their own as a flow of information? A related question may be asked of the Rushdie affair. Indian-British novelist Salman Rushdie became a *cause célèbre* following a *fatwa* pronounced against him in Iran in the 1980s, because of his alleged disrespect for Islam in *The Satanic Verses*. Religious authority clearly has ongoing power in the modern world. This case also raises questions about whether fundamentalism is merely a Western, Christian-based phenomenon or something more global in scope.

When the strong secularization thesis held sway it was fairly easy to ignore religious activities supposing them to be declining features of the social world. Today, that has changed, and the question now is, how are these pervasive and palpably religious activities best considered, sociologically speaking? In particular, is there a trend towards globalized religion in which increasing homogeneity and sameness is the order of the day? Or is religion dividing into localized fragments and sectarian splinters? Is difference multiplying? The view argued here is that neither position is particularly helpful on its own. Neither, by itself, explains the Toronto Blessing, the Heaven's Gate suicide, or the Rushdie affair. Rather, both local distinctiveness *and* global generality are simultaneously apparent, in interconnected ways.[3]

This seeming paradox may be explored using Roland Robertson's concept of "glocalization" to try to capture some of the complexities of the local–global theme.[4] The concept began life as a Japanese business technique – *dochakuka* – for adapting a global outlook to local conditions. Such micromarketing does not simply conform itself to local conditions, of course; it helps to *construct* consumers for commodities.[5] One could even say that glocalization encourages consumers to create themselves, to develop their own styles and tastes. Thus Disneyland Paris differs from its American counterparts – it serves wine in cafés, for instance – and Disneyland Tokyo caters for a Japanese clientele, offering time travel to earlier periods of Japanese history. Robertson extends the use of the glocalization concept into the cultural sphere, although he acknowledges that economics is more deeply bound up with the cultural than many have been prepared to admit.

Glocalization is in turn tightly tied to another process, the cultural shifts of postmodernity. These have to do, in part, with a global overproduction of images, differences, truths, and objects, which leads to a questioning of more conventional, taken-for-granted cultural realities. Because of time–space compression, discussed more fully in chapter 7, postmodernity also refers to an intensification of cultural contacts that help to erode older boundaries or raise doubts about traditional ways of doing things. The point is that these cultural shifts are bound up with glocalization, in which signs, individuals, and commodities travel more freely, to produce a blurring of boundaries.

It is not insignificant, either, that the local–global theme is also important within the sphere of religious discourses of various kinds. For instance, Japanese interest in the universal and particular, expressed today in *dochakuka*, is deep-seated and long-lived. And in the famous (sixth century BC) vision of Ezekiel, in which the "wheels within wheels" are attached to a kind of chariot-throne, the idea is that God, though universally mobile, nevertheless appears and acts locally. Again, the paradox is present that finds God in specific places and also everywhere. It is noteworthy that a means of movement is described, albeit in visionary terms: the chariot-throne. In what follows, particular attention is paid to the role of modern means of movement: now not only transport but also communication and information technologies (CITs).

In what follows, firstly, the conceptual groundwork is laid, in a discussion of glocalization, flows, and sacred landscapes. Secondly, the Toronto Blessing phenomena are used as a case study, in which these three concepts can be tried out and illustrated. This does, of course, skew the discussion towards Christian-based examples of glocalization, although this is partly rectified in the third section, on fundamentalisms associated with other faiths. Fourthly, some implications for further study of religion and globalization are considered. This refers back to emerging trends and to the challenges – both analytical and practical – of glocalization for religion.

Sacred landscapes

Three concepts offer some very useful ways of considering the theme of religion and the global–local debate. The first, glocalization, points up the interconnection between the local and the global. It punctures the inflated views of globalization as some mere macro-level socio-economic process involving world-systems that either do not touch the everyday lives of ordinary people in local places, or, if they do, merely impose alien pressures upon them. Rather, the local and the global are mutually dependent. This sets in place the broad analytical context.

The second, flows, is used effectively by Manuel Castells[6] when he tries to transcend traditional thinking about relatively fixed and stable systems – of economic life, especially – and stresses the sense of fluidity and flux in social analysis. Entrepreneurial networks, in which relationships flow between nodes, make place less economically, but not less socially, significant. Thus erstwhile decision centers lose autonomy in the network, creating a dysjuncture between the global economy and local communities. Arjun Appadurai,[7] who also uses the term "flows," talks as well of global cultural "scapes." These are the building blocks of "imagined worlds"[8] created by social groups of diverse kinds, from transnational corporations to ethnic neighborhoods. The concept of flows helps us move beyond the idea of "society" (as nation state), which was the taken-for-granted analytical sociological (and often historical) focus of modern times.

The third concept, "sacred landscapes," is used to make good an apparent gap in Appadurai's set of "scapes" (namely ethnoscapes, technoscapes, finanscapes, mediascapes, and ideoscapes). Although he does not elaborate the theme at length, Malcolm Waters observes that the great world religions, with their monotheism and universal claims, have had globalizing tendencies, as seen in the Ottoman Empire and in Christendom. But in modern times, processes such as the growth of individualism, the Western splitting apart of church and state, and the reduction of religion to Sunday and church have fostered new modes of religious activity – in Waters' view, ecumenist and fundamentalist.[9] What I call sacred landscapes Waters prefers to call "sacriscapes." Both terms refer to the same thing: flows of religious beliefs and practices.

The concept of glocalization helps to deflect attention from mere global*ism* as an approach. It is easy to see how the McLuhanesque global village might be seen as a product of burgeoning communication and information technologies, for, today, CITs are the single most significant means of breaking down barriers to communication, and thus of making the world a single place. Moreover, American CIT companies are world leaders, and, through them, only a few of the world's remotest places remain ignorant of Disney, McDonald's, and Coca-Cola. Forms of economic and cultural imperialism are undoubtedly visible here, and negative responses to them, as well as positive yearnings for them, are fully understandable.

Globalism often resonates with an economic triumphalism that rejoices each time a new franchise or outlet is opened in some previously untouched country.[10] It is thus newsworthy when McDonald's moves into Moscow as communism moves out, or when curried or kosher burgers appear in Delhi or Jerusalem, or when Disney debates with China over the relative merits of Hong Kong and Shanghai for a new theme park site. But the same kind of language is heard of global evangelism and church planting. Is this thinly veiled economic expansionism, or have corporations adopted a secular version of the evangelistic approach to those called "unreached peoples"? The answer is, neither; the different kinds of flow do not necessarily have the same patterns. They are dysjunctive.[11] At a World Evangelization Fellowship (WEF) meeting in Abbotsford, British Columbia in May 1997, Jun Vencer announced that "We've come to celebrate the globalization of the church."[12] But what exactly was being celebrated? It is clear from reports of the meeting that politically and culturally sensitive local initiatives, not some off-world vapor trails from jetsetting evangelists, were the focus of much discussion.

Globalism (and globalization) is misleading, for a number of reasons. The main one is that, as in Francis Fukuyama's "end of history" theorem, a certain complacent assumption prevails about having reached a single culminating point. This is curious in the light of the perceived sense of accelerating the rate of change. Even if global conditions are seen to be in tension, as in Benjamin Barber's graphic depiction of "Jihad vs McWorld," American influence is still considered predominant (in the McWorld symbol).[13] Yet other powerful impulses exist. The localism of Japanese marketing, even though it carries with it far fewer cultural images, directs an increasing number of transnational business strategies, well beyond Japan. And, as Mike Featherstone observes, "Brazilianization" could be seen as another important – albeit deplorable – trend, towards social zoning, and the dual cities of the very rich and the very poor.[14] Globalism seems to involve not only Westernization and Americanization, but Japanization and Brazilianization as well.

In more recognizably religious terms, certain grand themes may be discerned operating on a global level. Various authors have concluded that current trends produce an interest in what may be thought of as at least quasi-religious matters. The state, for instance, in taking responsibility for life-issues internally, and questions of human rights, national identities, and so on externally, confronts issues of human-ness directly.[15] Anthony Giddens takes this further, speculating that universal or global values are becoming important, particularly the survival of humanity or of the planet.[16] And Peter Beyer, in his study of religion and globalization, argues that a "global civil religion is both possible and likely,"[17] and that this could provide the context for local cultures.

But a closer analysis of cultural globalization reveals great diversity and difference, raising serious questions for the coherence of any so-called global society. Whether a Durkheimian normative integration or common cultural values could ever become dominant in a global setting is a very moot point. Global society, if such an entity exists, would relate to the rapid expansion of CITs, and their capacity to bind time and space, along with worldwide economic activity. But in local situations, these do not themselves necessarily promote cultural homogeneity. Indeed, just the opposite seems to be the case. As Featherstone observes, glocal marketing, dual cities and cultural syncretism suggest trends away from singularity and sameness.[18] A good case can be made for an oscillation between local and global – or at least panregional – influences in any given location.[19]

At the same time – and this highlights another weakness of some globalization theories as they apply to religion – the same kinds of glocalizing tendencies do not necessarily occur in every case. Far from it! As Hexham and Poewe point out, it is important to distinguish between a global culture rooted in a world religion and the global-ization of new religious movements. As they see it, "a global culture is a tradition that travels the world and takes on local colour."[20] Charismatic Christianity, some variants of which are discussed here, tends to remain true to the world tradition despite local adaptations, whereas in new religions what flows is fragments of traditions that are recombined in individual experiences. Diversity is positively valued, at least until the new religion has established itself locally by being grafted into a folk religion. This is the case, for instance, with the Unification Church, often known as the Moonies, which draws together fragments of Korean religious traditions, Christianity, science, secular philosophies,[21] and an intentional global consciousness.

There are other difficulties with the paradoxically ethnocentric nature of some globalization theories. Whereas once the West could count on having hegemonic control over a fairly large area of the globe, such is no longer the case. The shifting balance of power away from the West has allowed other voices to be heard, as postcolonial theory and analysis have demonstrated.[22] While voices from the margins have become more audible, their identities have also emerged as more mixed than was conventionally imagined. Black people, for instance, are both inside and outside Western, modern culture, whether in Europe or in North America. They stand partly as a product, partly as a denial of that Western, modern project.[23] Similarly, the aboriginal peoples of Canada or Australia are also in but not of the modern nation state. These increasingly audible other voices are heard, sometimes more frequently than Western social scientists like to acknowledge, speaking in religious tones.

It is by no means clear that Christian churches, as the predominant religious groupings of Western modernity, have come to terms with this situation. Liberation theology, during its heyday in the 1960s and 1970s, expressed some Christian anxieties about, and rejection of, colonialism (and was itself a partially globalized phenomenon). But liberation theologies themselves were often rooted in predominantly Western, modern soil and do not today seem to express the aspirations or cultural distinctiveness of peoples once touched by them. Certain forms of missiology, no doubt chastened by anthropological critique, provide sensitive accounts of how boundaries are crossed between faith and its absence.[24] But what may actually be found in Latin America, Africa, and the Pacific Rim are great varieties of local expression, often in syncretist forms. Cultural fragmentation and the "collapse of symbolic hierarchies"[25] seem rather to be the (dis)order of the day, especially, though not exclusively, as far as new religions are concerned. This confirms again the links between global and postmodern experiences.

But it is not clear, either, that sociologies and anthropologies of religion have come to terms with globalizing circumstances. Much writing still seems to assume that what occurs in the Western, especially Anglo-Saxon world is of prime significance, and that classic dilemmas that supposedly bedevil Western forms of religiosity return to haunt the global scene. Hence Malcolm Waters, among others, sees a growing dichotomy between ecumenist and fundamentalist religious forms in global contexts, an idea not so very far removed from the Bergerian quandary of modernity, between accommodation and resistance.[26] Christian religious forms in non-Western countries are often taken to be merely the products of Western imperialism. Yet where Christianity, especially in its Pentecostal forms, is growing most rapidly (Latin America, Africa, the Pacific Rim), it is indigenous growth, and the churches there send many more missionaries to other countries than they receive.[27]

The older, modernist construction of cultural order is melting like a frozen river in springtime. Fresh movements are breaking up the ice-pack, leaving fragments to float free, finding new but temporary attachments within the flows. In place of a fairly clear identification of members of nation states, of insiders and outsiders, and of social and cultural hierarchies, there is now much more ambivalence and ambiguity. There may be connections and networks, but these are much more fluid than fixed. Flows of influence, of common interests, and of cultural tastes may be discerned more readily than the categories of class or society that once characterized sociological analysis. These flows relate to what Benedict Anderson calls "imagined communities," in which there exists a sense of belonging and fellowship attached to certain symbols that are significant for forming a collective memory. Appadurai's flows involve ethnoscapes (people such as migrant workers, students, tourists, refugees), technoscapes (CITs, machines), finanscapes (stock-market data, money), mediascapes (TV, radio, satellites, newspapers, the Internet), and ideoscapes (political ideas). The kinds of social grouping that result are described by Michel Maffesoli in The Time of the Tribes.[28] Particularly in large metropolises, Maffesoli finds situations "swarming with heterogeneous values."

In the light of this palpable polytheism it is perhaps surprising that Appadurai says nothing of flows of religious beliefs and practices, although he does discuss fundamentalisms. Yet religious relationships and movements are also of increasing importance in today's world. Much secularization theory produced earlier in the twentieth century mistook the deregulation of religion for the decline of religion. Noting the falling rates of membership in, adherence to, and social influence of conventional organized religion in Western, industrial countries, such theorists often assumed that religious life in general was contracting. It became clear, however, that Christianity was, rather, being restructured. That term fitted well the US situation, at least. In some European countries and Canada, where churchgoing had fallen off since the 1960s, one could speak of "believing without belonging,"[29] hinting at a move away from "structure" altogether. Yet there may be scope for what Danièle Hervieu-Léger calls "affective parishes" – religious neo-tribes that have lost their connection to place but none the less operate as "community." Once again we see that religion in its post-institutional phase seems to have become more a cultural resource than a fixed identifiable entity.

Rather in the style of Beyer, Waters sees one response to post-modernizing and globalizing trends: the emergence of a humanistic ecumenism, the search for unifying principles and common religious culture. Planetary theology, Gaia, and other such movements may answer to this, but at a grassroots level other responses are much more likely. Indeed, the ecumenical turn could well be viewed by some as another evidence of the relativizing tendency of postmodernism. Cosmic universalism and credal vagueness go hand-in-hand. Such sacred landscapes would seem to offer some attractive possibilities, seen best in the varieties of New Age outlook, which are not incompatible with postmodern or metamodern culture.[30] They can also be appropriated by organizations – such as IBM – as a means of showing an appreciation of the spiritual, the human, or the natural, *within* the world of capitalist technoculture. This relates to another aspect of globalization, the location of high-technology business nodes in Pacific Asia, with explicitly religious aspects. The IBM tower in Singapore, for instance, features architectural openings, inspired by Feng Shui, to allow spirits to pass through, while the soaring Petronas twin towers in Kuala Lumpur are based on Malaysian Islamic designs.[31]

But contemporary sacred landscapes may just as easily challenge or resist postmodernizing trends. Against the disembedding of tradition and the (post)modern attenuation of meaning systems, fundamentalism offers some apparently solid alternatives. Fundamentalism also offers relief from the agonies of choice presented by consumer(ist) culture. Such sacred landscape flows may depend upon CITs – for the dissemination of voice, image, or music, or for the Catholic talk-booths that appear in some shopping malls – without necessarily endorsing other aspects of globalized culture. Fundamentalism may embrace such media, while simultaneously denying the pluralism of present-day cultures. So fundamentalisms may actually be fostered by postmodernizing trends. When not only formally religious verities but even the certainties offered by modernity seem to be breaking down, some means of reorganizing "all spheres of life in terms of a particular set of absolute values"[32] appear very attractive alternatives.

However, fundamentalisms both differ in type and are but one feature of global sacred landscapes. Conservative Islamic and Jewish movements may be seen as fundamentalisms, but they tend to be territorial and monopolistic, just as, to a lesser extent, Catholicism is.[33] But Protestantism (including fundamentalist varieties) seems to thrive where monopolies are breaking up, such as in Latin America. It has no obvious geographical hub, and in fact has many centers. It is important to differentiate between Protestantism in its various forms, because some seem to flourish more easily than others in new contexts. In Latin America, but also on the Pacific Rim, Pentecostalism, a variety of Evangelicalism, is growing fastest. And it is simplistic to equate either Evangelicalism or Pentecostalism with fundamentalism. Latin American Pentecostalism in particular may be considered a "walkout from all that belongs to the status quo, especially the corruptions of the political arena, in order to create a space where local people can run their own show,"[34] which hardly squares with authoritarian fundamentalism!

What evidence is there that glocalized religious activities are becoming more significant? After all, flows of religious ideas are nothing new. The universal thrust of the great religions depends on just such flows. Yet those earlier flows sometimes brought about much sameness, and a denial of local diversity. Although some Victorian missionaries were famed for going native, some cultural patterns were also exported (leading to incongruities like mitred bishops in the African bush), which would later fuel the anthropological critique of religion as promoter of Western culture.[35] Some such critiques, however, are notoriously cavalier, quite ignoring important evidence of indigenization, and of the limits of imperial or commercial involvement in missionary activity.[36] Glocalization would lead one to expect that today's flows would be much more diverse, locally flavored, and dependent, to a greater or lesser extent, on travel and communications media. Within them, no doubt one would also find elements of syncretism and experimentation, and also of attempts to contain or to channel change.

Glocalized blessings at Toronto

The Toronto Blessing may fruitfully be examined in terms of postmodernizing, glocalizing trends, as a flow, a sacred landscape. It is not a national phenomenon, although the particular airport call-sign is not insignificant. Nor does it fall neatly within older categories such as church, sect or denomination, although it could be construed as a new religious movement. On the other hand, it is not exactly global either. Although its influence has reached many countries, this is not deliberate policy (as "global marketing" would be) so much as the indirect effect of wishing to "share the blessing of God's love" with others from within a major international communications and transportation node. So the question may be posed: is this a glocalized blessing?

Airports figure prominently in contemporary accounts of the global postmodern intersection. Airports, like Disneyland, offer a profusion of such themes as simulation, sameness and difference, and high-technology promise. To take the most obvious, airports and Disneyworlds share the characteristic of sameness. Instead of the same lookalike world of Main Street and Mickey Mouse, or the technology shrine called EPCOT, the airport is a brightly lit, closed, self-referring system of steel and cement buildings. To take a flight one must trundle down long, glass-bound corridors, through customs, immigration, and security checks, past duty-free stores and gift boutiques and into the plane, via the gate lounge. After several fairly uncomfortable hours in limited seat space, one emerges into what appears to be exactly the same place: the airport. Was the flight real? Is this placeless space real?

How interesting, then, that one of the best-known religious phenomena of the 1990s occurs at an airport! The sense of movement and the consequent blurring of boundaries – of space, time, and difference – can be viewed through the prism of the airport. Airports are never somewhere else; they seem always to be here. At the same time, they are cultural conduits. They deliver passengers, eventually, into contexts that are recognizably different (assuming one gets beyond the ubiquitous strip malls, high rises, industry parks and suburban sprawls). Different currency must be used (assuming a credit card will not work for all purchases), and a different language or local dialect spoken (assuming English has not become the lingua franca here as well).

In 1994, an apparently new religious event took place in the warehousing area of Pearson International Airport at Toronto. Stories of strange behaviour hit the headlines, especially falling, and "holy laughter," and the huge crowds – including international travellers – that were quickly attracted to the scene. The church itself was then part of the California-based Vineyard network, and those headlines appeared first in the UK, starting with a *Sunday Telegraph* story in June 1994. The Canadian setting seemed, superficially, almost incidental to the action. By late 1995, however, the Vineyard churches dissociated from Toronto, and the renamed Toronto Airport Christian Fellowship went more or less amicably on its own way. The Toronto Blessing (hereafter the Blessing) became an indigenous, if widely networked local church.

The airport setting was significant, because it put the action neatly at a travel hub, of both international travel and ground transportation.

As John Lovelace suggests, the Blessing is the "jet-age version of the frontier camp meetings."[37] Out-of-town visitors come from many countries (over 25 in the first year) in droves (300,000 by mid-1996), 10 percent of whom were British.[38] In the UK, over 4,000 churches are said to be touched by the Toronto Blessing.[39] Indeed, it has been suggested that the Canadian context, defined by being "not American," may have given the Blessing a credibility in the UK that it might have lacked south of the border; perhaps the Canadian airport setting is more than incidental to its spread.

Mere accessibility, even with value-added Canadian credibility, does not explain satisfactorily the success of the Blessing. Rather, it has to be understood in the context of a broad constellation of factors, both global and (post)modern. These include issues of communication and of consumerism, each of which may be seen in both a positive and a negative light by those involved in or sympathetic to the Blessing. These issues are also in constant tension with each other, and are experienced differently in different cultural contexts. If, for instance, the charismatic experience epitomized in the Blessing is seen to break out of traditional authorities and structures of religious life (to establish a fresh market niche?), then the very use of CITs and certain fresh kinds of organization could eventually put constraints on the movement, routinizing it in ways classically analyzed by Max Weber.[40]

Without our slipping into a modernist-style reductionism, it is worth viewing the Blessing in the light of glocalizing consumer cultures. The deregulation of conventional religion may be seen as part of a more general expansion in the range of specialists and intermediaries who offer a variety of religious (along with other cultural) experiences. Life in the so-called advanced societies has become increasingly aestheticized – in music, art, and concern for the body – and new values, experiences, and modes of expression are constantly sought. While this has often been dismissed or attacked as anti-religious hedonism,[41] it may also be harnessed for religious ends.

The Blessing relies on CITs for contact and for a show-business style, focuses on the body as much as on words, and encourages visits to the airport or to local epicenters. An important epicenter is Holy Trinity Church, Brompton, in London, UK. The Leaders of the movement have attempted to downplay the spectacular and bizarre, especially the farmyard and jungle noises for instance. They have taken steps to reassure the wider Christian community of the Blessing's orthodoxy (Christ-centeredness), effectiveness (changing lives), and even historicity (such manifestations have precedents, from the first century to the eighteenth- and nineteenth-century revivals).[42] But the Blessing is none the less known for its unusual features.

CITs help to spread the word about the Blessing. Internationally, this may be seen in its website, which was voted in the top 5 percent of church websites for 1997.[43] This connects in obvious ways with glocalization – Internet sites are classic global non-places. Locally, CITs are visible in the style of worship, which uses electronic media, a master of ceremonies, and new and unconventional styles of music – "a blues-lovers' treat" is how the website describes one performer! Although this could have homogenizing effects (deflecting attention from indigenous traditions, such as Celtic Christianity for instance), this is open to empirical investigation.

It would be surprising if there were not also local reasons that the "fire" is "caught" more readily in some settings than in others, or, to maintain the earlier metaphor, that the flows follow some channels and not others. The Blessing may, for instance, touch certain groups that evidence few features of California-style Vineyard Fellowship, or even airport culture cosmopolitanism. In Pensacola, Florida, for example, the relevant sister church is, according to Margaret Poloma, much more like the more familiar old southern Pentecostalism, which suggests that the flames of the fire may burn quite differently in different locales, even though the spark may have come via Toronto. Of course, by the same token, Toronto itself could be seen as a special case of Pentecostalism. The Latin American connection reminds us that a much larger and more influential fire burns in the southern part of the Americas than in the northern.

Word of mouth from Blessing pilgrims helps publicity. Visitors return to their countries of origin and tell the story; others come to see for themselves. But perhaps "pilgrim" is the wrong word. In John Bunyan's classic hymn, the pilgrim shows steel-eyed determination to fulfill sacred vows and to "labour night and day to be a pilgrim." With the Blessing, things seem quite different. "Let's check it out" may be the first proposal,[44] thus linking the trip with experimentation and experience – like going to Graceland, home of Elvis, or returning to Woodstock after 25 years – rather than with the quest for a kingdom, citizenship of which yields identity and purpose. Once, moderns became "inner worldly pilgrims," still trying to make sense of life, but latterly they have encountered more and more difficulties along the way, as people and things have become less solid.[45] Today, the tourist replaces the pilgrim, as living-for-the-moment has replaced progress. Perhaps Toronto attracts tourists as well as pilgrims.[46]

Tourism also connects with bodily experiences, as fitness – "ready to go" anywhere – supersedes health. Bodily inhibition, characteristic of a more ascetic stage of capitalist development, has given way to a huge focus on and concern with the body in the present.[47] To be relatively freed from bodily constraints is to construct one's own identity, rather than to fit a mold. The body is not the natural, taken-for-granted object presented by modern ways of thinking. Today, it is more a cultural artefact, a setting for drama.[48] The Blessing, it seems, has a specific take on this, and one that sidesteps (but not necessarily denies) the conventional Protestant focus on the "word." The body falls, jerks, shakes, emits noises, and is used in extravagant demonstration as part of the deregulated religious experience. Here, non-verbal experience gives plausibility to the message. At the same time, regulation reappears; care is taken to ensure that only author-ized catchers cushion bodily falls, and only approved counsellors pray with the troubled, which is often accompanied by their touching of the body.

One other feature of the Blessing connects it with the glocaliza-tion debate: diversity and (overcoming) division. Leaders express the hope that denominational differences might be submerged, as "official religion" is transcended by "revival," and a united front is presented to the world.[49] Here we see the dream of global spiritual activity, with the Blessing as a first fruit. Yet alongside this vision, it must be noted that the reception of the Blessing in different contexts has been very mixed. Indeed, so far from some peaceable ecumenism emerging, in the UK it is the "divisiveness" of the movement that has dominated the headlines in the religious press. In the Internet discussions, too, questions have been raised about the theological appropriateness, the historical precedents, and the non-Christian analogs of the Blessing. Among the latter, it has been argued that the Blessing echoes many themes of the ancient occult energy practices of kundalini.

The Blessing may, then, be considered one channel for the flows of religious practices and, to a lesser extent, ideas, within the glocaliza-tion processes of the late twentieth century. This sacred landscape reveals the influences of postmodernizing cultures, with its focus on the spectacle, a lack of bodily inhibition, a varied and contemporary aesthetic, the extensive use of CITs, and the encouragement of spir-itual tourism. Local congregations, touched by the Blessing, are not discouraged from remaining local, but continued contact with the "virus" is assumed. Though there is also evidence of control – both external and internal – and of expressed desires to be orthodox, this is largely outside the bounds of conventional churches. Even the his-tory that is claimed for precedent is the history of the unusual, the extraordinary, not the history of the amazing, intact preservation of a sacred tradition.

Flowing together

The case of the Toronto Blessing is a good one to help us explore the dimensions of contemporary sacred landscapes, enabled by today's global circumstances. This particular flow of religious practices, and their associated but perhaps less significant beliefs, blurs national boundaries, using CIT-based media and spiritual tourism. One sees here both some tendencies towards supra-denominational cooperation, and towards local factionalism. Further studies of the reception of the Blessing in particular places would be necessary if we are to see how this works out in practice. But the cultural filters discussed by David Martin[50] with regard to local patterns of secularization would probably operate in similar ways within glocalizing processes. These would affect tendencies to sameness or diversity in given local settings.

Rather than see the social relations of religion merely in conventional terms of fixed or even flexible structural features such as are provided by the language of denomination or the nation state, I suggest that concepts such as flows and filters throw new light on what is going on today. Margaret Poloma, for instance, suggests that since the parting of the ways with the Vineyard movement, the partially blocked American conduit could offer new opportunities for a non-American Evangelical approach.[51] If we detach the Blessing from the major headquarters of Evangelical groups, while at the same time maintaining the global connections and channels, Christian renewal of a fresh type becomes possible. Such deregulation, one that allows flows to spill beyond time-honored boundaries of nation state and church structure, speaks at least of the relocation, rather than the mere decline, of religion in the postmodern world.

At the same time, challenges to religious practice, if not actual re-regulation, may well occur in these changing circumstances. When Anglican bishops from the so-called Third World – above all from African countries – call into question the acceptance of gays and lesbians as priests within the Episcopal Church in the USA, not only numerical but also moral strength appears to be shifting its center of gravity. Lest this be thought of as a form of reaction, however, calls for liberation are coming from the same quarter – geographically and theologically. At the WEF conference in Abbotsford, British Columbia, it was a Kenyan, Judy Mbugua, who argued most strenuously for women to be "released" for Christian ministry, and David Kima, from Papua New Guinea, who called for credible and compassionate social and political action among Evangelicals. What if this were to militate not only against Americanization, but also against the

Brazilianization mentioned above? Such flows, again enabled by contemporary conduits of communication, signal shifts in the currents of influence whose significance can at present only be dimly perceived.

On the other hand, certain phenomena are clear enough. For example, the power of Pentecostalism is underestimated by social scientists. This is true within Latin America, because few Pentecostals hold university positions, and because Pentecostalism may be seen as a threat to Catholic hegemony. And it is true outside Latin America, because most descriptive literature is in Spanish and Portuguese. But there can be little doubt that, since the 1980s, Pentecostalism has become a force to be reckoned with.[52] While Protestants comprise 10 percent of the Latin American population, or some 45 million people, two-thirds of them are Pentecostals. Brazil has the second-largest Evangelical group in the world, after the USA. Growth rates are accelerating in Brazil and Chile. For instance, in Greater Rio the number of Protestant places of worship exceeds that of Catholic churches and in the poorest districts the ratio rises to almost seven to one.

All this makes Featherstone's comments on Brazilianization even more interesting. For while Evangelicalism may be associated with the American middle classes and, to a limited extent, with the political New Right, in Latin America (especially in Brazil) it has been dubbed the "option of the poor." Although Brazilian Pentecostalism began as an American import, it must be remembered that it is comprised mainly of the Azusa Street – exuberant, black, "primal religiosity" – type, which has been quickly globalized through international networks of counter-establishment religion. So Pentecostalism came from the USA, but from its underside. Freston argues that this helps account for Pentecostalism's rapid spread in the Two-Thirds World; it is a "globalization from below." Here is no abstract theological cosmic Christ, or a quest for common ethical approaches to the environment, but a raw, earthy form of practical empowerment, based on conversion. As Martin says, this is an "indigenous Protestantism based in the hopes of the Latin American poor."[53]

Today, new opportunities present themselves for our understanding of the development of glocal sacred landscapes. On the one hand, within the history and sociology of religion, many more studies are available of actual practices, and forms of networking, as well as the more conventional denominational, parish, and biographical studies that characterize contemporary concern with the sacred. On the other hand, what might be called the cultural turn within sociology has highlighted a general proliferation of flows and scapes, often analyzed in terms redolent of religious language. The latter has also (re)opened debates about the relative autonomy of the cultural sphere, in ways that are illuminating for the sociology of sacred landscapes in particular. The work of Featherstone is especially pertinent here. He avoids both the scylla of economistic approaches to global culture that see it merely as an effect of capitalist production, or a Western export, and the charybdis of postmodern approaches that claim autonomy for culture, as if economy had nothing to do with Disney, Coca-Cola or, for that matter, Billy Graham.

In an early formulation of the globalization argument, Robertson suggested that several significant phenomena could be placed in this context; growing church–state tensions, the rise of new religious movements (NRMs) and the spread of fundamentalism.[54] Robertson suggested that the release from life in "society" provided by globalization generates concerns about world order, but also about human identity and selfhood. Growing out of these, he predicted increasing conflict on a "civil religion" axis, in which movements such as the fundamentalist New Right in the USA try to establish their world view as the civil religion of America. Such concerns, especially when they are seen in tension with "world civil religion" problems – the survival of the planet for example – would, he thought, lead to new religion–politics interactions, in both directions.

Global fundamentalisms

Robertson was, and is, a good guide. Since the mid-1980s a number of studies have appeared, examining the growth of globalized fundamentalisms. How they are understood depends partly on one's view of the relation of modernity to globalization. If globalization is seen as a product of modernity (as, for instance, Giddens[55] understands it), then the spread of the latter may be read as a threat to traditional social systems. In Iran, to take the case most frequently discussed, the arrival of modernity generates fundamentalistic reactions. If, on the other hand, the relation is reversed, such that modernity is seen as an outgrowth of increasing globality, to which Protestant Christianity contributed and contributes still, then the equation becomes more complex. It was Iran, after all, that provided some early fuel for the fire of secularization revisionism. Here was a country becoming more modern and more religious at one and the same time.

Fundamentalisms represent one of the most interesting, and puzzling, phenomena of the postmodernizing, globalizing world. They have been thrust to the forefront of international events at a time when many Western cultural observers imagined that religion would feature less, not more prominently, in world events. This means, among other things, that fundamentalisms are often interpreted in ways that are deaf to religious resonance, when it is precisely the religious aspect that is crucial to grasping what is going on. Fundamentalisms are a response of absolutes and fixity to a world of relativity and flows, but they depend upon the flows – of people, finance, ideas – for their visibility and for their modes of mobilization. And once the word fundamentalism became contemporary common currency, its use broadened to include both non-religious groups and religious groups – such as evangelicals – that frequently strive to distance themselves from fundamentalism.

Zygmunt Bauman argues that "Neo-tribal and fundamentalist tendencies, which reflect and articulate the experience of people on the receiving end of globalization, are as much legitimate offspring of globalization as the widely acclaimed 'hybridization' of . . . culture and the globalized top."[56] He fears the consequences of ongoing segregation and communication breakdown between these two groups, the "extraterritorial elites" and the "localized rest." More specifically, Manuel Castells sees fundamentalisms as a means of constructing "resistance identities" in the face of the globalized dissolution of legitimizing identities. His anxieties are more starkly put: "Fundamentalisms . . . will represent the most daring, uncompromising challenge to one-sided domination of informational, global capitalism. Their potential access to weapons of mass extermination casts a giant shadow on the optimistic prospects of the Information Age."[57]

While these fears may well be justified, they also hint at some of the classification difficulties that currently cause trouble in this area. There is no doubt, however, that one cause of the open fundamentalist challenge is the threat to traditional religious territory. As Appadurai says, "Deterritorialization, whether of Hindus, Sikhs, Palestinians, or Ukrainians, is now at the core of a variety of global fundamentalisms, including Islamic and Hindu fundamentalism."[58] A case in point concerns the murder in 1998 of a Vancouver publisher, Tara Singh Hayer, who was a leader of the moderate Canadian Sikh community. Although at the time of writing no suspects have been named, it is well known that Indian Sikh fundamentalists, led by Bhai Ranjit Singh, are contemptuous of the moderates who, they say, have defied official *hukam-namas* (edicts) that prescribe, among other things, that Sikhs should eat the community meal – *langar* – on the floor. British Columbia Sikhs use tables and chairs. The Indian Sikhs are under pressure from dominant Islamic and Hindu groups (from which Sikhism is derived) to maintain their identity, as they comprise only two percent of the population of India. As Appadurai notes (and this may be applied in the Canadian case), the "problem of cultural reproduction for Hindus abroad has become tied to the politics of Hindu fundamentalism at home."[59]

If the movement of people is an important catalyst for the growth of fundamentalisms, then so also is the movement of images and ideas. It is not just that mediascapes present a threat to cultures that feel themselves to be more victims than beneficiaries of globalization, but that fundamentalist movements also make use of CITs to provide vital organizational links. In discussing Islamic and Christian fundamentalisms, Castells repeatedly shows how dependent they are on high-technology links.[60] The latter highlight the flows between "virtual neighbourhoods" and "lived neighbourhoods" that make possible mobilizations of ideas, opinions, money, and social links. He cites the case of the destruction of the Babri Masjid in Ayodhya, India, by Hindu extremists in December 1992. The use of computer, fax, and related electronic networks "created very rapid loops of debate and information exchange between interested persons in the United States, Canada, England, and various parts of India."[61] Diasporas alter as they are enabled by new forms of electronic mediation.

Just as it is mistaken to think of globalization as producing some homogeneous sameness in cultures, so it is mistaken to think of specific products of globalization, like fundamentalisms, as being basically similar. They may have some common characteristics, such as reliance on the authority of sacred texts, which are a transcendent reference point. They also create boundaries between insiders and outsiders, which serve to reinforce identity. But they are also very diverse. In an interesting reversal of common practice in the study of religion, Gilles Kepel[62] uses the case of Islamic fundamentalism as paradigmatic for other fundamentalisms. He sees the religious basis for a social order built from below as an alternative way of constructing identity in a world whose modern meanings, imposed from above, have failed to satisfy. While this yields some important insights into Islamic fundamentalism, it is a mistake to imagine that the same kind of analysis will work automatically for Christian, Jewish, or Hindu fundamentalisms[63] any more than Christian-based analytical tools work straightforwardly for discussing Islam or other groups. Had Kepel offered the same kind of genealogical background to his discussion of other religious groups, his analysis would be the richer. He would also have avoided some misleading conclusions, at least regarding fundamentalists "saving America."

All too often, untenable assumptions are made about one fundamentalism or another. Appadurai points out how primordialism can lead to the conflation of issues such as ethnic violence and religious tradition.[64] Giddens' or Castells' fears about the violent tendencies clearly refer more, from their descriptions, to non-American, non-Christian fundamentalisms (for few of the latter have access to weapons of mass destruction, for example). Other authors indulge in categorizations that come dangerously close to simplistic dichotomies or suggestions that "revived tribalism" explains what is being witnessed at the turn of the century. Benjamin Barber's *Jihad versus McWorld* treads close to this trap, as does Samuel Huntington's *The Clash of Civilizations and the Remaking of World Order*.[65] Such ideas then become incorporated into official statements, such as the one from UN Secretary General Kofi Annan to the effect that religion is an "exclusionary identity" and a "force of fragmentation" that must be "confronted and restrained" lest it destroy "peace and progress."[66] But the conscious mobilization of cultural differences in pursuit of political ends is what is really going on. This involves identity construction of many different kinds, over against nation states, which are dependent on CITs and migrations. How to coexist with these real differences is a crucial issue for postmodern politics.

Thus fundamentalisms, whose recent expansion is an outgrowth of postmodern, global situations, represent an unavoidable religious dimension of contemporary cultural and political life. It is true, as Giddens reminds us, that much of what gets called fundamentalism has to do with how the truth of beliefs is defended or asserted.[67] But the beliefs themselves cannot be brushed aside easily. Against Giddens, it can be argued that most fundamentalisms are religious and, moreover, that religion is not an essentially *irrational* position, any more than it privileges reason. Giddens is right to associate religion with faith, but not faith with "a sort of emotional leap into belief."[68] Fundamentalisms deserve to be more carefully distinguished, especially if the kind of cosmopolitan dialogue sought by Giddens is to succeed. Caricatured fundamentalism can by definition contribute nothing to such dialogue.

Recognizing the reality of bedrock beliefs, acknowledging alternative reasons for faith, and exploring commonalities and differences strike me as a more likely way of pursuing cosmopolitan dialogue. Whatever else this may mean, in the United Nations or wherever, it suggests that religion may not safely be left out of the picture. This is at the heart of Charles Taylor's description of the "politics of recognition," in which informed respect and a "presumption of worth" are accorded to others' beliefs and practices.[69] Similarly, postcolonial literary critic Satya Mohanty argues that we must confront real disagreements, rather than fall for the "weak pluralist" and homogenizing position that somehow all cultures and beliefs are equally valuable.[70]

Some fundamentalists may have more to offer than a vague sense of unease or dissatisfaction with postmodern globalism. As Joel Carpenter hints in the case of Christian fundamentalism in the USA, whatever may be made of their sectarianisms or their legalisms, a desire for moral accountability and a sense of cultural direction may be their more lasting legacy.[71]

Places and spaces

The question of religion-and-politics, on a world scale, becomes more, not less significant than before. It takes myriad forms, although patterns are discernible. We have already seen that global circumstances have implications for secularization. As noted above, religious conservatism has appeared in several quarters over the past two or three decades, but with different dynamics, depending on their religious form. In Latin America, the old contending monopolies – Catholic and Enlightenment – have found their power eroding. This has permitted the expansion of Protestantism, among other things, in the cultural realm. Where once Puritanism offered the concept of calling that helped produce capitalism and bureaucracy, and Pietism a concept of calling that led to missions, now Pentecostalism offers a new kind of calling to mutual support, healing, and betterment, spread through story and song, in biography and migration. It is easier to export and adaptable enough to be indigenized, although as yet its political consequences are unclear. What seems indisputable is that as life itself becomes politicized, religion and power are reunited, and the political powers that be will increasingly have to take account of the religious factor.[72]

Similarly, in the matter of the increasingly central self, now cut loose from traditional social collectivities, we see glocalizing tendencies. The construction of identities in relation to more fluid social groupings appears to be a worldwide phenomenon, at least in places where consumer culture has taken a firm hold. This is seen in the New Age movement, for instance. We saw in the previous chapter how Christian, Hindu, and Romantic religious ideas could coexist in the thought of figures influenced by the New Age, such as the unfortunate Glenn Hoddle. Hervieu-Léger[73] also discusses this as the growing autonomy of believing subjects within high modernity, cut loose as they are from traditional constraints of regulated religion, and open to a cosmopolitan range of influences. She points to the emerging phenomenon of religious identities being constructed around a bricolage of beliefs, along with new forms of religious sociability.

The bricolage may be seen among certain religious groups in parts of Africa, Latin America, and the Pacific Rim, as well as in North America and Europe. In Korea, sports activities may be combined with Christian forms of religion. Within Pentecostalism, in several contexts, the expressive individualism of high or postmodern situations is contained and incorporated.[74] Of course, the bricolage may have ethnic aspects. While Bolivian Assemblies of God Pentecostals split away from that American denomination, in West Africa similar groups are known for their promotion of inter-ethnic marriage.[75] In other religious groups, different patterns may emerge. Muslim young people in Canada, for instance, increasingly identify with a global *umma* (religious community) rather than with ethnic or national groups, even though their parents' identities may be bound up with these.[76]

That such phenomena are glocal is clear from a number of studies. The use of contemporary music and CITs within Christian groups is visible not only in the Toronto Blessing movement, the Disneyfied Christian festivals, and theme parks in the North Atlantic region, but also in some Asian and Latin American countries. David Martin observes that the old Catholic monopoly has given way to a "lively pluralism and a huge variety of options" in an "open market."[77] The bricolage is visible here too; people move easily between the worlds of advanced technology and "healings, exorcisms and providential interventions." Equally, one finds in this postmodernizing context consumer- and leisure-oriented patterns of behavior among believers, but also patterns of control and constraint that rein them in. As Martin notes, the antecedent cultures still play a great part in determining local outcomes. The market overlays cultural deposits.

All of which returns us to the local. Theorists of globalization all too often fail to keep their feet on the ground. Indeed, some globalization theory is patently elitist, either in its obeisance to the supposed dictates of a global economy or in its stress on patterns of consumption, of travel, and tourism. It already assumes a certain standard of living and a desire to travel – not to mention an available visa. Yet much movement in today's world is that of migrant workers and refugees: the alien and marginalized Other. Just as secularization theories were often elitist, for example assuming forms of abstract rationality probably shared little beyond the (male) academics expounding the theories, so globalization theories can give a misleading, elitist impression.

In the end, religious flows and sacred landscapes originate in or at least connect with some place or places. And however far they travel, they are still experienced in particular places, where people live. Thus globalization is, as John Urry observes, "associated with the dynamics of relocalization."[78] However far-flung the charismatic neo-tribes or even the virtual (religious) community on the Internet, local, grass-roots manifestations of religious life still require careful study – albeit as part of the local–global nexus in conditions of post- or high-modern cultural change. The work of Nancy Ammerman on local congregations[79] is instructive here.

If local conditions and cultural patterns do still filter global flows, and if, as is increasingly the case, local groups are also aware of the effects of distant events, then resistance and receptivity are reflexive processes. The cultural hegemony of US media, for instance, is not everywhere passively absorbed, any more than religious hegemony is. Brazil has the second-largest Christian TV enterprise in the world, after the USA. What began as import substitution now offers independent networks. The CITs that mediate the postmodern and the global to polytheistic cultural groups may also lubricate the "wheels within wheels" that transport the universal-local Christian God.

In a Christian (Mennonite) study of French urban locales in Paris, Montreal, and Algiers, Frédéric de Coninck demonstrates a profound understanding of contemporary consumption and style, and of glocal Brazilianization, although without using that technical term. He also connects it with a discussion of religious groups demonstrating classic Christian concern for the marginalized, the homeless, the stateless, as incarnated "good news."[80] Thus here, in an advanced society setting, one finds an echo of the globalization from below that characterizes vibrant new religious movements in Two-Thirds World contexts. Such work, contextualized and appropriated locally, may contribute not only to the persistence but the radicalization of contemporary sacred landscapes.

7 Telescoped Time

Once, you rolled grandly into Toronto on the train, stopping at Union Station, that marvellous marble-clad monument to the age of the railway. As you looked out of the window beyond the Royal York Hotel, the skyline was dominated by steeples and church towers. Between them, you knew, were the workshops, markets, and homes of daily life.

Today, as you circle to land at Pearson International Airport, all you see is the soaring CN Tower, the Skydome sports arena, and the shining glass, steel, and cement bank buildings. Beyond, strung around endless suburban perimeters, you can pick out the mysteriously named centers dedicated to shopping. Much has changed, especially the speeded up transport and communications. The slower pace of the older city was reflected in the architecture and the street plan, the physical connections in which shopping was not "central," and the face-to-face relationships. Now the glass-faced tall-building architecture reflects its own observers while simultaneously sustaining connections with elsewhere, almost instantaneously reaching round the globe with financial, entertainment, and technoscientific information.

On the ground today, in Toronto as in many other cities, debates grind on as to how the city should be shaped for the future. A key aspect of this is how the city can reinforce its pull as a magnet for leisure and recreational activities. Skydome, the baseball arena, sits close to shopping areas, mass-transit stations, the soaring telecommunications tower, and the business core of Toronto. The Science Center is not far away, nor are the main museums. As far as sport is concerned, Wayne Gretsky, the retired champion of hockey, lends his name to a restaurant and a sports facility chain – Wayne Gretsky's

Iceland.[1] And in the museums, committed to the philosophy that learning is fun, edutainment has taken over. The more hands-on features, the more simulations, the more spectacular sites, the better. One thing is certain in plans for the city: speed is the *sine qua non*. Instant communications, fast food, rapid transit. It is not just times that are a-changing; time itself is transformed.

Here we see the Disneyization, and sometimes the Disneyfication, of urban space. What has occurred for decades in Main Street and World Showcase at Disneyland is now sought in every city. The goal is to recreate the past, as nostalgia and sentiment, and a sense of the future, as an optimistic Tomorrowland. Main Street USA symbolizes small-town America at the turn of the century, evoking warm and fuzzy feelings about the good old days, and minimizing social divisions and conflicts. Turning from past to future, the EPCOT Center places what is to come in the benevolent hands of technoscience, reassuring the world that tomorrow holds in store predictable progress towards a better life.[2] As for the present, Disneyland promotes this as a moment of choice and opportunity. More particularly, the celebration of past and future converges on the present, which is the moment to consume.[3] Time is telescoped into today.

Not only has the age-old puzzle of human temporality been reduced to history; history itself is recycled as nostalgia. Not only has hope been shrivelled into predictions about trends and tendencies; the predictions themselves are simulated and can be experienced virtually today. Not only have social relationships been uprooted from tradition; now they no longer enjoy even the ersatz life frameworks proffered by modernity. Nietzsche's reminder that we must in future live without the comfort of horizons is no longer a spur to active political engagement, or even to the mere revenge against present conditions that he rejected.[4] All horizons are now available for sale, their value is that of the market, and the sole duty remaining is to consume them.

Yet time horizons were once seen by broad swathes of the population as the conditions of human existence, within which everyday life was lived. In Europe and North America, the church calendar once revolved around the rhythm of the seasons and liturgy, with its regular repetitions, textured time as movement between creation and the return of Christ. Festivals and holy days reinforced this pattern, which linked life on earth with the God who was "our help in ages past, our hope for years to come."[5] Indeed, in Toronto such features framed daily life until after the turn of the twentieth century.[6] Religious life now, as then, involves an awareness of both the limits and the modes of transcending those horizons. The Christian ritual of Eucharist expresses this well. Jesus' words unite past and future with the present; "Do this, in remembrance of me, until I come."[7] Memory connects present to past. Hope links present with future.

But those horizons were dismantled by modernity, then reappropriated, to reappear in modern guise. Modernity swung the focus away from the past and towards the future. The past was demoted except as a paean of praise to progress, which thrusts attention forward to the future. In comparison with the early modern balance between past and future, modernity is weighted to the future. The postmodern in a sense completes the task, by disassembling even the replacement horizons such as, above all, the idea of progress. Thus even the frame is discarded now, leaving little but nostalgia where the past once was. But this does not happen in some abstract realm of theory or of speculation. As George Grant noted in the 1960s, it happens in "what is immediately present to all of us." He went on, "When I drive on the highways around Hamilton and Toronto, through the proliferating factories and apartments, the research establishments and supermarkets; when I sit in the bureaucracies in which the education for the technocracy is planned . . . it is then that the conception of time as history is seen in its blossoming."[8]

The same urban spaces still contain religious sites, of course. Venerable worship edifices are still visible in all the cities of the world, both ancient and relatively modern. But in Europe and North America they frequently find their most faithful visitors are tourists. Cathedrals are under new management. Such church buildings often stand as symbolic sentinels, museums marking the sites of old practices, quaint relics of a bygone era. Even here, memory has succumbed to nostalgia. If camera-clicking pilgrims do find a religious ritual, ceremony, or service in progress, they may be forgiven for thinking, from the dress and language, that they have stumbled into a living museum where old ways are dramatically reproduced by seasonal staff, acting parts.[9] Except that Disney does it better.

Does Disneyization affect the conditions that once encouraged religious hope and religious memory? In today's urban settings such conditions seem to be absent or obscured. The postmodern social and cultural context, in which an increasing proportion of the world's population finds itself, appears to re-frame time as well as space. On the one hand, it corrodes shared concepts for thinking about history and time.[10] On the other, less formally, but probably more influentially, it decomposes older daily practices that held people's lives together over time. Because these two processes go hand in hand, perhaps the postmodern should be considered not so much a time of crisis – as some intellectuals see it – as a crisis of time.

Today's postmodern world is one of high technology – computers to clones – of an explosion of electronic media, of a pervasive consumer culture, and of globalized relations of all kinds. The world of cyberspace and consumerism lives under the sign of fluidity and flux, and time itself is flexible. The temporal horizon, which once offered a context, and constraints, on social life, was first transmuted into progress and then started to shrink from consciousness altogether. Time is no longer of the essence, as space starts to obtain the upper hand. Along with space, time is one of the chief coordinates of human social existence, and much is being transformed as time and space are reconfigured by changing institutions and practices.[11] Time, as a forward movement into the future, is giving way to the instant and the simultaneous, just as space, as definable, governable territory, is giving way to flows and to virtuality. The connection with Disneyland is clear. Theme park cities provide a placebo past that is nostalgic, plucked selectively from history with a view to consumption, and a future folded into the present. For the future, too, has everything to do with the products of corporations; it is little more than an extended present.[12]

To read the signs of the times, to grasp some dimensions of the massive changes characterizing our times, attention must be paid to these shifts in modernity, and to the new time-organizing concepts and everyday practices they have generated. Exploring this may yield some of the clues regarding the prospects for reconnecting memory and hope, beyond Disneyfied nostalgia and optimism. If the previous chapter relates mainly to the spatial, with its focus on the global and the local, this one refers mainly to the temporal, past, present, and future. Needless to say, as social processes and personal biographies exist at the intersection of the two – time and space – the difference between the two chapters is really one of emphasis. Time and space fold into each other in everyday experience.

Compressing time

It is a commonplace observation that the pace of life seems to have speeded up. At the same time, those distant from us seem closer when they can be contacted instantly by phone or e-mail, or visited by intercontinental flights. Our temporal and spatial worlds have been rapidly compressed, in ways that sometimes seem overwhelming. As David Harvey says, "The experience of time–space compression is challenging, exciting, stressful, and sometimes deeply troubling, capable of sparking, therefore, a diversity of social, cultural, and political responses."[13] This is partly because, while space can be covered more quickly, the frequency and density of increased communication "makes for less time for communication and its effects to last." Peter Beyer, whose observation this is, also points up the result: "a greater immediacy of otherness and a greater immediacy of change."[14] This has immense implications for the religious.

Of course, the process of time–space compression is a modern one, accented by the ubiquitous clock, and the timetables of railways, factories, prisons, and schools, which served to knit together the social fabric of time and space.[15] But the old categories of time and space, which seemed to serve modernity so well, tend to evaporate in present conditions. In the most obvious case, cyberspace, the only spaces are virtual ones. There is no place to this space. Yet cyberspace has so-called sites that are visited and many other synthetic reminders of physical space. And time is also transformed. Global time zones are only just over a century old. When they were set up, time-organizing concepts had to adjust to the possibility of communication without transportation. With the invention of the telegraph, messages no longer had to be carried physically. Today, however, we have a dizzying range of shifts to cope with.

In the world of electronic communications, for instance, distinctions must be made between "real time" and the asynchronous experiences of e-mail and the Internet. For the last two decades of the twentieth century, the felt sense of time–space compression intensified, as new technologies allowed capitalist enterprises to restructure the processes of production, consumption, and exchange. Production has become more flexible, while consumption and exchange have gone electronic in many ways, perhaps most obviously through the widespread use of plastic money. As an early British advertising slogan crowed about credit cards, they "take the waiting out of wanting." At a personal level, such an acceleration of encounters, both direct and indirect, means that relationships are brief but intense. As Paul Virilio shows, high-paced interconnectivity is becoming a substitute for the slower intersubjectivity that once characterized more traditional relationships.[16] This is a fast world.

All this connects with the emergence of the postmodern. Life is sensed as volatile and ephemeral, as not only fashions, but also modes of working life, leisure activities, forms of entertainment, and even political and philosophical ideas, mutate with remarkable rapidity. Everything, it seems, has to be instant – such as "fast-food" – and disposable – or, now, at least for some items, recyclable. When everything seems temporary, as Georg Simmel and, later in the twentieth century, Alvin Toffler noted, a blasé attitude develops, along with "myopic specialization, reversion to image of a lost past (hence the importance of mementoes, museums, ruins), and excessive simplification (either in the presentation of self or in the interpretation of events)."[17] If anything is Disneyesque, it is this. Short-term plans, short-term gains, become the order of the day, and advertising becomes a major industry for manipulating tastes and desires, so that signs and images become as important, if not more so, than the commodities themselves. Indeed, as image becomes central, so image services spring up, offering creation, consultancy, and personalized designs for the right image.

The replication of everything from buildings to voices brings the simulacrum to center stage, in which telling the difference between the original and the reproduction becomes increasingly difficult. For example, an exhibition at the Museum of Civilization in Ottawa depicts artefacts from ancient Egypt, in the time of Tutankhamun. But only a few of the items displayed are genuine; many cleverly constructed pieces are actually made for the exhibition (although the lack of glass cases and guards helps the museum visitor guess which is which). Simulated age is apparently as acceptable as a genuinely ancient artefact. The successful Disneyfication of such sites places past and present together as items for consumption. Temporal distance is thus diminished, leaving only artificial horizons to frame a history.[18]

As in Disneyland, time is telescoped. In World Showcase, not only are some of the world's most famous places available, but also their connections in time are confused. Past, present, and future appear not as a line, but as a *mélange*, a collage. Disney's planned "Historyland" park would take this even further. Recently, in a public discussion, the authenticity of Disney's America was affirmed in these words: "Disney always does things first-class, and . . . they'll hire the best historians money can buy . . . to create a completely plausible, completely believable appearance of American history."[19] Thus the telescoping of time also entails historical revision, which is also a Disneyfied feature of Microsoft's CD-ROM histories. The latter vary subtly, depending on the countries in which they are marketed. Seemingly, *dochakuka* has temporal as well as spatial dimensions.

The details matter little, it seems. Mere dates and locales are incidental to Disney's "history." If nostalgia can be generated and tourism stimulated, then history can be created, customized, and consumed. And Disneyfication can be taken anywhere. In 1997, for example, elaborate celebrations marked the 500th anniversary of the North American landfall of Giovanni Caboto – John Cabot – in Bona Vista, Newfoundland. Why the tourist trail led there, rather than, say, somewhere in Nova Scotia (with its equally plausible landfall sites), has to do more with which province could obtain financial support for the event than with the accuracy of historical detail. To the much greater chagrin of many Canadians, Disney has now bought the "Mountie" image of the Royal Canadian Mounted Police. The results of that remain to be seen, for the history as well as the future of that force.[20]

Disneyland is both an expression of, and a vehicle for, time–space compression. One encounters in concentrated form both the dizzying sense of "implosion" – this is McLuhan's global village – and some of its effects: the volatile, fragmented, simulated experience of commodified culture. At the same time, Disneylands help to create the conditions suitable for carrying this culture elsewhere. Disneyization is a conduit for accelerated time–space compression.

Timeless time

Clock time is a crucial ingredient of classic modernity. Life run by the clock, in which the sequencing of tasks in a particular order that is measurable and predictable, is vital if one is to catch a plane, make an international phone call at a sociable hour, or even just buy one's groceries before the store closes. And not any clock will do. We can safely forget the medieval clock, the urban toy that boasted only an hour hand. Digital watches, which tell the time in second-fractions and remind us of engagements, are *de rigueur* today. In postmodern times, of course, the clock is still essential, but the social meaning of time is exploding. As Castells argues, this transformation is a profound one: "it is the mixing of tenses to create a forever universe, not self-expanding but self-maintaining, not cyclical but random, not recursive but incursive: timeless time, using technology to escape the contexts of its existence, and to appropriate selectively any value each context could offer the ever-present."[21] For Castells, "timeless time" is the emerging dominant form of social time. And although Castells does not major on this, it should also be noted that, just as clock-time was imbricated with the religious dimensions of social life, this new temporality has implications for religious life today.

Some of the religious implications are brought out most clearly in the work of Anthony Giddens, for whom time sociology is central to understanding modernity. Whereas in premodern situations time and space were linked through place, the modern world was characterized more and more by their separation. Space pulled away from place, while time was "emptied," thus facilitating the "lifting out" of social relationships from their traditional locales.[22] In traditional settings, which are often local, people's lives are organized in terms of a past, present, and future that is stable and within which they have a fairly consistent mode of being. Their continuing security, their sense of what counts as appropriate behavior, derives from this and lends a sense both of identity and of meaning in life. Explicitly religious ideas, practices, and institutions are involved in this.[23]

Modernity's substitution of rationalized regimes and routines, along with the necessary tokens of trust between strangers, has done little to compensate for the loss of "ontological security" as time empties itself. In what Giddens calls conditions of late modernity, even those substitutes are destabilized. "What was due to become a social and physical universe subject to increasingly certain knowledge and control instead creates a system in which areas of relative security interlace with radical doubt and with disquieting scenarios of risk."[24] In his view, this accounts for the "new forms of religious sensibility and spiritual endeavor" so evident today. It shows particularly why fundamentalisms would have such an appeal. But more generally, these movements represent the "return of the repressed, since they directly address issues of the moral meaning of existence which modern institutions tend so thoroughly to dissolve."[25] While this explanation does not pretend to be complete, it is none the less a suggestive, partial one.

Unlike Harvey, who finds capitalist accumulation at the root of the trend towards timeless time, Castells sees a broader independent role for culture, even though he does rightly highlight ways in which global capital is implicated within new temporalities. Electronically managed capital markets around the world create what Castells calls a "global casino," in which time becomes quintessentially the source of value. The speed of transactions is crucial to their profitability, and computers are often programmed to make almost instantaneous decisions, some of which have caused notorious instability in financial markets. The very idea of "futures markets," which trade on developments yet to take place, shows how time is compressed and absorbed in new ways. These processes in turn have impacts within the enterprise, generating needs for new flexibilities in management, higher production schedules, and faster turnover. Production is networked and time is managed, processed as a resource, rather than as a fixed factor.

At a personal level, this is a major disorientation. Paid working time still structures social life for many people. Thus, as changes occur in the number of hours worked and their distribution in the day, month, and life cycle, great differences are made to experiences of social life, positively and negatively. Whereas standardization and harmonization of working times were once the order of the day, now huge diversity exists between countries, firms, and types of organization. The large-scale entry of women into the labor force, variable job assignments, and flexible time-schedules lead to what French sociologist Frédéric de Coninck calls a "social shattering," as competing and contradictory temporalities shake and splinter previous patterns of sociality.[26] The uprooting (*déracinement*) from local communities that accompanied the first industrial revolution is now more than matched by a temporal uprooting, which increasingly undermines the sense of belonging that comes from telling the same "story."

The flexible worker learns to be disposable. The expectation of lengthy training for a lifelong career is not well founded today. And, given currently rising divorce rates in most advanced societies, the expectation of lifelong relationships may be equally dubious. The cancellable arrangement, one that lasts only until further notice, is rather the order of the day. The episodic, the fleeting, the uncertain come to characterize social and cultural life in more and more spheres. This situation may ideally suit the world of transnational corporations, for whom the paramount need is a flexible labor force. But its social and personal consequences have yet to be seen. It is already clear that, combined with greater geographical mobility, time flexibility generates a need for tokens of trust (such as credit cards or driver licences) to compensate for the fact that more and more of our dealings are with strangers.[27]

Castells proposes that the life cycles themselves are becoming blurred as essential biological and social rhythms of life are disrupted by timeless time. For not only is work-life affected by new technologies; reproductive and life-span-affecting technologies are also making an impact. Times of birth and death are subject to attempted calculation and control. Existential choices and decisions, concerning the profoundest matters of life and death, confront human beings as never before. Castells calls its effects "social arrhythmia." It culminates in the denial of death, which has become a commonplace in contemporary advanced societies. The denial is achieved either through placing unprecedented – and, one might add, unwarranted – faith in medical technology, or through the trivializing of death through endless repetition in the mass media.[28]

Beyond this theme, Castells also comments on two other matters – instant war, with its "technologically induced temporality,"[29] and "virtual time," with its twin characteristics of simultaneity and timelessness. The former, involving technologically sophisticated professionals who conduct war remotely – as occurred, classically, in the Gulf War – and the equally careful management of news for domestic consumption, is the privilege of the powerful, technologically dominant nations. News management, which creates a culture simultaneously ephemeral and eternal, is based on a new media "temporal collage, where not only the genres are mixed, but their timing becomes synchronous in a flat horizon, with no beginning, no end, no sequence."[30] Both of these are aspects of the general perturbation of time, in which temporality is evacuated of older concepts and experiences of time, to become the "timeless time" of the present.

This timeless time, which creates an extended present, also has the effect of making the future disappear. Whereas the premodern world was characterized by a fairly stable temporal order, which was replaced by the quantified and commodified time of modernity, the accelerated time of postmodernity produces simultaneity and a foreshortening of the future. Helga Nowotny puts it like this: "A present geared to accelerated innovation is beginning to devour the future. Problems which could formerly be deferred into the future reach into the present for their part, press for solutions which admittedly may not be on the agenda until tomorrow but demand to be dealt with today."[31] Nowotny foresees some dire social consequences of this, in that "short-term interactions negate time, and where time is neglected, responsibility also dwindles."[32] The contexts of care for the Other contract as, literally, people have no time for each other. Loving one's neighbor, a classic ethical demand of Jewish and Christian traditions, may be harder in postmodern times.

To disrupt time is to generate uncertainties, to loosen anchors, to dissolve meanings. Although Nowotny has little to offer on this front, more than one author points out ways in which growing ephemerality stimulates quests for new moorings, new bearings. Even David Harvey, who sees little autonomous role for the cultural, acknowledges that time–space compression has recently coincided with religious revivals, a search for authenticity and authority in politics, a re-emphasis on home as haven and local community as a source of roots, and the importance of photographs and music to yield a "sense of self that lies outside the sensory overloading of consumerist culture and fashion."[33] Castells, probing beyond the materialist base, finds a new culture, which installs "individual dreams and collective representations in a no-time mental landscape."[34] New Age music exemplifies this for Castells, with its "electronic spiritualism" that attempts to fuse the biological individual into the cosmological whole, to bring together the net and the self.

The end of history

The routines of everyday life may well be punctuated only by brief moments of intense time. But on a larger scale questions are still asked about history and the future. What for some may be playful, depthless time that takes no serious account of what was or what is to come poses for others new questions about the end of history. As Krishan Kumar observes, social theory itself could almost be said to have started with biblically rooted end-time ideas.[35] Both the Hebrew scriptures and the New Testament indicate a culminating episode for human history, in the coming, or the second coming, of the Messiah. Hegelian and Marxist thought in particular was predicated on a rupture between the conditions of the present and the conditions of a renewed future, which depend for inspiration on a version of millennialism when time shall be no more.

It is hardly surprising that, as the year 2000 approached, both political events and academic theorizing focussed attention on the significance of the millennium. Millennial anxieties were attached to events such as the Oklahoma government building bombing (in 1997) and the Sarin gas attacks on the Tokyo subway (in 1993 and 1997). The coming of the millennium spawned both dire warning and confident assertion. Or at least, these symptoms appear coincidentally with the twenty-first century. On the one hand, history is viewed as being volatile, ready to blow in some apocalyptic blast. The "millennium rage"[36] exponents expect something pretty explosive. Their evidence is activities such as the attacks by the Sons of Gestapo, the Unabomber, the conflagration at the Branch Dravidians site at Waco, Heaven's Gate "cult" suicides, and so on. On the other hand, Francis Fukuyama's version of the end of history is much nearer a whimper than a bang. For him, the collapse of the Berlin Wall and the close of the Cold War usher in an era in which battling ideologies are no more. So-called liberal democracy has triumphed, he claims, as the "final form of human government."[37] Henceforth, relentless calculation, problem-solving, and consumer satisfaction will bring boredom to all. Fukuyama did not claim that, as it were, nothing would happen any more. Rather, history as an arena for ideological conflicts would come to an end now that Western civilization has brought liberal capitalist democracy to all. With what Fukuyama calls the "big questions" settled, mere concern with the best means to fulfill the promise of the reigning paradigm would take over.

The controversy surrounding the Fukuyama thesis has been out of proportion to the technical significance of his work. But clearly he struck a chord. A number of factors leave his ideas open to serious question. His notion of liberal democracy leaves little room for the massive – and frequently bloody – upsurges of nationalism appearing throughout the world. Nor does it account for the diverse beliefs which are all too often lumped together as Asian values that have risen to prominence in Pacific Asia. Singapore, Indonesia, Malaysia, and Korea, to give relevant examples, hardly count as liberal democracies in quite the sense that Fukuyama intends. More left-wing-oriented versions of liberal democracy also continue to be available, throwing down a gauntlet to the free-market version espoused by Fukuyama. And, lastly, his thesis does not account for those events that may break into history, such as ecological disaster, genocide, and refugee migrations.

Notably, in his end-of-history thesis Fukuyama has little to say about religion. This is odd, given the role that, say, Augustine has in forming at least Western ideas of history (and of which Hegel and Marx were in part heirs), not to mention the huge and continuing influence of religion on world history. Whether conventional or otherwise, religion will still be implicated in changes occurring on the far side of the millennium.[38] How could Fukuyama not discuss fundamentalisms at least? Such movements have taken on tremendous – if sometimes exaggerated – political importance at the end of the century.

Perhaps Fukuyama does not discuss the realm of religion, of faith, and of valuing because he is blind to the extent to which the Western viewpoint he espouses itself represents what might be thought of as a faith position. Like secularization theory, when used as a meta-narrative, Fukuyama's assumptions seem to exclude religious considerations. His is an overarching commitment to what remains of the Enlightenment project, which many Westerners like him continue to think is worth exporting, globally. Yet, as Baudrillard observes with somewhat apocalyptic abandon, "what the West wants to impose on the world is . . . its lack of values. This terrorism is not the result of fundamentalism but of an unfounded culture. It is the [intégrisme] of emptiness . . ."[39]

In *The End of History and the Last Man* Fukuyama does not appear to grasp either the significance for ordinary people of the habits of the heart or the ways in which his viewpoint also betrays a religious direction(lessness). In its sequel, however, Fukuyama seems to compensate for this by bringing religion into what he calls *The Great Disruption*.[40] His faith in liberal democracy is such that the challenges of militant fundamentalisms are still downplayed, although he does acknowledge that what he thinks of as milder varieties of religion may reappear in the West, starting in the USA. These, he says, are responses to a desire for community and to felt "hunger" for ritual and cultural tradition in a world where social ties have become more transient.

An alternative view to Fukuyama's is that the future is a positive pressure cooker, ready to explode with conflict. Reference was made in chapter six to the ideas of Samuel Huntington and Benjamin Barber, each of whom foresees heightened tensions on a global scale.[41] Huntington observes that many forms of authoritarianism, nationalism, corporatism, and market capitalism exist in different countries. More significant, he insists, are religious differences. These are the central means of motivation and mobilization today. "The more fundamental divisions of humanity in terms of ethnicity, religions, and civilizations remain and spawn new conflicts."[42] Huntington reads Fukuyama's evidence not as the denouement but as the decline of the West. It is, as Baudrillard says, an illusion of the end.[43]

Barber's view is that the interdependent forces of Jihad and McWorld are the cockpit of struggle today. This is the divided, duelling future, which may also be seen in the work of Castells, of Bauman, and of Robert Kaplan.[44] The basic asymmetries of the globe are on an axis dividing the "net" and the "self," "globals" and "locals," "affluence and security," and "poverty and violence" respectively. Here, once more, is a more apocalyptic version of future events. It is, moreover, one that stresses the destructive rather than the revelatory aspects of apocalypse. It has in its favor a larger repository of realism than Fukuyama's vision, but it hardly holds out hope for the third millennium.

Curiously enough, both versions of "the future" may be found in explicitly religious contexts. Perhaps this is not so surprising, given the Janus-faced nature of apocalypse, with its judgment and its disclosure. In the previous chapter we noted the rise of an ecumenist vision of global religious harmony, or at least of a common quest for understanding. Given the majoritarian Christian antipathy towards state communism that prevailed in most of Eastern Europe until 1989, it is no accident that unreflective support for the market economy and Western democracy appears as the natural alternative in some quarters. Various Christian groups have warned about this as a "false eschatology" however, including some evangelical and reformed groups which declared that they reject "the Messianic Western dream . . . selfish secular materialism pursues its own economic growth irrespective of the need to preserve the environment and to serve the development of the poorer nations. It is characterized by self-absorbed individualism and insensitive affluence, which are incompatible with Christian let alone truly human values."[45] Such views fit well with those of Richard Fenn, who argues that the religious impulse may do much to thwart the spread of fascism. It is the lack of ritual, he insists, that opens the door to unjust and undemocratic regimes.[46]

On the other hand, a strong streak of apocalypticism does attend some religious pronouncements on the future, including those on destructive doomsdays. Often echoing futurological forecasts, but now relying on speculative biblical exegesis rather than statistical extrapolation of trends, current events are interpreted within a frame that has more than a whiff of nationalism. Hal Lindsay's bestselling *Late, Great Planet Earth*, for instance, plays on millennial apprehensions and ideas such as the "great tribulation" to give a sense of the future as predictable and insurable, given the right religious responses. As one commentator says, this is "hardly an eschatology that may serve as an answer to the present crisis of modernity and the evolving postmodern paradigm."[47]

It seems that the primary postmodern alternatives involve either denying the present and accepting the past or denying the past and accepting the present. The former may be reduced to Disneyfied nostalgia, the latter to consumption in an endless present. The utopian vision of a globalized American future is probably seen less as something yet to occur than as an automatic outcome of the present. And as for the apocalyptic, it has no place in the Disney scheme. But information-sated regimes that favor forgetting, or that reassure us that events yet to occur can be risk-managed, are poor providers of ontological security or ongoing identity, let alone of a sense of priorities for facing the future. The very notions of memory and hope – so central to most religious outlooks – seem to have lost some salience in postmodern times.

Memory and hope

This is the current crisis of time. The focus of the foregoing, on the ways that communication technologies and consumerism are contributing to a postmodernizing world, raises time perturbation as a serious question. Zapping with the TV remote and fast food may sound like trivial examples, but they are symbolic signs of our times. Although the word cyberspace suggests location or place, one could equally argue that drastically reduced communication time is what the Internet is all about. The instantaneous has pulled us into the gravitational field of a permanent present. We are prisoners of the immediate, trapped between past and present.[48] The end of history for Paul Virilio is the "upper speed limit" of accelerating time. He quotes a Holocaust survivor, who sees the "breathtakingly frantic pace" and "dizzying kaleidoscope" of history as favoring "the rise to power of forgetting."[49]

All this helps to create an unwelcoming environment for the religious life, at least as that life was known in modernity. If, as Danièle Hervieu-Léger argues,[50] religion operates within "communities of memory," then disruptions to memory, through collective amnesia and, for that matter, selective amnesia – the Disneyfied collage approach to history – pose a challenge of some magnitude. In her work, religion relates to a believing community with a distinct genealogy. Past and future are significant for the present existence of the community, which is held together by shared symbols, ideas, and social practices. Maintaining a living memory as a source of meaning for the present and hope for the future is difficult, to say the least, in postmodernizing conditions. Yet in the Jewish scriptures, for instance, this is exactly what goes on, as the most ancient records show. The exiled and diasporic Jews of Nehemiah's time, found again their future hope in God through retracing the line of collective memory to promises made to Abraham, and beyond, right back to Creation.

In the modern world, memory and hope were steadily uncoupled. Today, Disney culture plays tricks with both. A sense of history is often reduced to commodified heritage, while the future is in the high-tech hands of the futuristic EPCOT, the idol of silicon-simulated worlds. Here again is a secularized religious chronotope that emphasizes the story of a good past and a rosy future, but in which the redemptive dynamic is in human hands alone. Communities of memory, among which the religious are the strongest and the longest lasting, have been dominated in the West by detraditionalization and deinstitutionalization. Religious symbols and stories are, like so much else in contemporary culture, cut loose, free-floating, fluid. They do not disappear. Rather, they reappear as cultural resources. Little surprise, then, that such surrogates tend towards the bricolage, the smorgasbord, the mixing and melding of once different elements. With religion deregulated, it seems, anything goes.

Or does it? In fact, one still finds patterns of belief, some sense of memory, a quest for coherence, even in situations where the postmodern tendencies are pronounced. In some Latin American churches, for instance, in which conventional Christian commitments mingle cheerfully with electronically enhanced worship and postmodern pastiche-style patter, there is marked growth (and no sense of incongruity).[51] The deinstitutionalization and deregulation of religion allows for fresh growth, new directions, and sometimes surprising strategic alliances. This of course obliges at least Christian believers to confront the awkward question, posed by Jesus himself, of how far, in times past, believers have mistaken mere human traditions for the demands of God. The "chain of memory" (to use Hervieu-Léger's term) or of believing can remain intact even if certain conventional links are replaced or removed altogether. But the process is far from automatic or assured.

At any rate, it is clear that contemporary conditions make problematic the time dimension of social life, which has strong implications for the religious realm and for its faith practices. The postmodern is marked by an evacuation of traditional time from daily temporality, and ramifications are seen not only in the relatively trivial instantaneity of today's cultural forms but also in the disturbed patterns of sociality, starting in the workplace, and moving steadily into all other spheres. Social arrhythmia and its cultural aspects affect all that is touched by the flexible and fluid world of postmodernity. The endless present denies any future but that provided by more technology, more consumption, while at the same time offering even the past as another object for consumption, or as a focus for nostalgic longing (or both). The Disneyfication of the whole process serves only to reinforce the time-perturbation, despite the faint and distorted echoes of historicity and hope in the Disney narratives. Where then can any sense of continuity and of shared commitments – the essence of that chain of memory, and thus of hope – be found?

8 Faith's Future

Jesus in Disneyland is a metaphor for religious life in postmodern times. It is, of course, a very Christian metaphor, in that Jesus is far less central to Islam and Judaism, let alone to other religious faiths, than to Christianity. And it is a very American-sounding metaphor, even though Disney has been successfully globalized. But the metaphor speaks of democratized and commodified cultures that now form the context within which faith has to find fresh footholds. And it alludes to relationships that are more and more electronically mediated, in which symbols and images have become centrally important, bringing society and culture ever closer together. It is a reminder that the basic coordinates of social life – time and space – are being reconfigured, decomposed from their modern lines and shapes into flows and fragments that will alter radically life in the twenty-first century. The metaphor is also meant as a warning of a Disneyfied world in which, as Baudrillard says, "reality itself becomes a spectacle, where the real becomes a theme park" and in which we all become film extras in our own world.[1] Including our religious worlds.

Religion or, rather, spirituality has undoubtedly become a consumer item. New sources of meaning are sought that include prominently the figure or at least the name of Jesus. In Canada, to take the example with which I am most familiar, Jesus has become an icon of choice on T-shirts and tote-bags and appears in rap music lyrics and in bestselling books. But this is equally and undoubtedly a postmodern Jesus. As theologian Henry Maier comments, while a personal relationship with God is sought, people want "an easier, faster, no-fuss, microwavable God." The cross remains a major stumbling block for many – as it always will – but, in Maier's estimation, Jesus is popular because "he's a pluralist, he welcomes outsiders, he welcomes women, he is against organized religion, he's for economic justice. Jesus comes dressed up in the clothes of our own culture."[2]

In this book I have tried to explain something of the sociological background to the present postmodernizing conditions that are so quickly altering cultural landscapes across the globe. Faith is in ferment; new beliefs are brewing. To try to grasp some of the major trends is crucial, not just from the viewpoint of those who hold to some conventional commitments, but from the perspective of all who wish meaningfully to participate in the pluralist, mediated, globalizing information age for which I use the shorthand "postmodernity." This final chapter does three things. First, it retraces our steps through the book. Secondly, it argues that to consider religious life in postmodern contexts obliges us also to reconsider how sociological analysis proceeds; sociology is in no way exempt from or external to the challenges presented by postmodernity. Thirdly, I comment a little more directly than hitherto on some implications of the foregoing analysis for specifically Christian living in the present.

Recollecting

Secularization as a metanarrative is dead. Or rather, the popular interpretations of Max Weber – those that ignore the new possibilities for polytheisms, prophets, or alternative rationalities, and that focus only on the prospects for the "polar night of icy hardness" as the steel cage of secular instrumental rationalization closes in – are dead. Just as the ending of Christendom did not seal the fate of institutional religiosity, so the deregulation of religion that followed Christendom's demise does not portend its final doom, or its social and cultural irrelevance. Granted, organized religion, especially in its modern, denominational forms, is not generally in healthy shape in the affluent Western societies, especially in Europe. In so far as this is the case, properly limited reference to secularization still makes sociological sense. Having said that, of course, where the cognate equivalents to Western Christianity exist in other parts of the world, often they are flourishing. Conventional, mainline religious groups may have fallen on hard times, but the curtain has yet to fall on faith, spirituality, and the quest for transcendence.

The simple dichotomies that bedevilled modern analyses of religion no longer work, if indeed they ever did. While resistance to postmodernizing conditions may harden into fundamentalistic reaction, that can at times even be tinged with violent edges; and where accommodation to present conditions may evacuate the very core of meaning from major world religions, these are not the only choices left open for today's seekers. The cultural resources of religiosity are drawn on in diverse ways, and some orthodox religious groups perpetuate themselves through a process of negotiation and navigation through the unfamilar tides and currents of the postmodern. As we have seen, groups and individuals with clear religious identities engage in a continuing process of adaptation *and* resistance in respect to contemporary conditions.

As to the nature of these contemporary conditions, it is important to see them as structural alterations in the ways that human lives are lived in the twenty-first century. I have stressed the somewhat tentative nature of these postmodern premonitions. But the very debate about postmodernity – along with that concerning an "information age" or "globalization" – is evidence of a widespread sense of the seismic social changes that are currently occurring. Without our drifting into determinism, either technological or economic, it can safely be assumed that two factors are crucial to the rise of postmodernity: the diffusion of communication and information technologies, and the decisive shift towards consumer capitalism and consumer lifestyles. Social interaction and organization take on a new cultural pattern, which is, as Castells says, "why information is the key ingredient of our social organization and why flows of messages and images between networks constitute the basic threads of our social structure."[3] It is also why choice, rather than constraint, has become such a central "value," and thus also a marker of social divisions.

These factors, above all, throw up both the new challenges and the new opportunities for contemporary religion, faith, and spirituality. Cultural expression is now integrated with all other electronic communication systems, with several profound consequences. The symbolic power of traditional senders of messages is weakened in so far as those messages are vulnerable to mixing, dilution, and distortion. And unless their senders find fresh means of recoding the messages they are liable to be sidelined. Old authorities are thus even more questionable than under previous conditions, which also exhibit increased culture contact through migration and tourism. And as such sources of meaning become obscured or less apparently available, so self-identity moves steadily into a more central social-cultural position. Identities are constructed either to resist felt threats or as projects to try to overcome them, or both at once. Consumer cultures affect the choices made in the fields of faith and spirituality, in both resistance and project forms of identity construction, often but not always with inherently mutable and unstable outcomes. The already existing cultural conditions affect those outcomes too, so that both local and global dynamics will play a part in the extent to which project or resistance identities predominate.

Time and space, which in modern times seemed so measurable, so predictable, and which provide the warp and woof of social life, are also in flux. The social fabric is thus patterned in novel ways, with new dimensions. Time–space compression creates a global village, but the village is both everywhere and nowhere. Global flows of many kinds yield the new fluidity to patterns of social interaction on an international plane, while they simultaneously limit "locals" within "places" with both positive and negative effects. Time also implodes into an endless present, which has the dangerous potential of attenuating memory and foreclosing hope. The world of the instant and the immediate is at the same time the world of drastically disturbed rhythms. Not only have seasons and day-and-night lost much of their salience for sociality; even the artificial divisions of the nine-to-five and the life-cycle prospect culminating in retirement at 65 are subject to rescheduling.

Within modernity, the religious meanings of time and space could more straightforwardly be worked out, given the close connections between the modernist spirit and certain forms of Christianity. Even so, while the overdone secularization thesis reigned, much was made of both the churches' failure properly to respond to modern conditions and its having responded to them all too fully. Churches in modern, bureaucratic guise were clearly influenced by the dominant mode of organization, the limited company. Doctrinal capital could thus be accumulated and transmitted, even when the denomination seemed to lose its beating heart or its sense of direction. But from time to time revival has come to even the most moribund ecclesiastical forms, a situation seldom foreseen by those looking through the spectacles of secularization. Equally, while specific forms of time-space organization may cast for a period at least a shadow of spirit, they may not be the right places to look in the long term. In the words of the Australian Aboriginal story told earlier, the river may now be flowing elsewhere.

Although unintended consequences abounded within modern situations, there was at least a general sense of congruence between, on the one hand, created space as an opening for development, or time as an arena for discipline and redemption and, on the other, territorial expansions or organizational regimes that came to characterize the power containers of modernity. Postmodern time–space compression, by contrast, is induced by large-scale technological forces which, although they are not autonomous, have no hint of causal connection with outworked faith – except faith in technology – or religious routines. Contemporary cultural formations thus exist on the edge of uncertainty. Such a situation offers simultaneously opportunities for the retrieval of alternative conceptions of space and time, and threats of condemnation to continual fracturing and fragmentation that deny all wholeness and harmony to human existence. Retrievals, however, would involve deliberate resistance, privileging place over the spaces of flows, for instance, or relativizing time in relation to eternity.

Does this mean, then, that when all is said and done the prognoses of the strong secularization thesis may still be fulfilled? What I have written here weighs heavily against such a conclusion. Even in modern conditions, far too much was expected of the strong secularization thesis. It mistook the limited European uncoupling of church and state for a universal process. It failed to note that the impact of urbanism and industrialism varied from place to place, and that these processes themselves were a mere passing phase of modern capitalist development. It often overestimated the extent to which in everyday life people think in strictly scientific terms. And, of course, it tended to assume that science itself is somehow unreligious at the level of its basic assumptions. In other words, the sociology that spawned secularization as a high-level explanation of religious attenuation in the modern world was, as a product of the same world, also limited in its vision.

If secularization as a metanarrative is vulnerable to criticism in its original modern European setting, it must be said that it sits even less comfortably in the increasingly postmodern, global world of communication and information technologies and consumerism. These emergent features alter the social and cultural landscape in ways that make very doubtful any merely linear development from, say, secularization into hypersecularization. The modern is still present, of course, with many of its influences still intact. But modernity's contradictions are now more openly evident, and the ambiguities of its effects on religion are much better known. Rivers of conventional religion still flow, but deregulated religion has long since spilled out into a delta of streams and channels. New networked modes and globalized currents of religious activity constantly create surprises, from Pentecostalism's globalization from below to the reappearance of politically potent public religions, or to the sometimes salutary eruption of fundamentalisms.

Rethinking

The study of religion in postmodern times calls for fresh perspectives. It is not enough to argue for a new paradigm as an alternative to

tired, Eurocentric secularization theories, even though this is a significant first step. Nor is it sufficient to suggest that religion be rethought,
not as organizational form, but as cultural resource, although, once
again, this is a liberating and illuminating move. A further step must
be taken, one in which the sociology of religion recognizes more
candidly, more openly, its own role in the situations it purports to
study. There are good philosophical reasons for this. But in line with
the rest of the analysis in this book, I wish to suggest that there are
equally good reasons presented by the sociological realities that are
under discussion. Sociology, whether it explores religion or anything
else, cannot pose as an innocent bystander or a detached observer of
social and cultural trends.

The stance of clinical separateness of observer and observed is a
fading dream of Enlightenment. It is fading not just because other,
more recent philosophical arguments are ousting it, but because the
conditions of knowledge-production themselves are changing. In the
conditions elaborated above, knowledge has undergone considerable
change. In the information age, knowledge is at once raw material,
process, and product of production. Knowledge acts on knowledge
to produce new knowledge. Sociological knowledge serves to inform
social activity itself, making sociologists – or at least those who succeed in making themselves heard – the co-authors of the drama for
which they are also interpreters and critics. Sociological knowledge
circulates with the other symbols and images of the age, to be drawn
upon by groups, organizations, and individuals in the process of self-
understanding, identity construction, and goal formation.

It should be stressed that this emphasis on the reflexive character of
the discipline does not necessarily signal a relapse into relativism, even
though some of postmodernistic bent have allowed or even encouraged
it to do so. As understood here, such reflexivity is consistent with
relational (not relativistic) knowledge, with realism (which simultaneously asserts the reality of and the connections between "individual"
and "society"), and also with social responsibility (rather than indif-
ference).[4] In the sociology of religion, this means several things, including becoming aware of how sociology is perceived and used both by
relatively powerful groups in education, media, and government, but
also by religious organizations and groups, and seeking to acknowledge, as far as possible, the assumptions and faith implications of
the kinds of explanation that such sociologies put forward.

Sociology has spent many decades escaping from the clutches of an
impossible dream of perfect knowledge, and it has not fully loosened
the shackles. But the way out, as I see it, is for us to admit the short-
comings of empiricism and positivism without falling into the morass

of relativism. All attempts at explanation – social theory – are under-determined by the facts, and, equally, all facts are theory-laden. What this means, according to Mary Hesse, is that normative assumptions enter the process of theory construction.[5] These are a part of the theory but may not be arrived at through empirical observation or methodological explanation. In the sociology of religion, such assumptions may include the ideas that human social life is irreducibly religious and that faith-orientations both are an aspect of social action and also structure that activity.

This in turn adds weight to the notion that affirmative rather than merely skeptical approaches to the postmodern are available to sociological practice. Where skeptical postmodern*ism* would chronically defer all meaning, the approach taken here relies also on retrieval. Some shared meanings are, after all, part of the very conditions of human existence.[6] Following the work of Emmanuel Levinas, care for the Other has become a major theme of contemporary social ethics, one that has strong resonance with some basic religious understandings.[7] But not all meanings are shared, by any means, and a reflexively responsible sociology of religion is also fine-tuned to those differences, as well as to the commonalities of existence. And as long as sociology has not itself succumbed to the historical lobotomy that simultaneously enervates hope, then both transformation (on the basis of commonalities) and tolerance (of difference) may effectively be sought, as reasons for engaging in sociological analysis.

Reshaping

Religious life in postmodern times demands not only to be understood differently, but also to be lived differently. Religious practices, which are in any case constantly revised, may be revised in more and less informed ways. Sociology certainly does not have all the answers, and this should not for a moment be construed as a call for sociological expertise to engineer religious responses to the postmodern. On the other hand, sociology does offer some insights, which may inform believers as well as those more reticent about their deepest commitments. In this book, Christian examples have featured most prominently, for the simple reason that I have been dealing with cultures profoundly affected by Christianity. But it is also the case that my own faith commitments are Christian commitments, and readers will get the best sense of some implications of my analysis of religion in postmodern times by considering some Christian situations that I have offered as examples.

To continue in the same vein as in the previous section, then, it is not enough to go beyond new paradigms for the study of religion. Sociology should resituate itself within the postmodern. This means, among other things, that sociology should embrace reflexivity without relativism, reject the legislative mode, but not basic commitments, focus on Otherness, but seek commonalities, and seek appropriate transformative purposes for the discipline. But beyond this, a religious reading of what I have written may draw out certain ramifications for faith and spirituality in the twenty-first century. A full treatment of this would require another book. So the following comments are suggestive rather than in any way comprehensive.

Christianity faces a curious conjunction: the crisis of modernity. Modernity is a social-cultural formation of major, world-changing dimensions, which Christianity helped to generate, and from whose unintended consequences it has tried, with varying degrees of success, to extricate and exempt itself. The crisis of modernity is an aspect of postmodern conditions. For a long time, many Christians essayed to accept what is still salvageably Christian from the modern project, while at the same time displaying hesitation or opposition towards those features deemed inimical or at least indifferent to Christian practice. Thus, for example, during the twentieth century Christian groups in the West played a prominent role in the formation of welfare states but also became increasingly uneasy about the extent of bureaucratic control over the poor exercised by such apparatuses. To take another example, some found Christian warrant for a "just war" compatible with the defence of democratic freedoms, but balked at the later products of industrialized warfare that introduced nuclear and virtual engagement.

New situations present both new challenges and new opportunities, just as they did in the heyday of modern times. Then the problem was often construed in the West as a post-Christendom crisis. One major difference, however, is that today, with the shrinking of institutional religiosity, the burden of choice falls far more squarely on individual shoulders. But part of the thrust of this book has been to stress the ambivalence of current situations. Although I have not minimized the genuine threats to Christian spirituality and social action, this is not another lament for a lost past, or a weary warning about the postmodern menace. As I have argued, the "postmodern menace" viewpoint owes much to some too philosophical fears. Such nervousness overlooks the significance of everyday life activities as the real arena of the social, and also underestimates the capacity of knowledgeable (religious) agents – not to mention God! – to recognize situations for what they are, and to make a difference.

With regard to the central significance of CITs, the challenge is quite clear. The groups that will find a voice will be those that are able to encode their messages, their symbols, in ways that adapt them for the new media. How far this can be achieved with integrity is a question all religious groups must face, but it is clear that groups without such media capacity will by that fact limit their ability to communicate within the mainstream of cultural currents. Those that, for whatever reason, resist that route, choosing, for instance, not to sully themselves by association with the global flows of elite power, may also relieve themselves of a potential anxiety attending involvement with the new media. For to engage with digital and electronic communication systems, even if it is done by the most diehard fundamentalist groups, is to enter the fray, not with authoritative utterance, but as one competing voice among many.

A similar quandary awaits all who acknowledge the religious significance of the postmodern consumer culture. As we saw in an earlier chapter, to recognize the salience of religious competition for the vitality of religious groups need not translate into a policy recommendation that ailing churches should upgrade their marketing techniques or immediately set up e-spirituality sites on the web. The hazards of consumerism become ironically visible at this point. Choice is broadened for the majority, although this takes place in a world of diminishing resources for making the kinds of moral and "risk society" choices that confront us today. But it opens up a fresh role for religious groups, offering guidance, for example, with those agonizing life-and-death choices that are increasingly presented by the unrestricted development of technoscience, but for which moral resources seem distressingly sparse.

On the other hand, the very making of choices in a postmodern world is the privilege of consumers. "Locals," who are often discarded, "flawed consumers," have far fewer chances to make choices. Moreover, choices made in a consumer culture may all too easily be made by default according to criteria arising from within that culture, which may thus by definition fail to take the transcendent into account. As consumerism continues to expand in importance, things will continue to change rapidly, because customers have been carefully taught never to be satisfied. This fact militates against all the religious practices that take their cue from divine requirement rather than from mere human need or human capacities. And it sharpens the distinction between guiltless (and enjoyable) consuming and the new cultural drive and political mandate to consume without limits that I have designated consumerism.

This raises some acute questions, which, frankly, appear not to have been faced with much seriousness, and which make some intellectual worries about the postmodern pale by comparison. The challenge of consumerism contains a directly spiritual dimension connected with the classic incompatibility of "serving God and Mammon"[8] but is also implicated in basic Christian injunctions to care for Creation and to love our neighbors. To take the second of these, as we have also seen, the increase of indirect relations in the society of strangers makes the "neighbor" less visible. Mere propinquity, of course, was never in question. The point, as Derrida, Bauman, and others have shown more recently, is to take responsibility for the Other wherever she or he is encountered.[9] How this is worked out in the society of strangers, living under the sign of mobility, is a crucial question for the present. Christian agencies are still prominent in the world of homelessness and humanitarian aid,[10] but the everyday challenge of consumerism has yet to be fully acknowledged by most Christian communities.

Time–space compression also defies conventional Christian practices. The space-weighted example used here, of globalization, contains many paradoxes for Christians. It is fairly easy to propose that religious globalization from above occurs from the control-cockpits of the wealthy megachurches, with their themed premises, multimedia studios, Starbucks coffee outlets, and cinnamon-scented, sacred-musak-lulled bookstores. Religious globalization from below, on the other hand, grows like wild flowers in the cracks in the concrete in the shanties of São Paulo or Manila, exuberant tongues of fire that offer meaning and hope for apparently "choiceless" locals, the socio-economic *alter egos* of the elite global villagers. These contrasting social realities of religious life coexist uneasily as exemplars of the same commitments. But in both cases, at least one paradox remains: the message is global in scope, its recipients local.

Christians realized – sometimes a little late in the day – that a key challenge of modernity was to defend particularity against totalizing instrumental reason, which stood as a monumental, would-be universal "truth." Hence, to allude again to the welfare state example, it was the condition of individuals rendered vulnerable by the economic machine of industrial capitalism that prompted Christian action in the first place. And the same individual vulnerability, but this time subject to dependency-inducing, welfare-trap bureaucracies, later inspired some Christian arguments against the coerciveness of state welfare. Poverty, of course, has not vanished in postmodern times, although its character is altered, and its incidence more systematically globalized. That is one new challenge. But another is the postmodern tendency to glorify particularity, to the extent of denying universals. The politics of identity, which in its extreme forms loses all sense of who might truly be a "victim," offers both challenges and new opportunities in this regard. Christian insistence on universals that embrace particularity may fall on deaf ears, but such insistence offers a cogent alternative to both modern minimizing of particularity and postmodern doubts about universality.

Changing patterns of time also present ambivalent possibilities. The tyranny of time was often seen as a less than desirable product of modernity,[11] subverting spirituality through its timetables, schedules, and rigid routines. And, although the endless present of postmodern times may at first appear to fulfill some modern promises of the technologically enabled leisure society, it is far from clear that the day of gentler sequences and more relaxed rhythms is about to arrive. Freedom from some clock-bound regimes, enabled by the new flexibilities of time-space organizing, does not necessarily spell freedom to enjoy a calmer pace of life. Indeed, as the commodification of time is intensified within consumer capitalism, old tyrannies are likely to persist. Deliberately loosening the ties to time-bound schedules and choosing slow-paced alternatives to the dominant fast world may be another positive contribution that Christian communities can make today.

It is interesting that Castells, who discusses the contemporary timelessness of time, also sees environmental movements as a harbinger of alternative time patterning. Where compressed time produces the instant world, and where discontinuous time (as in cyberspace) eliminates old sequences, a felt need arises to bridge the gap between ephemerality and eternity. Environmentalism, he claims, offers another concept of "glacial time."[12] This assumes a long-term relation between humans and nature, and requires a return to "natural" rhythms and thus a resistance to the increasingly alien control of time. The "intergenerational solidarity" that results from this approach, argues Castells, is such because it emphasizes the unity – and, for that matter, continuity – of the human species.[13] This clearly accords with the turn towards "native spiritualities," especially in North America. While this turn has obvious merit, it also leaves open the question of how exactly it could be translated into a mode of temporality for those *already* involved, if not enveloped, in the world of timeless time. It is a challenge with which believers who have already survived modernity might do well to contend.

Such a challenge also connects several themes of this book. To refer again to the Christian "care for creation" motif, it might be said that this offers two related opportunities: one, distinctive contributions that stress, for instance, the common destiny of bodily human persons and the painfully "groaning"[14] planet, and, two, the chance to co-operate strategically with others from different religious traditions and spiritualities, crossing the boundaries of difference to present a front against the futility of insatiable desire and the environmental destructiveness of constantly escalating consumerism. If such a challenge does not come from those with recognizable religious commitments, it is difficult to see where else it might originate. The more radical the green movement, the more likely it is to show religious roots in its outlook.

Something similar may be said, too, about changing understandings of the body – another gauntlet defiantly thrown down in postmodern times. Like time, the body was subjected to precise regimes of measurement, discipline, and regulation within modernity. Some of these – also like modern time regimes – had their origins in biblically inspired practices, such as the desire to understand human anatomy as a work of God. But the body is now an object of consumption, and of endless manipulation, for the right image or for fitness. The old, fixed boundaries are now fuzzy, not only those between the human body and the animal body, but also those between the human and the machine. As Sampson says, "From being the object of scientific regulation, the body has become the site of style."[15] As we have seen, within more than one Christian tradition the body is being rediscovered in worship, thus sidestepping the modern dichotomy between spiritual experience and bodily repression. Here again, postmodern conditions give rise to new freedoms as well as to new questions, that Christians, among others, are obliged to confront.

It may be that in earlier times revivals and reformations were easier to pinpoint and to prepare for, or perhaps they are only ever recognized as such in retrospect. At any rate, all I have attempted here is some hints about what appear to me to be crucial areas for Christian consideration and action. Postmodern conditions are by definition unstable and volatile, and accelerated globalization only accentuates these features more. But so far from foreclosing the possibilities for appropriate Christian living, these conditions actually open the door to new variations, new combinations of authentic and responsible action. The demise of Christendom reduces radically the temptations of power, clearing space for the old story to be retold, just as processes such as religious globalization from below are a reminder that genuine growth can occur without the aid of Western evangelists or the English language. The old story, after all, recounts how the most significant initiatives are not human ones, and that ironic reversals – life out of death, strength in weakness, richness in poverty – are the real stuff of history.

Jesus and Disneyland

"Jesus in Disneyland" is a metaphor, no more, no less. The phrase is intended to be suggestive rather than offer the promise of some crucial interpretive key to the present. Inasmuch as postmodern conditions are appearing, they reflect features of the Disney environment. They enlarge the scope of certain characteristics of modernity, above all in CITs and consumerism, without somehow transcending the modern conditions that preceded them. But the postmodern, Disneyesque environment is the one in which more and more people find themselves, or from which they find themselves excluded, for better or for worse, in both cases. And it is also the context within which the religious sphere is mutating, and sometimes even metamorphosing.

Christians may well find themselves in an abrasive relation with the Disneyfied world. The creeping colonization of the globe by Mickey Mouse and all his hosts is achieved by tantalizingly trojan means. In so far as it trivializes truth, simplifies suffering, and sucks us into its simulated realities as extras in the spectacle, it can hardly expect to go unchallenged. In so far as it excludes the eternal, and colludes with consumerism as the highest good, it calls forth critique. But at the same time Christians may feel ambivalent about Disneyized domains. For if they recall the significance of storytelling, or remind us about the place of emotion and even of spirituality in fractured and coldly rationalized societies, they simply join the protest against a narcissistic modernity, in love with its own image. Theming, dedifferentiation, merchandizing, and emotional labor are not necessarily noxious.

How faith finds new forms, how spirituality finds new modes of expression, within postmodern conditions, cannot be predicted. The point is not prediction (even if it was for some modernist sociologies) but the tracing of trends, the mapping of everyday experiences. Sociology cannot come to the rescue of religion, any more than it can make the world a better place. Human beings do, however, construct their identities and channel their dreams using whatever resources are available for self- and social understanding. There are some resources – such as the sense of "eternity in the heart", or the moral demands inscribed within creation itself, or the scandal of the crucified saviour – to which sociology can add nothing. Other resources – including revelation – can be further illustrated by the sorts of stories that sociologists tell. That is the hope in which I have told this one.

Notes

Preface

1. David Lyon (1985) *The Steeple's Shadow: On the Myths and Realities of Secularization*, London: SPCK; Grand Rapids: Eerdmans, 1987.
2. David Lyon (1994) *Postmodernity*, Buckingham: Open University Press; Minneapolis: University of Minnesota Press. Revised and Expanded second edition, 1999.
3. "How very different we are," *McLean's* magazine, November 1996. David Lyon and Marguerite Van Die (eds) (forthcoming) *Rethinking Church, State, and Modernity: Canada between Europe and the USA*, Toronto: University of Toronto Press.

Chapter 1   Meeting Jesus in Disneyland

1. Jean Baudrillard (1988) *America*, London and New York: Verso, p. 104.
2. *Church around the World* (1996), 26:10, Carol Stream, IL: Tyndale House.
3. Apparently Napoleon repeated Laplace's remark to another mathematician, Lagrange, who responded, "Ah, but it is such a fine hypothesis. It explains so many things."
4. Bryan Turner (1994) *Orientalism, Postmodernism, and Globalism*, London and New York: Routledge, chapter 14.
5. *The National Post* (Canada), March 6, 1999.
6. Paul Ioro, "Has Disney taken over America?," *Spy*, September/October 1994, pp. 56–63.
7. Chris Rojek (1993) "Disney Culture," *Leisure Studies*, 12:2, p. 130.
8. Rojek, p. 134.

9 Umberto Eco (1986) *Travels in Hyperreality*, New York: Harcourt Brace Jovanovich, p. 58.
10 Neil Postman (1985) *Amusing Ourselves to Death*, New York: Viking.
11 Alan Bryman (1999) "The Disneyization of Society," *Sociological Review*, 47:1, p. 26.
12 Bryman, p. 33.
13 Bryman, p. 40.
14 George Ritzer (1993) *The McDonaldization of Society*, Thousand Oaks, CA: Pine Forge; and (1998) *The McDonaldization Thesis*, London and Beverly Hills, CA: Sage.
15 Manuel Castells (1996, 1997, 1998) *The Information Age* (in three volumes), Oxford and Malden MA: Blackwell.
16 Zygmunt Bauman (1992) *Intimations of Postmodernity*, London and New York: Routledge; and (1998) *Work, Consumerism and the New Poor*, Buckingham: Open University Press.
17 I argue this in *Postmodernity*, revised edition, 1999.
18 Gianni Vattimo (1985) *The End of Modernity*, Cambridge UK: Polity Press; Baltimore MD: Johns Hopkins University Press.
19 Jean-François Lyotard (1981) *The Postmodern Condition*, Minneapolis: University of Minnesota Press.
20 Max Weber (1976) *The Protestant Ethic and the Spirit of Capitalism*, London: Allen and Unwin.
21 Steve Bruce (ed.) (1992) *Religion and Modernization*, Oxford and New York: Oxford University Press, p. 21.
22 Zygmunt Bauman (1997) *Postmodernity and Its Discontents*, Cambridge UK: Polity Press; New York: New York University Press, pp. 2, 180.
23 See Robert Wuthnow (1988) *The Restructuring of American Religion*, Princeton NJ: Princeton University Press, pp. 282–6.
24 James Beckford (1989) *Religion and Advanced Industrial Society*, London: Unwin-Hyman, pp. 171–2.
25 Max Weber (1958) "Science as a vocation" in Hans Gerth and C. Wright Mills (eds) *From Max Weber: Essays in Sociology*, London: Routledge.
26 Benjamin Woolley (1992) *Virtual Worlds*, Oxford: Blackwell.
27 Rojek, p. 131.
28 Umberto Eco (1986) *Faith in Fakes*, London: Secker and Warburg.
29 Quoted in Richard Schickel (1998) "Disney," *Time* magazine, 152:23, December, p. 7.
30 Alan Bryman (1995) *Disney and his Worlds*, London and New York: Routledge, p. 162f.
31 Compare this with a similar scheme that informs Danièle Hervieu-Léger (1997) "Le Transmission religieuse en modernité," *Social Compass*, 44:1.
32 Michael Crawford (1992) "The world in a shopping mall" in Michael Sorkin (ed.) *Variations on a Theme Park*, New York: Noonday, p. 16.
33 John Hannigan (1995) "The postmodern city: A new urbanization," *Current Sociology*, 43:1.
34 Val Ross (1998) "We don't wanna grow up," *Globe and Mail*, Toronto, October 31, C1.

35 I Corinthians 13:11.
36 Anthony Giddens (1990) *The Consequences of Modernity*, Cambridge UK: Polity Press.
37 Samuel Huntington (1996) *The Clash of Civilizations and the Remaking of World Order*, New York: Simon and Schuster.
38 Danièle Hervieu-Léger (1993) *La Religion pour mémoire*, Paris: Cerf, p. 241.
39 Jean Baudrillard (1983) *Simulations*, New York: Semiotext(e), p. 25.
40 Rojek, p. 133.
41 Paul Heelas (1996) *The New Age Movement*, Oxford UK and Cambridge MA: Blackwell, p. 151.
42 William Romanowski (1996) *Pop Culture Wars*, Downers Grove: Inter-Varsity Press, p. 292.
43 The term "social actors" in sociology is a coded reminder that the "players" in the social "drama" are conscious, deliberating, intending persons.
44 David Ley and K. Olds (1988) "Landscape as spectacle: World's Fairs and the culture of heroic consumption," *Environment and Planning D: Society and Space*, 6, pp. 191–212.
45 Jonathan Sacks (1991) *The Persistence of Faith: Religion, Morality and Society in a Secular Age*, London: Weidenfeld and Nicolson, p. 8.
46 Grace Davie (1994) *Religion in Britain Since 1945: Believing without Belonging*, Oxford: Blackwell.
47 In this context I think of George Rawlyk (1996) *Is Jesus your Personal Saviour*, Montreal and Kingston: McGill-Queen's University Press, or of Eileen Barker (1984) *The Making of a Moonie: Brainwashing or Choice*, Oxford: Blackwell.
48 Nancy Ammerman (1994) "Telling congregational stories," *Review of Religious Research*, 35:3, p. 290.

Chapter 2 Faith's Fate

1 Matthew Arnold (1954) *Poetry and Prose*, London: Hart-Davis, p. 144.
2 Peter and Sue Kaldor (1988) *Where the River Flows*, Homebush West NSW: Anzea, p. xvii, quoted in Alister McGrath (1993) *The Renewal of Anglicanism*, Harrisburg PA: Morehouse Publishing, pp. 7–8.
3 Nancy Ammerman (1987) *Bible Believers*, New Brunswick NJ and London: Rutgers University Press, p. 2.
4 Anthony Giddens (1990) *The Consequences of Modernity*, Cambridge UK: Polity Press, p. 109.
5 See Grace Davie (ed.) (1999) *Religion in Modern Europe: A Memory Mutates*, Oxford: Oxford University Press.
6 See Stejpan Meštrović (1997) *Postemotional Society*, London and Thousand Oaks CA: Sage.
7 Elizabeth Brusco (1993) "The reformation of machismo: Asceticism and masculinity among Colombian Evangelicals" in Virginia Garrard-Burnett

and David Stoll (eds) *Rethinking Protestantism in Latin America*, Philadelphia, Temple University Press, pp. 143–58.

8   Robert Bellah et al. (1985) *Habits of the Heart*, Berkeley CA: University of California Press.

9   Peter Beyer (1998) "The city and beyond as dialogue: Negotiating religious authenticity in global society," *Social Compass*, 45:1, pp. 67–79.

10   Peter L. Berger (1999) "The desecularization of the world" in *The Desecularization of the World: Essays on the Resurgence of Religion in World Politics*, Grand Rapids MI: Eerdmans. See also his *A Far Glory: The Quest for Faith in an Age of Credulity*, New York: Viking, 1992.

11   Peter L. Berger (1967) *A Rumour of Angels*, Garden City NY: Doubleday.

12   See, for instance, Richard Robison and David S. G. Goodman (eds) (1996) *The New Rich in Asia: Mobile phones, McDonald's and Middle-class Revolution*, London and New York: Routledge. Matters religious do not appear in the index, even though it is acknowledged that Pacific Asian societies reject the "secular" model of Western societies.

13   Jeffrey Hadden (1987) "Towards desacralizing secularization theory," *Social Forces*, 65:3, March, pp. 587–611.

14   Steve Bruce (1996) *Religion in the Modern World: From Cathedrals to Cults*, Oxford: Oxford University Press.

15   See, for example, Douglas John Hall (1997) *The End of Christendom and the Future of Christianity*, Valley Forge PA: Trinity Press International.

16   See, for example, James Beckford (1989) *Religion in Advanced Industrial Society*, London: Unwin-Hyman.

17   Émile Durkheim (1922) *The Division of Labour in Society*, Glencoe NY: Free Press.

18   Beckford, p. 46.

19   Bryan Wilson (1975) *Contemporary Transformations of Religion*, Oxford: Oxford University Press.

20   Bruce, *passim*.

21   Karel Dobbelaere (1981) *Secularization: A Multi-Dimensional Concept*, published as a trend report in *Current Sociology*, 29, pp. 3–213.

22   José Casanova (1994) *Public Religions in the Modern World*, Chicago IL: University of Chicago Press, p. 6.

23   Manuel Castells (1997) *The Power of Identity*, Oxford and New York: Blackwell, p. 354.

24   Richard Fenn (1982) *Liturgies and Trials*, Oxford: Blackwell.

25   Beckford, p. 110.

26   Peter L. Berger (1967) *The Sacred Canopy*, New York: Anchor-Doubleday. This is one of the books that Berger now questions. The thesis was repeated in modified form in many other places, however, such as in James Davison Hunter (1987) *American Evangelicalism: Conservative Religion in the Quandary of Modernity*, New Brunswick NJ: Rutgers University Press.

27   Danièle Hervieu-Léger (1986) *Vers un nouveau christianisme*, Paris: Cerf.

28 I have in mind studies such as Robert Wuthnow (1988) *The Restructuring of American Religion*, Princeton NJ: Princeton University Press, and, in Canada, John Stackhouse (1994) *Canadian Evangelicalism in the Twentieth Century*, Toronto: University of Toronto Press.

29 Robert Wuthnow (1994) *Sharing the Journey: Support Groups and America's New Quest for Community*, New York: Free Press. See also Robert Wuthnow (1998) *Loose Connections: Joining Together in America's Fragmented Communities*, Cambridge MA: Harvard University Press.

30 Nancy Ammerman (1994) "Telling congregational stories," *Review of Religious Research*, 35:4, p. 296.

31 Peter L. Berger, Brigitte Berger, and Hansfried Kellner (1974) *Homeless Minds*, Harmondsworth: Penguin.

32 Daniel Bell (1977) "The return of the sacred? The argument on the future of religion," *British Journal of Sociology*, 28, pp. 419–49.

33 Paul Heelas (1996) *The New Age Movement*, Oxford: Blackwell.

34 See, for example, Tony Walter (1999) *Mourning for Diana*, Oxford and New York: Berg.

35 Bruce, p. 234.

36 Reginald Bibby (1993) *Unknown Gods: The Ongoing Story of Religion in Canada*, Toronto: Stoddart.

37 David Martin (1996) "Religion, secularization, and postmodernity: Lessons from the Latin-American case" in Pål Repstad (ed.) *Religion and Modernity: Modes of Co-existence*, Oxford: Scandinavian University Press.

38 David Martin.

39 Hervieu-Léger (1986, 1993).

40 Gilles Kepel (1994) *The Revenge of God*, Cambridge UK: Polity Press, p. 13.

41 Paul Freston (1998) "Evangelicalism and globalization: General observations and some Latin American dimensions" in Mark Hutchinson and Ogbu Kalu (eds) *A Global Faith: Essays on Evangelicalism and Globalization*, Sydney: Centre for the Study of Australian Christianity, p. 70.

42 See, for example, Vicki Noble (1991) *Shakti Woman: Feeling Our Fire, Healing Our World, the New Female Shamanism*, San Francisco CA: Harper and Row; Vivienne Crowley (1989) *Wicca: The Old Religion in the New Age*, Wellingborough: Aquarian Press.

43 Robert Wuthnow (1988), p. 10.

Chapter 3   Postmodern Premonitions

1 Anthony Giddens (1990) *The Consequences of Modernity*, Cambridge UK: Polity Press.

2 Danièle Hervieu-Léger (1993) *La Religion pour mémoire*, Paris: Cerf.

3 Manuel Castells (1996, 1997, 1998) *The Information Age* (in three volumes), Oxford and Malden: Blackwell.

4 Zygmunt Bauman (1992) *Intimations of Postmodernity*, London and New York: Routledge.

5 Manuel Castells (1996) *The Rise of the Network Society*, Oxford and Malden MA: Blackwell, p. 201.

6 Bauman, p. 49.

7 Thoughts in this paragraph were stimulated by comments from Philip Sampson.

8 Zygmunt Bauman (1997) *Postmodernity and its Discontents*, New York: New York University Press.

9 Gilles Kepel (1994) *The Revenge of God*, Cambridge UK: Polity Press.

10 Jean-François Lyotard (1981) *The Postmodern Condition*, Minneapolis: University of Minnesota Press.

11 Zygmunt Bauman (1995) *Life in Fragments*, Oxford and New York: Blackwell.

12 Raymond Lemieux (1996) "La Religion au Canada: Synthèse et problématiques," *Social Compass*, 43:1, pp. 135–58.

13 Peter L. Berger (1992) *A Far Glory: Faith in an Age of Credulity*, New York: Viking.

14 Hervieu-Léger.

15 Mike Featherstone (1995) *Undoing Culture*, London: Sage, p. 3.

16 Richard Fenn (1990) "Premodern religion in a postmodern world: A reply to Professor Zylerberg," *Social Compass*, 37:1, p. 100.

17 Fenn, p. 103.

18 John O'Neill (1988) "Religion and postmodernism: The Durkheimian bond in Bell and Jameson," *Theory, Culture, and Society*, 5:2–3, p. 501.

19 Fenn, p. 105.

20 The London, UK, based organization INFORM exists to offer independent and accurate information and advice about new religious movements. The CESNUR website offers a similar service on-line.

21 Massimo Introvigne (1999) "Misinformation, religious minorities and religious pluralism," a statement to the Organization for Security and Cooperation in Europe meeting on March 22. <http://www.cesnur.org/vienna.htm>.

22 James Davison Hunter (1991) *Culture Wars: The Struggle to Define America*, New York: Basic Books.

23 Hunter, p. 49.

24 James Davison Hunter (1996) *The State of Disunion* (the Postmodernity Project), Ivy VA: In Media Res Educational Foundation.

25 See John H. Simpson (1994) "The structure of attitudes towards body issues in the American and Canadian populations: An elementary analysis" in Ted G. Jelen and Martha A. Chandler (eds) *Abortion Politics in the United States and Canada: Studies in Public Opinion*, Westport CT: Praeger.

26 Philip Mellor and Christopher Shilling (1997) *Re-forming the Body*, London: Sage.

27 Manuel Castells (1997) *The Power of Identity*, Oxford and New York: Blackwell, p. 254.

28 Castells (1996), p. 477.
29 Dave Tomlinson (1995) *The Post Evangelical*, London: SPCK Triangle.
30 Mike Riddell (1998) *Threshold of the Future: Reforming the Church in the Post-Christian West*, London: SPCK.
31 This jibe came from Randolph Williamson, a pastor in Swarthmore, PA. See Katrina Burger (1997) "Willow Creek: The flock that rocks," *Forbes* magazine, May 5.
32 Bong Rin Ro (1998) "Bankrupting the prosperity gospel," *Christianity Today*, November 16, pp. 59–61.
33 Alain Touraine (1988) *Return of the Actor: Social Theory in Postindustrial Society*, Minneapolis: University of Minnesota Press.
34 Charles Taylor (1991) *The Malaise of Modernity*, Toronto: Anansi, p. 14.
35 Robert Wuthnow (1989) *The Struggle for America's Soul*, Grand Rapids MI: Eerdmans, p. 116.
36 Pierre Bourdieu (1977) *Outline of a Theory of Practice*, Cambridge UK and New York: Cambridge University Press.
37 Nancy Ammerman (1997) "Religious choice and religious vitality" in Lawrence A. Young (ed.) *Rational Choice Theory and Religion: Summary and Assessment*, New York and London: Routledge.
38 Ammerman, p. 205.
39 Danièle Hervieu-Léger (1997) "La Transmission religieuse en modernité," *Social Compass*, 44:1.
40 See, for example, Nancy Nason-Clark (forthcoming) "The steeple or the shelter? Family violence and church and state relationships in contemporary Canada" in David Lyon and Marguerite Van Die (eds) *Rethinking Church, State, and Modernity: Canada between Europe and the USA*, Toronto: University of Toronto Press.
41 Alessandra Stanley (1998) "Pope's encyclical assails decline of faith," *Globe and Mail* (Toronto), October 16, A1, 2.
42 John Milbank (1990) *Theology and Social Theory: Beyond Secular Reason*, Oxford UK and Cambridge MA: Blackwell, p. 261.
43 Milbank, p. 433.
44 Pauline Marie Rosenau (1992) *Post-modernism and the Social Sciences*, Princeton NJ: Princeton University Press, p. 15.
45 Rosenau, p. 16.

Chapter 4　Signs of the Times

1 <www.afa.net>.
2 Graham Murdock (1997) "The re-enchantment of the world" in Stewart Hoover and Knut Lundby (eds) *Rethinking Media, Religion, and Culture*, London: Sage.
3 Stewart Hoover and Knut Lundby (1997) "Introduction" in Hoover and Lundby.

4   On religious boundary negotiation, see the fascinating account by Richard Fenn (1978) *Toward a Theory of Secularization*, Storrs CN: Society for the Scientific Study of Religion.

5   James Davison Hunter (1991) *Culture Wars: The Struggle to Define America*, New York: Basic Books, p. 160 (italics in original).

6   Hunter, p. 170.

7   Manuel Castells (1996) *The Rise of the Network Society*, Oxford and New York: Blackwell, p. 375.

8   Peter Beyer (1994) *Religion and Globalization*, London: Sage, p. 5.

9   Gabriel Herbert (1935) *Liturgy and Society: The Function of the Church in the Modern World*, London: Faber and Faber, p. 7.

10 Richard Fenn (1982) *Liturgies and Trials*, Oxford: Blackwell, p. xiv.

11 Kieran Flanagan (1991) *Sociology and Liturgy*, London: Macmillan, p. 57.

12 G. S. Goodhardt, A. S. C. Ahrenberg, and M. A. Collins (1987) *The Television Audience*, London: Gower.

13 David Martin (1990) *Tongues of Fire: The Explosion of Protestantism in Latin America*, Oxford and New York: Blackwell.

14 Salem Alaton (1997) "Praise the Lord and pass the hankies," *Globe and Mail* (Toronto), January 4, D7.

15 Quentin Schultze (1991) *Televangelism and American Culture*, Grand Rapids MI: Baker Book House.

16 Schultze, p. 248.

17 Gianni Vattimo (1992) *The Transparent Society*, Cambridge UK: Polity Press; Baltimore MD: Johns Hopkins University Press.

18 Vattimo, p. 3.

19 Akbar Ahmed (1992) *Islam, Globalization, and Postmodernity*, London and New York: Routledge, p. 260.

20 Jean Baudrillard (1993) *The Transparency of Evil*, London: Verso.

21 See Philip Mellor and Chris Shilling (1997) *Reforming the Body*, London: Sage, p. 169.

22 Joshua Cooper Ramo (1996) "Finding God on the web," *Time*, December 16, pp. 44–50.

23 Joan Connell (1998) "Searching for God in cyberspace," on the *High Tech and Macumba* site: <www.goethe.de/br/sap/macumba/conelsho.htm>.

24 Lorne L. Dawson and Jenna Hennebry (1999) "New religions and the Internet: Recruiting in a new public space," *Journal of Contemporary Religion*, 14:1, p. 31.

25 William Gibson (1994) *Neuromancer*, New York: Ace.

26 Mike Featherstone (1991) *Postmodernism and Consumer Culture*, London: Sage, p. 3.

27 *The Globe and Mail* (Toronto), August 3, A1.

28 Paul Virilio (1997) "Cyberwar, God, and television" in Arthur and MarieLouise Kroker (eds) *Digital Delirium*, Montreal: New World Perspectives, p. 45.

29 Virilio, p. 45.

30 Howard Rheingold (1993) "A slice of my life in virtual community" in Linda Harasim (ed.) *Global Networks*, Cambridge MA: MIT Press, p. 61.

31 Benjamin Woolley (1992) *Virtual Worlds*, Oxford: Blackwell, p. 9.
32 This is a basic insight of Harold Adams Innis (1964) *The Bias of Communication*, Toronto: University of Toronto Press.
33 See, for example, Kevin Robins (1996) *Into the Image: Culture and Politics in the Field of Vision*, London and New York: Routledge, chapter 4.
34 Barry Wellman (ed.) (1999) *Networks in a Global Village*, Boulder CO: Westview Press.
35 D. Holmes (1997) *Virtual Politics: Identity and Community in Cyberspace*, London: Sage, p. 16.
36 See Kenneth Bedell (1998) "Religion and the Internet: Reflections on research strategies," paper presented to the meetings of the Society for the Scientific Study of Religion, Montreal, November.
37 Jay Kinney (1995) "Religion, cyberspace, and the future," *Futures*, 27:7, p. 773.
38 George Chryssides (no date) "The Internet and new religions" at <www.goethe.de/br/sap/macumba/crysiinte.htm>.
39 Ramo.
40 This is considered in Dawson and Hennebry, p. 34. The theorists whose work stimulates such reflections are generally favorably disposed to rational choice or market theories of religion, and include, for instance, the analysis of Rodney Stark (1996) *The Rise of Christianity: A Sociologist Reconsiders History*, Princeton NJ: Princeton University Press.
41 Stewart Hoover (1988) *Mass Media Religion*, London and Beverly Hills CA: Sage.
42 Manuel Castells (1996) *The Rise of the Network Society*, Oxford and New York: Blackwell, p. 375.

Chapter 5   Shopping for a Self

1 Quoted in *The Times*, January 30, 1999, and requoted in *Globe and Mail* (Toronto), February 5, 1999, A1.
2 Andrew Nickolds (1999) "Verily, he hath lost the plot," *Guardian* (London), February 2, p. 2.
3 Madeleine Bunting (1999) "What is he on?" *Guardian* (London), February 2, p. 3.
4 See, for example, M. J. Donahue (1993) "Prevalence and correlates of New Age beliefs in six Protestant denominations," *Journal for the Scientific Study of Religion*, 32:2, pp. 177–84; Tony Walter and Helen Waterhouse (1999) "A very private belief: Reincarnation in contemporary England," *Sociology of Religion*, 60:2, pp. 187–97.
5 Bunting, p. 2.
6 Phenomena such as these were discussed in the 1970s under the rubric of "common religion," see, for example, Robert Towler (1974) *Homo Religiosus*, London: Constable; and, in the 1990s, under that of "implicit

religion," see Edward Bailey (1998) *Implicit Religion*, London: Middlesex University Press. In a North American context, Wade Clark Roof discusses experiential spiritualities in (1996) "God is in the details: Reflections on religion's public presence in the United States in the mid-1990s," *Sociology of Religion*, 57:2, pp. 149–62.

7   The phrase comes from James B. Twitchell (1999) *Lead us into Temptation: The Triumph of American Materialism*, New York: Columbia University Press.

8   Robert Bocock (1993) *Consumption*, London and New York: Routledge, p. x.

9   Daniel Bell (1976) *The Cultural Contradiction of Capitalism*, London: Heinemann.

10 Peter L. Berger (1967) *The Sacred Canopy*, New York: Anchor-Doubleday.

11 Laurence Iannacone "The consequences of religious market structure," *Rationality and Society*, 3, pp. 156–77; Lawrence Young (ed.) (1997) *Rational Choice Theory and Religion: Summary and Assessment*, London and New York: Routledge.

12 Reginald Bibby (1987) *Fragmented Gods*, Toronto: Irwin.

13 Reginald Bibby (1993) *Unknown Gods*, Toronto: Stoddart.

14 Stephen Warner (1993) "Work in progress toward a new paradigm for the sociological study of religion in the United States," *American Journal of Sociology*, 98:5, p. 1077.

15 Mike Featherstone (1991) *Consumer Culture and Postmodernism*, London: Sage.

16 Featherstone, p. 63.

17 Zygmunt Bauman (1992) *Intimations of Postmodernity*, London: Routledge, p. 49.

18 Mary Douglas (1982) "The effects of modernization on religious change," *Daedalus*, 111:1, p. 16.

19 Bauman, p. 50.

20 This is discussed in David Lyon (1994) *The Electronic Eye: The Rise of Surveillance Society*, Cambridge UK: Polity Press, and in Oscar Gandy (1993) *The Panoptic Sort: A Political Economy of Information*, Boulder CO: Westview Press.

21 The term "social orchestration" is my attempt to encapsulate the non-coercive character of consumer seduction by database marketing. It points to the collusion of data-subjects in the ways they are influenced by companies or, conversely, to the creation of subjects by such systems. See David Lyon (forthcoming) *Surveillance Society: Monitoring Everyday Life*, Buckingham, Open University Press.

22 Zygmunt Bauman (1998) *Work, Consumerism, and the New Poor*, Buckingham and Philadelphia: Open University Press, p. 38.

23 Philip Sampson (1994) "The rise of postmodernity" in Philip Sampson, Vinay Samuel, and Chris Sugden (eds) *Faith and Modernity*, Oxford: Regnum Lynx, p. 31.

24 Featherstone (1991), pp. 112–28.

25 José Casanova (1994) *Public Religions in the Modern World*, Chicago: University of Chicago Press.
26 Featherstone (1991), p. 114.
27 Daniel Bell (1976), p. 156.
28 Robert Bellah et al. (1985) *Habits of the Heart*, Berkeley: University of California Press, p. 74.
29 Paul Heelas (1994) "The limits of consumption and the post-modern religion of the New Age" in Russell Keat, Nigel Whiteley, and Nicholas Abercrombie (eds) *The Authority of the Consumer*, London: Routledge, p. 112.
30 Featherstone, p. 119.
31 Featherstone, p. 126.
32 Featherstone, p. 126.
33 See Kenneth Richard Jacobsen (1997) "Prophecy, performance, and persuasion: Sermon art and dramatic art in England 1575–1630," PhD thesis, Queen's University, Kingston, Ontario.
34 R. Laurence Moore (1994) *Selling God: American Religion in the Marketplace of Culture*, New York: Oxford University Press, p. 10.
35 Moore, p. 275.
36 Moore, p. 276.
37 Bibby (1987).
38 John Webster Grant (1972) *Religion in the Canadian Era*, Toronto: McGraw-Hill Ryerson.
39 Bibby (1987), p. 82.
40 Bibby (1993), p. 169.
41 Peter Beyer (1997) "Religious vitality in Canada: The complementarity of religious market and secularization perspectives," *Journal for the Scientific Study of Religion*, 36:2, p. 286.
42 Grace Davie (1994) *Religion in Britain since 1945: Believing without Belonging*, Oxford: Blackwell, p. 199.
43 Davie, p. 76.
44 Davie, p. 199.
45 Fundamentalism is discussed more fully in chapter 6.
46 See Nancy Ammerman (1997) "Religious choice and religious vitality" in Lawrence A. Young (ed.) *Rational Choice Theory and Religion: Summary and Assessment*, New York and London: Routledge, pp. 119–32.
47 Warner, p. 1050.
48 James Beckford (1989) *Religion in Advanced Industrial Society*, London: Unwin-Hyman, p. 172.
49 Wade Clark Roof (1993) *A Generation of Seekers: The Spiritual Journeys of the Baby Boom Generation*, New York: HarperCollins, p. 5.
50 Robert Wuthnow (1998) *After Heaven: Spirituality in America Since the 1950s*, Berkeley CA: University of California Press.
51 Bocock, p. 109.
52 Bocock, p. 110.
53 Ray Pahl (1995) *After Success: Fin de Siècle Anxiety and Identity*, Cambridge UK: Polity Press, p. 120.

54 Pahl, p. 120.
55 Anthony Giddens (1991) *Modernity and Self-identity*, Cambridge UK: Polity Press, p. 215.
56 Manuel Castells (1997) *The Power of Identity*, Oxford and New York: Blackwell.
57 Pahl, p. 149.
58 Zygmunt Bauman (1997) *Postmodernity and its Discontents*, New York: New York University Press.
59 Danièle Hervieu-Léger (1997) "La Transmission religieuse en modernité," *Social Compass*, 44:1.
60 Raymond Lemieux (1996) "La Religion au Canada: Synthèse des problématiques," *Social Compass*, 43:1, 149.
61 R. Susman (1979) "Personality and the making of twentieth century culture" in J. Higham and P. K. Conkin (eds) *New Directions in American Cultural History*, Baltimore MA: Johns Hopkins University Press, p. 220.
62 Philip Rieff (1966) *The Triumph of the Therapeutic: Uses of Faith after Freud*, New York: Harper and Row.
63 This theme is discussed, for example, by Bernice Martin (1982) *A Sociology of Contemporary Cultural Change*, London: Macmillan, and by Paul Heelas (1996) "Detraditionalization of religion and self: New Age and postmodernity" in Kieran Flanagan and Peter Jupp (eds) *Postmodernity, Sociology, and Religion*, London: Macmillan, and New York, St Martin's Press.
64 Philip Mellor and Chris Shilling (1997) *Re-Forming the Body: Religion, Community, and Modernity*, London and Beverly Hills CA: Sage, p. 126.
65 Margaret Rodgers (1997) "Same-sex unions: The debate heats up," *Southern Cross*, July, 3:6.
66 The Disney Project (1995) *Inside the Mouse: Work and Play at Disneyworld*, Durham NC: Duke University Press, p. 111.
67 Bauman, p. 183.
68 Gilles Kepel (1994) *The Revenge of God*, Cambridge UK: Polity Press.
69 The Disney Project, p. 107.
70 On this, see Linda Woodhead (1999) "Theology and the fragmentation of the self," *International Journal of Systematic Theology*, 1:1. Woodhead uses a typology somewhat different from the one presented here, but its aim, of distinguishing different types of "fragmented self," is very similar.
71 Bocock, p. 118.
72 Bocock, p. 119.

Chapter 6   A Global Spirit

1 Margaret Poloma (1996) "By their fruits . . . A sociological assessment of the Toronto Blessing" in *The Toronto Report*, Wiltshire UK: Terra Nova Publications.

2 Jack Kapica (1997) "Heaven's Gate thrown open to the world," *Globe and Mail* (Toronto), April 4, p. A7.

3 John Urry (1994) *Consuming Places*, London and New York: Routledge, 152–62.

4 Roland Robertson (1995) "Glocalization: Time-space and homogeneity–heterogeneity" in Mike Featherstone et al. (eds) *Global Modernities*, London: Sage.

5 On this, see Arjun Appadurai (1996) *Modernity at Large: Cultural Dimensions of Globalization*, Minneapolis: University of Minnesota Press, p. 42.

6 Manuel Castells (1989) *The Informational City*, Oxford and New York: Blackwell; (1996) *The Rise of the Network Society*, Oxford and New York: Blackwell.

7 Appadurai, *passim*.

8 Benedict Anderson (1993) *Imagined Communities: Reflections of the Origins and Spread of Nationalism*, London: Verso.

9 Malcolm Waters (1995) *Globalization*, London and New York: Routledge.

10 Zygmunt Bauman (1998) *Globalization: The Human Consequences*, Cambridge UK: Polity Press, and New York: Columbia University Press.

11 Appadurai, p. 37.

12 *Christian Week* (Canada) (1997), May 27.

13 Benjamin Barber (1995) *Jihad versus McWorld*, New York: Times Books.

14 Mike Featherstone (1995) *Undoing Culture*, London: Sage, p. 9.

15 See, for example, Robertson.

16 Anthony Giddens (1990) *The Consequences of Modernity*, Cambridge UK: Polity Press.

17 Peter Beyer (1994) *Religion and Globalization*, London: Sage, p. 227.

18 Featherstone, pp. 9–14.

19 Terence Ranger (1993) "The local and the global in Southern African religious history" in Robert W. Hefner (ed.) *Conversion to Christianity*, Berkeley CA: University of California Press.

20 Irving Hexham and Karla Poewe (1997) *New Religions as Global Cultures*, Boulder CO: Westview Press, p. 41.

21 Eileen Barker (1984) *The Making of a Moonie*, Oxford: Blackwell, pp. 74–93.

22 See also Gianni Vattimo (1988) *The End of Modernity*, Cambridge UK: Polity Press.

23 Featherstone, p. 11.

24 Mark Noll (1996) "The challenges of contemporary church history, the dilemmas of modern history, and missiology to the rescue," *Missiology*, 24:1.

25 Featherstone, p. 13.

26 Waters, *passim*.

27 See Mark Hutchinson (1998) "It's a small church after all," *Christianity Today*, November 16, p. 48.

28   Michel Maffesoli (1995) *The Time of the Tribes*, London: Sage.
29   Grace Davie (1994) *Religion in Britain since 1945: Believing without Belonging*, Oxford and New York: Blackwell.
30   See David Lyon (1993) "A bit of a circus: Notes on postmodernity and the New Age," *Religion*, 23:2.
31   See "Building the Biggest," *Scientific American*, 277, p. 6.
32   Frank Lechner (1992) "Against modernity: Anti-modernism in global perspective" in P. Colomy (ed.) *The Dynamics of Social Systems*, London: Sage.
33   David Martin (1990) *Tongues of Fire: The Explosion of Protestantism in Latin America*, Oxford and New York: Blackwell, p. 293.
34   David Martin (1996) "Religion, secularization and postmodernity: Lessons from the Latin-American case" in Pål Repstad (ed.) *Religion and Modernity: Modes of Co-existence*, Oxford: Scandinavian University Press.
35   Andrew Walls (1996) *The Missionary Movement in Christian History: Studies in the Transmission of Faith*, New York: Orbis Books.
36   See, for instance, the critique offered by David Bebbington (1998) "Of this train, England is the engine: British Evangelicalism and globalization in the long nineteenth century" in Mark Hutchinson and Ogbu Kalu (eds) *A Global Faith: Essays on Evangelicalism and Globalization*, Sydney: Centre for the Study of Australian Christianity, pp. 122–39.
37   Quoted in Bruce Hindmarsh (1995) "The 'Toronto Blessing' and the Protestant Evangelical awakening of the eighteenth century compared," *Crux*, December, 31:4, pp. 5–13.
38   See Faith and Order Committee (1996) *The Toronto Blessing*, London: Methodist Publishing House.
39   Hindmarsh, p. 4.
40   See the discussion in Poloma.
41   See, for instance, William Romanowski (1996) *Pop Culture Wars*, Downers Grove: Inter-Varsity Press.
42   See the account in Guy Chevreau (1994) *Catch the Fire*, London: Marshall-Pickering.
43   The address is <www.tacf.org/index.html>.
44   See *The Toronto Blessing* (note 38 above).
45   Bauman.
46   See also the discussions in Ian Reader and Tony Walter (eds) (1993) *Pilgrimage in Popular Culture*, London: Macmillan. This chapter was written before I found Martyn Percy (1998) "The morphology of pilgrimage in the Toronto Blessing," *Religion*, 28, pp. 281–8.
47   See Mellor and Shilling, *passim*.
48   Philip Sampson (1996) "Die Repräsentation des Körpers," *Kunstforum International*, Bd. 132, pp. 94–111.
49   Hindmarsh, p. 6.
50   David Martin (1978) *A General Theory of Secularization*, Oxford and New York: Blackwell.

51 Margaret Poloma (1996) "The spirit and the bride: The Toronto Bless-ing and church structure," *Evangelical Studies Bulletin*, 13:4, Winter, pp. 1–5.

52 The data used in this section are from Paul Freston (1997) "Evangelical-ism and globalization: General observations and some Latin American dimensions" in Mark Hutchinson and Ogbu Kalu (eds) *A Global Faith: Essays on Evangelicalism and Globalization*, Sydney: Centre for the Study of Australian Christianity.

53 Martin (1990), p. 5.

54 See also Roland Robertson (1998) *International Sociology*, 13:1.

55 Giddens, *passim*.

56 Bauman, p. 3.

57 Manuel Castells (1998) *End of Millennium*, Oxford and New York: Blackwell, p. 355.

58 Appadurai, p. 38.

59 Appadurai, p. 38.

60 A point underscored by Appadurai as well.

61 Appadurai, p. 196. .

62 Gilles Kepel (1994) *The Revenge of God: The Resurgence of Islam, Christianity and Judaism in the Modern World*, Cambridge: Polity Press.

63 Danièle Hervieu-Léger (1991) Review of Kepel's "La Revanche de dieu," *Archives des Sciences Sociales de Religion*, avril–juin, pp. 263–4.

64 Appadurai, p. 140.

65 Samuel Huntington (1996) *The Clash of Civilizations and the Remak-ing of World Order*, New York: Simon and Schuster.

66 United Nations, New York, September, 15 1997.

67 Anthony Giddens (1999) "Globalization," The Reith Lectures of the BBC, broadcast April, and also at <http://news.bbc.co.uk/hi/english/static/events/reith_99/week3/lecture3.htm>.

68 Giddens, lecture 3, p. 5.

69 Charles Taylor (1992) *Multiculturalism and the Politics of Recognition*, Princeton NJ: Princeton University Press, p. 70–3.

70 Satya Mohanty (1995) "Colonial legacies, multicultural futures: Rela-tivism, objectivity, and the challenge of otherness," *Publications of the Modern Languages Association of America*, 110:1, p. 113.

71 Joel Carpenter (1998) *Revive Us Again: The Reawakening of American Fundamentalism*, New York and Oxford: Oxford University Press.

72 Roland Robertson (1989) "Globalization, politics, and religion" in James Beckford and Thomas Luckmann (eds) *The Changing Face of Religion*, London and Beverly Hills CA: Sage.

73 Danièle Hervieu-Léger (1997) "La Transmission religieuse en modernité," *Social Compass*, 44:1.

74 Martin (1996).

75 Freston.

76 Ali Zaidi (1998) International Sociological Association, Montreal.

77 Martin (1996).

78   John Urry (1994) *Consuming Places*, London and New York: Routledge.
79   Nancy Ammerman (1996) *Congregation and Community*, New Brunswick NJ and London: Rutgers University Press.
80   Frédéric de Coninck (1996) *La Ville: Notre Territoire, nos appartenances*, Quebec: La Clairière.

Chapter 7   Telescoped Time

1   See John Hannigan (1998) *Fantasy City: Pleasure and Profit in the Postmodern Metropolis*, London and New York: Routledge, p. 143.
2   Alan Bryman (1995) *Disney and his Worlds*, London and New York: Routledge, p. 136.
3   M. Billig, referred to in Bryman, p. 136.
4   On this, see George Grant (1969) *Time as History*, Toronto: CBC Learning Systems, p. 44.
5   These words come from a Christian hymn, "O God our help in ages past," by Isaac Watts (1674–1748). It is a paraphrase of Psalm 90.
6   See, for example, William Westfall (1999) "The Church of England in Victorian Canada: An ongoing establishment," paper given at "Religion and Public Life" conference, Queen's University, Kingston, and forthcoming in Marguerite Van Die (ed.) *Religion and Public Life*, Toronto: University of Toronto Press.
7   By these words I paraphrase the essential elements of the institution of the Eucharist from I Corinthians, chapter 11.
8   Grant, p. 9.
9   See Mike Featherstone (1995) *Undoing Culture*, London: Thousand Oaks CA, and New Delhi: Sage, p. 96.
10   Such concepts are called "chronotopes" in the work of Mikhail Bakhtin (1981) *The Dialogical Imagination*, Austin TX: University of Texas Press. I have followed loosely his meaning, without using the word.
11   See Graham Murdock (1993) "Communications and the constitution of modernity," *Media, Culture and Society*, 15, pp. 521–39.
12   Bryman, pp. 135–42.
13   David Harvey (1989) *The Condition of Postmodernity*, Oxford and New York: Blackwell, p. 240.
14   Peter Beyer (1998) "The city and beyond as dialogue: Negotiating religious authenticity in global society," *Social Compass*, 45:1, p. 68.
15   On this, see the excellent treatment by Anthony Giddens (1985) *The Nation State and Violence*, Cambridge UK: Polity Press.
16   James Der Derian (1998) *The Virilio Reader*, Oxford UK and Malden MA: Blackwell, p. 5.
17   Harvey, p. 286.
18   I owe this illustration to the work of a graduate student at Queen's, Leighann Neilson.
19   David Lowenthal (1996) *The Heritage Crusade and the Spoils of History*, New York: Viking, p. 167.

20 See the discussion in Michael Dawson (1998) *The Mountie: From Dime Novels to Disney*, Toronto: Between the Lines.

21 Manuel Castells (1996) *The Rise of the Network Society*, Oxford and New York: Blackwell, p. 433.

22 Anthony Giddens (1991) *Modernity and Self-identity*, Cambridge UK: Polity Press, and Stanford CA: Stanford University Press, pp. 17–18.

23 Giddens (1991), p. 48.

24 Giddens (1991), p. 207.

25 Giddens (1991), p. 207.

26 This is discussed throughout Frédéric de Coninck (1995) *Travail intégré, société éclatée*, Paris: Presses Universitaires de France.

27 On this, see the discussions of trust in Giddens (1991) (I think that Giddens was first to speak of "tokens of trust"); David Lyon (1994) *The Electronic Eye: The Rise of the Surveillance Society*, Cambridge UK: Polity Press, and Minneapolis: University of Minnesota Press; Richard Ericson and Kevin Heggarty (1997) *Policing the Risk Society*, Toronto: University of Toronto Press.

28 Zygmunt Bauman (1992) *Mortality, Immortality and Other Life Strategies*, Cambridge: Polity Press; Tony Walter (1996) *The Eclipse of Eternity: A Sociology of the After Life*, London: Macmillan, and New York: St Martin's Press.

29 Castells, p. 461.

30 Castells, p. 462.

31 Helga Nowotny (1994) *Time: The Modern and Postmodern Experience*, Cambridge UK: Polity Press, p. 11.

32 Nowotny, p. 14.

33 Harvey, p. 292.

34 Castells, p. 463.

35 Krishan Kumar (1999) "Living at the end: Theories of post-history" in Gary Browning, Abigail Halcli, and Frank Webster (eds) *Theory and Society: Understanding the Present*, London: Sage.

36 Philip Lamy (1996) *Millennium Rage: Survivalists, White Supremacists, and the Doomsday Prophecy*, New York: Plenum.

37 Francis Fukuyama (1992) *The End of History and the Last Man*, New York: Free Press.

38 See Asa Briggs (1996) "The final chapter" in Asa Briggs and Daniel Snowman (eds) *Fins de Siècle*, New Haven CT: Yale University Press.

39 Jean Baudrillard (1996) "The West's Serbianization" in Thomas Cushman and Stejpan Meštrović (eds) *This Time We Knew: Western Responses to Genocide in Bosnia*, New York: New York University Press. I have been unable to check the original French of this quotation, so I have inserted what I suspect is the correct word, *intégrisme* – referring to fundamentalist forms of Catholicism – in place of "integrationism."

40 Francis Fukuyama (1999) *The Great Disruption: Human Nature and the Reconstitution of Social Order*, New York: Free Press.

41 Samuel Huntington (1996) *The Clash of Civilizations and the Remaking of World Order*, New York: Simon and Schuster; Benjamin Barber (1994) *Jihad versus McWorld*, New York: Ballantine Books.
42 Huntington, p. 67.
43 Jean Baudrillard (1994) *The Illusion of the End*, Cambridge UK: Polity Press.
44 Robert Kaplan (1997) *The Ends of the Earth*, London: Macmillan.
45 "Evangelism and Social Responsibility. An Evangelical Commitment," a report of a consultation in Grand Rapids MI, and Exeter UK: Paternoster Press, 1982, pp. 36–7.
46 Richard Fenn (1997) *The End of Time*, London: SPCK.
47 Tormod Engelsviken (1994) "Modernity and eschatology" in Philip Sampson et al. (eds) *Faith and Modernity*, Oxford: Regnum Lynx, p. 172.
48 Jean Cheseneux (1996) *Habiter le temps*, Paris: Bayard.
49 Paul Virilio in Der Derian (ed.), p. 158.
50 Danièle Hervieu-Léger (1993) *La Religion pour memoire*, Paris: Cerf.
51 David Martin (1996) "Religion, secularization, and postmodernity: Lessons from the Latin-American case" in Pål Repstad (ed.) *Religion and Modernity: Modes of Co-existence*, Oxford: Scandinavian University Press.

Chapter 8   Faith's Future

1 Jean Baudrillard (1996) "Disneyworld Company," *Liberation* (Paris), translated in *C-Theory*, <http://www.ctheory.com/e25-disneyworld_comp.html>, by François Debrix.
2 Stephanie Nolen (1999) "Give them Jesus, but hold the theology," *Globe and Mail*, January 2, pp. A1, A6.
3 Manuel Castells (1996) *The Rise of the Network Society*, Oxford and New York: Blackwell, p. 477.
4 See Tim May (1998) "Reflections and reflexivity" in Tim May and Malcolm Williams (eds) *Knowing the Social World*, Buckingham: Open University Press.
5 Mary Hesse (1980) *Revolutions and Reconstructions in the Philosophy of Science*, Notre Dame IN: University of Notre Dame Press.
6 Scott Lash (1994) in Ulrich Beck, Anthony Giddens, and Scott Lash (eds) *Reflexive Modernization*, Cambridge UK: Polity Press, p. 146.
7 See David Lyon (1997) "Sliding in all directions: Social hermeneutics from suspicion to retrieval" in Roger Lundin (ed.) *Disciplining Hermeneutics*, Grand Rapids MI: Eerdmans, pp. 109–13.
8 This is a reference to Christ's warning against a divided heart: to try to serve both God and Mammon – the personified symbol for merely material gain – is a basic contradiction. See Matthew 6: 24.
9 See, for example, Zygmunt Bauman (1993) *Postmodern Ethics*, Oxford and New York: Blackwell.

10　Agencies with strong Canadian roots would include Habitat for Humanity, the Mennonite Central Council, and World Vision.
11　See, for example, Robert Banks (1983) *The Tyranny of Time*, Exeter: Paternoster Press.
12　The concept comes from Scott Lash and John Urry (1995) *Economies of Signs and Space*, London: Sage.
13　Manuel Castells (1997) *The Power of Identity*, Oxford and New York: Blackwell, p. 126.
14　See Romans 8: 20–5.
15　Philip Sampson (1994) "The rise of postmodernity" in Philip Sampson, Samuel Vinay, and Chris Sugden (eds) *Faith and Modernity*, Oxford: Regnum Lynx, p. 20.

Bibliography

Ahmed, Akbar (1994) *Islam, Globalization, and Postmodernism*, London and New York: Routledge

Albrow, Martin (1996) *The Global Age*, Cambridge UK: Polity Press

Ammerman, Nancy (1987) *Bible Believers*, New Brunswick NJ and London: Rutgers University Press

Ammerman, Nancy (1994) "Telling congregational stories," *Review of Religious Research*, 35:4, pp. 289–99

Ammerman, Nancy (1996) *Congregation and Community*, New Brunswick NJ and London: Rutgers University Press

Ammerman, Nancy (1997) "Religious choice and religious vitality" in Lawrence A. Young (ed.) *Rational Choice Theory and Religion: Summary and Assessment*, New York and London: Routledge

Anderson, Benedict (1983) *Imagined Communities: Reflections on the Origins and Spread of Nationalism*, London: Verso

Appadurai, Arjun (1996) *Modernity at Large: Cultural Dimensions of Globalization*, Minneapolis: University of Minnesota Press

Arnold, Matthew (1954) *Poetry and Prose*, London: Hart Davis

Bailey, Edward (1998) *Implicit Religion*, London: Middlesex University Press

Bakhtin, Mikhail (1981) *The Dialogical Imagination*, Austin TX: University of Texas Press

Banks, Robert (1983) *The Tyranny of Time*, Exeter: Paternoster Press

Barber, Benjamin (1995) *Jihad vs McWorld*, New York: Times Books

Barker, Eileen (1984) *The Making of a Moonie: Brainwashing or Choice?*, Oxford: Blackwell

Baudrillard, Jean (1983) *Simulations*, New York: Semiotext(e)

Baudrillard, Jean (1988) *America*, London and New York: Verso

Baudrillard, Jean (1993) *The Transparency of Evil*, London: Verso

Baudrillard, Jean (1994) *The Illusion of the End*, Cambridge UK: Polity Press

Baudrillard, Jean (1996) "Disneyworld Company" *Liberation* (Paris), translated in *C-Theory*, <http://www.ctheory.com/e25-disneyworld_comp.html>, by François Debrix

Baudrillard, Jean (1996) "The West's Serbianization" in Thomas Cushman and Stejpan Meštrović (eds) *This Time We Knew: Western Responses to Genocide in Bosnia*, New York: New York University Press

Bauman, Zygmunt (1992) *Mortality, Immorality, and Other Life Strategies*, Cambridge UK: Polity Press

Bauman, Zygmunt (1992) *Intimations of Postmodernity*, London and New York: Routledge

Bauman, Zygmunt (1993) *Postmodern Ethics*, Oxford and New York: Blackwell

Bauman, Zygmunt (1995) *Life in Fragments*, Oxford and New York: Blackwell

Bauman, Zygmunt (1996) "From pilgrim to tourist: Or a short history of identity" in Stuart Hall and Paul du Gay (eds) *Questions of Cultural Identity*, London: Sage

Bauman, Zygmunt (1997) *Postmodernity and its Discontents*, Cambridge UK: Polity Press, and New York: New York University Press

Bauman, Zygmunt (1998) *Globalization: The Human Consequences*, Cambridge UK: Polity Press, and New York: Columbia University Press

Bauman, Zygmunt (1998) *Work, Consumerism and the New Poor*, Buckingham and Philadelphia: Open University Press

Bebbington, David (1998) "Of this train, England is the engine: British Evangelicalism and globalization in the long nineteenth century" in Mark Hutchinson and Ogbu Kalu (eds) *A Global Faith: Essays on Evangelicalism and Globalization*, Sydney: Centre for the Study of Australian Christianity

Beckford, James (1989) *Religion in Advanced Industrial Society*, London: Unwin-Hyman

Bedell, Kenneth (1998) "Religion and the Internet: Reflections on research strategies" paper presented to the meetings of the Society for the Scientific Study of Religion, Montreal, November

Bell, Daniel (1976) *The Cultural Contradictions of Capitalism*, London: Heinemann

Bell, Daniel (1977) "The return of the sacred? The argument on the future of religion," *British Journal of Sociology*, 28, pp. 419–49

Bellah, Robert, et al. (1985) *Habits of the Heart*, Berkeley CA: University of California Press

Berger, Brigitte, Peter Berger, and Hansfried Kellner (1974) *Homeless Minds*, Harmondsworth: Penguin

Berger, Peter L. (1967) *Faith in Angels*, Garden City NY: Doubleday

Berger, Peter L. (1967) *The Sacred Canopy*, New York: Anchor-Doubleday

Berger, Peter L. (1980) *The Heretical Imperative*, New York: Anchor

Berger, Peter L. (1992) *A Far Glory: The Quest for Faith in an Age of Credulity*, New York: Free Press

Berger, Peter L. (1999) "The desecularization of the world" in Peter L. Berger (ed.) *The Impact of Religious Conviction on the Politics of the Twenty-first Century*, Grand Rapids MI: Eerdmans

Beyer, Peter (1994) *Religion and Globalization*, London: Sage

Beyer, Peter (1997) "Religious vitality in Canada: The complementarity of religious market and secularization perspectives," *Journal for the Scientific Study of Religion*, 36:2, pp. 272–88

Beyer, Peter (1998) "The city and beyond as dialogue: Negotiating religious authenticity in global society," *Social Compass*, 45:1, pp. 67–79

Bibby, Reginald (1987) *Fragmented Gods: The Poverty and Potential of Religion in Canada*, Toronto: Stoddart

Bibby, Reginald (1993) *Unknown Gods: The Ongoing Story of Religion in Canada*, Toronto: Stoddart

Bocock, Robert (1993) *Consumption*, London and New York: Routledge

Bourdieu, Pierre (1977) *Outline of a Theory of Practice*, Cambridge UK and New York: Cambridge University Press

Briggs, Asa (1996) "The final chapter" in Asa Briggs and Daniel Snowman (eds) *Fins de Siècle*, New Haven CT: Yale University Press

Bruce, Steve (ed.) (1992) *Religion and Modernization*, New York and Oxford: Oxford University Press

Bruce, Steve (1996) *Religion in the Modern World: From Cathedrals to Cults*, Oxford: Oxford University Press

Brusco, Elizabeth (1993) "The reformation of machoism: Asceticism and masculinity among Columbian Evangelicals" in Virginia Garrard-Burnett and David Stoll (eds) *Rethinking Protestantism in Latin America*, Philadelphia, Temple University Press

Bryman, Alan (1995) *Disney and his Worlds*, London and New York: Routledge

Bryman, Alan (1999) "The Disneyization of Society," *Sociological Review*, 47:1, pp. 25–47

Calhoun, Craig (1994) *Social Theory and the Politics of Identity*, Oxford: Blackwell

Carpenter, Joel (1998) *Revive Us Again: The Reawakening of American Fundamentalism*, New York and Oxford: Oxford University Press

Casanova, José (1994) *Public Religions in the Modern World*, Chicago IL: University of Chicago Press

Castells, Manuel (1989) *The Informational City*, Oxford: Blackwell

Castells, Manuel (1996) *The Rise of the Network Society*, Cambridge MA and Oxford UK: Blackwell

Castells, Manuel (1997) *The Power of Identity*, Oxford and New York: Blackwell

Castells, Manuel (1998) *The End of Millennium*, Oxford and New York: Blackwell

Cheseneux, Jean (1996) *Habiter le temps*, Paris: Bayard

Chevreau, Guy (1994) *Catch the Fire*, London: Marshall Pickering

Coninck, Frédéric de (1995) *Travail intégré, société éclatée*, Paris: Presses Universitaires de France

Coninck, Frédéric de (1996) *La Ville: Notre Territoire, nos appartenances*, Quebec: La Clairière

Crawford, Michael (1992) "The world in a shopping mall" in Michael Sorkin (ed.) *Variations on a Theme Park*, New York: Noonday

Crowley, Vivienne (1989) *Wicca: The Old Religion in the New Age*, Wellingborough: Aquarian Press

Davie, Grace (1994) *Religion in Britain since 1945: Believing without Belonging*, Oxford: Blackwell

Davie, Grace (1999) "Europe: The exception that proves the rule" in Peter L. Berger (ed.) *The Impact of Religious Conviction on the Politics of the Twenty-first Century*, Grand Rapids MI: Eerdmans

Davie, Grace (forthcoming) *Religion in Modern Europe: A Memory Mutates*, Oxford: Oxford University Press

Dawson, Lorne L. and Jenna Hennebry (1999) "New religions and the Internet: Recruiting in a new public space," *Journal of Contemporary Religion*, 14:1, pp. 17–39

Dawson, Michael (1998) *The Mountie: From Dime Novels to Disney*, Toronto: Between the Lines

Derian, James Der (1998) *The Virilio Reader*, Oxford UK and Malden MA: Blackwell

Disney Project, The (1995) *Inside the Mouse: Work and Play at Disney World*, Durham NC: Duke University Press

Dobbelaere, Karel (1981) *Secularization: A Multi-dimensional Concept*, a Trend Report published as *Current Sociology*, 29, pp. 3–213

Donahue, M. J. (1993) "Prevalence and correlates of New Age beliefs in six Protestant denominations," *Journal for the Scientific Study of Religion*, 32:2, pp. 177–84

Douglas, Mary (1982) "The effects of modernization on religious change," *Daedalus*, 111:1, pp. 1–19

Durkheim, Émile (1922) *The Division of Labour in Society*, Glencoe: Free Press

Eco, Umberto (1986) *Travels in Hyperreality*, New York: Harcourt Brace Jovanovich

Eco, Umberto (1986) *Faith in Fakes*, London: Secker and Warburg

Engelsviken, Tormod (1994) "Modernity and eschatology" in Philip Sampson, Vinay Samuel, and Chris Sugden (eds) *Faith and Modernity*, Oxford: Regnum Lynx

Ericson, Richard and Kevin Heggarty (1997) *Policing the Risk Society*, Toronto: University of Toronto Press

Evangelism and Social Responsibility: An Evangelical Commitment, a report of consultation in Grand Rapids MI, and Exeter UK: Paternoster Press, 1982, pp. 36–7

Faith and Order Committee (1996) *The Toronto Blessing*, London: Methodist Publishing House

Featherstone, Mike (1991) *Postmodernism and Consumer Culture*, London: Sage

Featherstone, Mike (1995) *Undoing Culture*, London, Thousand Oaks CA and New Delhi: Sage

Featherstone, Mike, Scott Lash, and Roland Robertson (eds) (1995) *Global Modernities*, London: Sage

Fenn, Richard (1978) *Toward a Theory of Seculariazation*, Storrs CN: Society for the Scientific Study of Religion

Fenn, Richard (1982) *Liturgies and Trials*, Oxford: Blackwell

Fenn, Richard (1990) "Pre-modern religion in the postmodern world: A reply to Professor Zylerberg," *Social Compass*, 37:1, pp. 97–105

Fenn, Richard (1997) *The End of Time*, London: SPCK

Flanagan, Kieran (1991) *Sociology and Liturgy*, London: Macmillan

Flanagan, Kieran and Peter Jupp (eds) (1996) *Postmodernity, Sociology and Religion*, London: Macmillan

Freston, Paul (1998) "Evangelicalism and Globalization" in Mark Hutchinson and Ogbu Kalu (eds) *A Global Faith: Essays on Evangelicalism and Globalization*, Sydney: Centre for the Study of Australian Christianity

Fukuyama, Francis (1992) *The End of History and the Last Man*, New York: Free Press

Fukuyama, Francis (1999) *The Great Disruption: Human Nature and the Reconstitution of Social Order*, New York: Free Press

Gandy, Oscar (1993) *The Panoptic Sort: A Political Economy of Information*, Boulder CO: Westview Press

Gibson, William (1984) *Neuromancer*, New York: Ace

Giddens, Anthony (1985) *The Nation-state and Violence*, Cambridge UK: Polity Press

Giddens, Anthony (1990) *The Consequences of Modernity*, Cambridge UK: Polity Press, and Stanford CA: Stanford University Press

Giddens, Anthony (1991) *Modernity and Self-identity*, Cambridge UK: Polity Press

Goodhardt, Gerald Joseph, A. S. C. Ehrenberg, and M. A. Collins (1987) *The Television Audience*, London: Gower

Grant, George (1969) *Time as History*, Toronto: CBC Learning Systems

Grant, John Webster (1972) *Religion in the Canadian Era*, Toronto: McGraw-Hill Ryerson

Hadden, Jeffrey (1987) "Towards desacralizing secularization theory," *Social Forces*, 65:3, March, pp. 587–611

Hall, Douglas John (1997) *The End of Christendom and the Future of Christianity*, Valley Forge PA: Trinity Press International

Hannigan, John (1995) "The postmodern city: A new urbanization?" *Current Sociology*, 43:1, pp. 151–217

Hannigan, John (1998) *Fantasy City: Pleasure and Profit in the Postmodern Metropolis*, London and New York: Routledge

Haraway, Donna (1997) *Modest_Witness@Second_Millennium.Female_Man_ meets_OncoMouse*, London and New York: Routledge

Harvey, David (1989) *The Condition of Postmodernity*, Cambridge MA and Oxford UK: Blackwell

Heelas, Paul (1994) "The limits of consumption and the post-modern religion of the New Age" in Russell Keat, Nigel Whiteley, and Nicholas Abercrombie (eds) *The Authority of the Consumer*, London: Routledge

Heelas, Paul (1996) "Detraditionalization of religion and self: New Age and postmodernity" in Kieran Flanagan and Peter Jupp (eds) *Postmodernity, Sociology, and Religion*, London: Macmillan, and New York: St. Martin's Press

Heelas, Paul (1996) *The New Age Movement*, Oxford UK and Cambridge MA: Blackwell

Hefner, Robert W. (ed.) (1993) *Conversion to Christianity*, Berkeley CA: University of California Press

Herbert, Gabriel (1935) *Liturgy and Society: The Function of the Church in the Modern World*, London: Faber and Faber

Hervieu-Léger, Danièle (1986) *Vers un nouveau christianisme*, Paris: Cerf

Hervieu-Léger, Danièle (1991) Review of Kepel in *Archives des Sciences Sociales de Religion*, avril–juin, pp. 263–4

Hervieu-Léger, Danièle (1993) *La Religion pour memoire*, Paris: Cerf.

Hervieu-Léger, Danièle (1997) "La Transmission religieuse en modernité," *Social Compass*, 44:1, pp. 131–43

Hervieu-Léger, Danièle (1998) "The transmission and formation of socio-religious identities in modernity: An analytical essay on the trajectories of identification," *International Sociology*, 13:2 pp. 213–28

Hesse, Mary (1980) *Revolutions and Reconstructions in the Philosophy of Science*, Notre Dame IN: University of Notre Dame Press

Hexham, Irving and Karla Poewe (1997) *New Religions as Global Cultures*, Boulder CO: Westview Press

Hindmarsh, Bruce (1995) "The 'Toronto Blessing' and the Protestant Evangelical awakening of the eighteenth century compared," *Crux*, December, 31:4, pp. 5–13

Holmes, D. (1997) *Virtual Politics: Identity and Community in Cyberspace*, London: Sage

Hoover, Stewart M. (1988) *Mass Media Religion*, London and Beverly Hills CA: Sage

Hoover, Stewart M. and Knut Lundby (eds) (1997) *Rethinking Media, Religion, and Culture*, London, Thousand Oaks CA, and New Delhi: Sage

Hunter, James Davison (1987) *American Evangelicalism: Conservative Religion in the Quandary of Modernity*, New Brunswick NJ: Rutgers University Press

Hunter, James Davison (1991) *Culture Wars: The Struggle to Define America*, New York: Basic Books

Hunter, James Davison (1996) *The State of Disunion* (the Postmodernity Project), Ivy VA: In Media Res Educational Foundation

Huntington, Samuel P. (1996) *The Clash of Civilizations and the Remaking of World Order*, New York: Simon and Schuster

Hutchinson, Mark and Ogbu Kalu (eds) (1998) *A Global Faith: Essays on Evangelicalism and Globalization*, Sydney: Centre for the Study of Australian Christianity

Iannaconne, Laurence (1990) "Religious practice: A human capital approach," *Journal for the Scientific Study of Religion*, 29, pp. 297–314

Iannaconne, Laurence (1991) "The consequences of religious market structure," *Rationality and Society*, 3, pp. 156–77

Innis, Harold Adams (1964) *The Bias of Communication*, Toronto: University of Toronto Press

Introvigne, Massimo (1999) "Misinformation, religious minorities and religious pluralism," a statement to the Organization for Security and Cooperation in Europe meeting on March 22, <http://www.cesnur.org/vienna.htm>

Ioro, Paul (1994) "Has Disney taken over America?" *Spy*, September/October, pp. 56–63

Jacobson, Kenneth Richard (1997) "Prophecy, performance, and persuasion: Sermon art and dramatic art in England" *1575–1630*, PhD thesis, Queen's University, Kingston, Ontario

Kaldor, Peter and Sue Kaldor (1988) *Where the River Flows*, Homebush West NSW: Anzea

Kaplan, Robert (1997) *The Ends of the Earth*, London: Macmillan

Kepel, Gilles (1994) *The Revenge of God*, Cambridge UK: Polity Press

Kingwell, Mark (1996) *Dreams of Millennium*, Toronto: Viking

Kinney, Jay (1995) "Religion, cyberspace, and the future," *Futures*, 27:7, pp. 763–76

Kroker, Arthur (1994) *Data Trash*, Montreal: New World

Kumar, Krishan (forthcoming) "Living at the end: Theories of post-history" in Gary Browning, Abigail Halcli, and Frank Webster (eds) *Theory and Society: Understanding the Present*, London: Sage

Lamy, Philip (1996) *Millennium Rage: Survivalists, White Supremacists, and the Doomsday Prophecy*, New York: Plenum

Lash, Scott (1994) in Ulrich Beck, Anthony Giddens, and Scott Lash (eds) *Reflexive Modernization*, Cambridge UK: Polity Press

Lash, Scott and John Urry (1995) *Economies of Signs and Space*, London: Sage

Lechner, Frank (1992) "Against modernity: Anti-modernism in global perspective" in P. Colomy (ed.) *The Dynamics of Social Systems*, London: Sage

Lemieux, Raymond (1996) "La Religion au Canada: Synthèse et problématiques," *Social Compass*, 43:1, pp. 135–58

Ley, David and K. Olds (1988) "Landscape as spectacle: World's Fairs and the culture of heroic consumption," *Environment and Planning D: Society and Space*, 6, pp. 191–212

Lowenthal, David (1996) *The Heritage Crusade and the Spoils of History*, New York: Viking

Lyon, David (1985) *The Steeple's Shadow: On the Myths and Realities of Secularization*, London: SPCK, and Grand Rapids MI: Eerdmans, 1987

Lyon, David (1993) "A bit of a circus: Notes on postmodernity and New Age," *Religion*, 23:2, pp. 117–26

Lyon, David (1994) *The Electronic Eye: The Rise of Surveillance Society*, Cambridge UK: Polity Press

Lyon, David (1994) *Postmodernity*, Buckingham: Open University Press, and Minneapolis: University of Minnesota Press; revised and expanded edition, 1999

Lyon, David (1996) "Religion and the postmodern: Old problems, new prospects" in Kieran Flanagan and Peter Jupp (eds) *Postmodernity, Sociology and Religion*, London: Macmillan, and New York: St Martin's Press

Lyon, David (1997) "Sliding in all directions: Social hermeneutics from suspicion to retrieval" in Roger Lundin (ed.) *Disciplining Hermeneutics*, Grand Rapids MI: Eerdmans, pp. 109–13

Lyon, David (forthcoming) "The net, the self, and the future," *Prometheus*

Lyon, David (forthcoming) *Surveillance Society: Monitoring Everyday Life*, Buckingham: Open University Press

Lyon, David and Marguerite Van Die (eds) (forthcoming) *Rethinking Church, State, and Modernity: Canada Between Europe and the USA*, Toronto: University of Toronto Press

Lyotard, Jean-François (1981) *The Postmodern Condition*, Minneapolis: University of Minnesota Press

McGrath, Alister (1993) *The Renewal of Anglicanism*, Harrisburg PA: Morehouse Publishing

Maffesoli, Michel (1995) *The Time of the Tribes*, London: Sage

Martin, Bernice (1982) *A Sociology of Contemporary Cultural Change*, London: Macmillan

Martin, David (1965) "Towards eliminating the concept of secularization" in Julius Gould (ed.) *Penguin Survey of the Social Sciences*, Harmondsworth: Penguin, pp. 169–82

Martin, David (1978) *A General Theory of Secularization*, Oxford and New York: Blackwell

Martin, David (1990) *Tongues of Fire: The Explosion of Protestantism in Latin America*, Oxford and New York: Blackwell

Martin, David (1996) "Religion, secularization and postmodernity: Lessons from Latin-America" in Pål Repstad (ed.) *Religion and Modernity: Modes of Co-existence*, Oxford: Scandinavian University Press

Martin, David (1997) *Reflections on Sociology and Theology*, Oxford: Clarendon Press

May, Tim (1998) "Reflections and reflexivity" in Tim May and Malcolm Williams (eds) *Knowing the Social World*, Buckingham: Open University Press

Mellor, Philip and Christopher Shilling (1997) *Re-forming the Body*, London: Sage

Městrovíc, Stejpan (1997) *Postemotional Society*, London and Thousand Oaks CA: Sage

Milbank, John (1990) *Theology and Social Theory: Beyond Secular Reason*, Oxford UK and Cambridge MA: Blackwell

Mohanty, Satya (1995) "Colonial legacies, multicultural futures: Relativism, objectivity, and the challenge of otherness," *Publication of the Modern Languages Association of America*, 110:1, p. 113

Moore, R. Laurence (1994) *Selling God: American Religion in the Marketplace of Culture*, New York and Oxford: Oxford University Press

Murdock, Graham (1997) "The re-enchantment of the world" in Stewart Hoover and Knut Lundby (eds) *Rethinking Media, Religion, and Culture*, London: Sage

Noble, Vicki (1991) *Shakti Woman: Feeling Our Fire, Healing Our World, the New Female Shamanism*, San Francisco CA: Harper and Row

Noll, Mark (1996) "The challenges of contemporary church history, the dilemmas of modern history, and missiology to the rescue," *Missiology*, 24:1, January

Nowotny, Helga (1994) *Time: The Modern and Postmodern Experience*, Cambridge UK: Polity Press

O'Neill, John (1988) "Religion and postmodernism: The Durkheimian bond in Bell and Jameson," *Theory, Culture and Society*, 5:2–3, pp. 493–508

Pahl, Ray (1995) *After Success: Fin-de-Siècle Anxiety and Identity*, Cambridge UK: Polity Press

Poloma, Margaret (1996) "By their fruits . . . a sociological assessment of the Toronto Blessing," *The Toronto Report*, Wiltshire UK: Terra Nova Publications

Poloma, Margaret (1996) "The spirit and the bride: The Toronto Blessing and Church Structure," *Evangelical Studies Bulletin*, 13:4, Winter, pp. 1–5

Postman, Neil (1985) *Amusing Ourselves to Death*, New York: Viking

Ranger, Terence (1993) "The local and the global in Southern African religious history" in Robert W. Hefner (ed.) *Conversion to Christianity*, Berkeley CA: University of California Press

Rawlyk, George (1996) *Is Jesus Your Personal Saviour?* Montreal and Kingston: McGill-Queen's University Press

Reader, Ian and Tony Walter (eds) (1993) *Pilgrimage in Popular Culture*, London: Macmillan

Rheingold, Howard (1993) "A slice of life in my virtual community" in Linda Harasim (ed.) *Global Networks*, Cambridge MA: MIT Press

Riddell, Mike (1998) *Threshold of the Future: Reforming the Church in the Post-Christian West*, London: SPCK

Rieff, Philip (1996) *Triumph of the Therapeutic: Uses of Faith after Freud*, New York: Harper and Row

Ritzer, George (1993) *The McDonaldization of Society*, Newbury Park, CA: Pine Forge

Ritzer, George (1998) *The McDonaldization Thesis*, London and Beverly Hills CA: Sage

Robertson, Roland (1985) "Humanity, globalization and worldwide religious resurgence: A theoretical exploration," *Sociological Analysis*, 46:3, pp. 219–42

Robertson, Roland (1989) "Globalization, politics and religion" in James Beckford and Thomas Luckmann (eds) *The Changing Face of Religion*, London and Beverly Hills CA: Sage

Robertson, Roland (1993) "Community, society, globality, religion" in Eileen Barker et al. (eds) *Secularization, Rationalism and Sectarianism*, New York and Oxford: Oxford University Press

Robertson, Roland (1995) "Glocalization: time-space and homogeneity–heterogeneity" in Mike Featherstone et al. (eds) *Global Modernities*, London: Sage

Robertson, Roland (1998) "Discourses of globalization: Preliminary considerations," *International Sociology*, 13:1, 25–40

Robins, Kevin (1996) *Into the Image: Culture and Politics in the Field of Vision*, London and New York: Routledge

Robison, Richard and David S. G. Goodman (eds) (1996) *The New Rich in Asia: Mobile Phones, McDonald's and Middle-class Revolution*, London and New York: Routledge

Rojek, Chris (1993) "Disney culture," *Leisure Studies*, 12:2 pp. 121–35

Romanowski, William (1996) *Pop Culture Wars*, Downers Grove: Inter-Varsity Press

Roof, Wade Clark (1993) *A Generation of Seekers: The Spiritual Journeys of the Baby Boom Generation*, New York: HarperCollins

Roof, Wade Clark (1996) "God is in the details: reflections on religion's public presence in the United States in the mid-1990s," *Sociology of Religion* 57:2, pp. 149–62

Rosenau, Pauline Marie (1992) *Post-modernism and the Social Sciences*, Princeton NJ: Princeton University Press

Sacks, Jonathan (1991) *The Persistence of Faith: Religion, Morality and Society in a Secular Age*, London: Weidenfeld and Nicolson

Sampson, Philip (1994) "The rise of postmodernity" in Philip Sampson, Vinay Samuel, and Chris Sugden (eds) *Faith and Modernity*, Oxford: Regnum Lynx

Sampson, Philip (1996) "Die Repräsentation des Körpers," *Kunstforum International*, Bd. 132, pp. 94–111

Sampson, Philip, Vinay Samuel, and Chris Sugden (eds) (1994) *Faith and Modernity*, Oxford: Regnum Lynx

Schultze, Quentin (1991) *Televangelism and American Culture*, Grand Rapids MI: Baker Book House

Simpson, John H. (1994) "The structure of attitudes towards body issues in the American and Canadian populations: An elementary analysis" in Ted G. Jelen and Martha A. Chandler (eds) *Abortion Politics in the United States and Canada: Studies in Public Opinion*, Westport CT: Praeger

Stackhouse, John (1994) *Canadian Evangelicalism in the Twentieth Century*, Toronto: University of Toronto Press

Stark, Rodney (1996) *The Rise of Christianity: A Sociologist Reconsiders History*, Princeton NJ: Princeton University Press

Susman, Warren (1979) "Personality and the making of twentieth century culture" in John Higham and Paul Keith Conkin (eds) *New Directions in American Intellectual History*, Baltimore MD: Johns Hopkins University Press

Taylor, Charles (1991) *The Malaise of Modernity*, Toronto: Anansi

Taylor, Charles (1992) *Multiculturalism and the Politics of Recognition*, Princeton NJ: Princeton University Press

Tomlinson, Dave (1995) *The Post Evangelical*, London: SPCK Triangle

Touraine, Alain (1988) *Return of the Actor: A Social Theory in Postindustrial Society*, Minneapolis: University of Minnesota Press

Towler, Robert (1974) *Homo Religiosus*, London: Constable

Turner, Bryan (1994) *Orientalism, Postmodernism, and Globalism*, London and New York: Routledge

Twitchell, James B. (1999) *Lead Us into Temptation: The Triumph of American Materialism*, New York: Columbia University Press

Urry, John (1995) *Consuming Places*, London and New York: Routledge

Van Die, Marguerite (ed.) (forthcoming) *Religion and Public Life*, Toronto: University of Toronto Press

Vattimo, Gianni (1985) *La fina della modernità*, Garzanti Editore; ET Jon R. Snyder, *The End of Modernity*, Cambridge UK: Polity Press, and Baltimore MD: Johns Hopkins University Press (1988)

Vattimo, Gianni (1992) *The Transparent Society*, Cambridge UK: Polity Press, and Baltimore MD: Johns Hopkins University Press. ET of *La società transparente*, Garzanti Editore (1989)

Virilio, Paul (1997) "Cyberwar, God and television," interview in Arthur and Marielouise Kroker (eds) *Digital Delirium*, Montreal: New World Perspectives

Walls, Andrew (1996) *The Missionary Movement in Christian History: Studies in the Transmission of Faith*, New York: Orbis Books

Walter, Tony (1996) *The Eclipse of Eternity: A Sociology of the After Life*, London: Macmillan, and New York: St Martin's Press

Walter, Tony (ed.) (1999) *Mourning for Diana*, Oxford and New York: Berg

Walter, Tony and Helen Waterhouse (1999) "A very private belief: Reincarnation in contemporary England," *Sociology of Religion*, 62:2, pp. 187–97

Warner, Stephen (1993) "Work in progress toward a new paradigm for the sociological study of religion in the United States," *American Journal of Sociology*, 98:5, pp. 1044–93

Waters, Malcolm (1995) *Globalization*, London and New York: Routledge

Weber, Max (1958) "Science as a vocation" in Hans Gerth and C. Wright Mills (eds) *From Max Weber: Essays in Sociology*, London: Routledge

Weber, Max (1976) *The Protestant Ethic and the Spirit of Capitalism*, London: Allen and Unwin

Wellman, Barry (ed.) (1999) *Networks in the Global Village*, Boulder CO: Westview Press

Westfall, William (1999) "The Church of England in Victorian Canada: An ongoing establishment", paper given at "Religion and Public Life Conference," Queen's University, Kingston, Ontario, and forthcoming in Van Die and Lyon

Wilson, Bryan (1975) "The debate over secularization," *Encounter*, 45:10, pp. 77–83

Wilson, Bryan (1976) *Contemporary Transformations of Religion*, Oxford: Oxford University Press

Woodhead, Linda (1999) "Theology and the fragmentation of the self," *International Journal of Scientific Theology*, 1:1

Woolley, Benjamin (1992) *Virtual Worlds*, Oxford: Blackwell

Wuthnow, Robert (1988) *The Restructuring of American Religion*, Princeton NJ: Princeton University Press

Wuthnow, Robert (1989) *The Struggle for America's Soul*, Grand Rapids MI: Eerdmans

Wuthnow, Robert (1994) *Sharing the Journey: Support Groups and America's New Quest for Community*, New York: Free Press

Wuthnow, Robert (1998) *Loose Connections: Joining Together in America's Fragmented Communities*, Cambridge MA: Harvard University Press

Wuthnow, Robert (1998) *After Heaven: Spirituality in America Since the 1950s*, Berkeley CA: University of California Press

Young, Lawrence (ed.) (1997) *Rational Choice Theory and Religion: Summary and Assessment*, London and New York: Routledge

Zaidi, Ali (1998) (1997) "Revitalization of the Ummah: some implications for socio-cultural theory," paper presented at the Canadian Sociology and Anthropology Association, June.

Subject Index

Name Index